Existential
Semiotics

Advances in Semiotics
EDITED BY THOMAS A. SEBEOK

Existential
Semiotics

Eero Tarasti

Indiana
University
Press

BLOOMINGTON AND INDIANAPOLIS

This book is a publication of

Indiana University Press
601 North Morton Street
Bloomington, IN 47404-3797 USA

HTTP://WWW.INDIANA.EDU/~IUPRESS

Telephone orders 800-842-6796
Fax orders 812-855-7931
Orders by e-mail iuporder@indiana.edu

MANUFACTURED IN THE UNITED STATES OF AMERICA

Library of Congress Cataloging-in-Publication Data

Tarasti, Eero.
Existential semiotics / Eero Tarasti.
p.   cm. — (Advances in semiotics)
Includes bibliographical references and index.
ISBN 0-253-33722-4 (alk. paper) — ISBN 0-253-21373-8 (pbk. : alk. paper)
1. Semiotics—Philosophy.   I. Title.   II. Series.
P99.T29 2000
401'.41—dc21
00-026810
1 2 3 4 5   05 04 03 02 01 00

CONTENTS

PREFACE *As an Introduction*   vii

Part One *Philosophical Reflections*

1. On the Paths of Existential Semiotics   3
2. Signs and Transcendence   17
3. Endo-/Exogenic Signs, Fields, and Worlds   37
4. Understanding, Misunderstanding, and Self-Understanding   57
5. Signs of Anxiety; or, The Problem of the Semiotic Subject   76

Part Two *In the Forest of Symbols*

6. From Aesthetics to Ethics: Semiotic Observations on the Moral
   Aspects of Arts, Especially Music   87
7. The "Structural" and "Existential" Styles in Twentieth-Century Arts 98
8. On the Authenticity and Inauthenticity of Art   112

Part Three *The Social and Cultural Field of Signs*

9. On Post-colonial Semiosis   137
10. Semiotics of Landscapes   154
11. Poetics of Place (Particularly in Music)   164
12. Walt Disney and Americanness: An Existential-Semiotical Exercise   172
13. " . . . and you find the right one": A Narratological Analysis of an
    Advertising Film   191
14. Senses, Values—and Media   209

INDEX   215

PREFACE

As an Introduction

It is certainly true that semiotics can no longer be what it was in the age of "classical semiotics," that is, in the writings of Peirce and Saussure through Lévi-Strauss to Greimas, Barthes, Foucault, or the early Kristeva and Eco. Some semioticians have turned to "hard sciences" such as computer-assisted technological models and cognitive research, whereas others have become prophets of postmodernism or engaged with various social and gender issues. Some semioticians, such as Thomas A. Sebeok with his new writings on biosemiotics, belong to the timeless core of semiotics for every period. Among some European semioticians, of which I am one, the turn to phenomenology and hermeneutics has been obvious.

In these essays, I sketch a new philosophical basis for semiotic inquiry and try to test it using applications to various fields. I hope that music is not too foregrounded in these applications, in spite of my alter ego as a musicologist.

As to my new theory, I am not yet able to offer the reader any well-established, axiomatic system. I have been inspired by certain continental philosophers from Hegel to Kierkegaard and Heidegger to Sartre; therefore I call my new approach "existential semiotics." However, this does not mean a return to an earlier phase. For instance, with respect to Hegel and Kierkegaard I am not primarily interested in their ideas related to romanticism, but rather in their methods of reasoning. I am occupied by processes, temporality, signs in flux, and particularly in the states before fixation into a sign, or what I call "pre-signs."

By no means do I want to reject the findings of classical semiotics—they have to be preserved as an essential part of the semiotic heritage to the new millennium. But as is so often true in the life of sciences, they prove to be special cases, valid in certain limited areas, whereas the new research strategies may be proceeding along entirely new avenues. The strength of semiotics has always been its extraordinary flexibility and context sensitivity.

Only in this way will the science of signs also be the science of future.

Helsinki, November 15, 1999

PART ONE

Philosophical Reflections

1

On the Paths of Existential Semiotics

Very seldom do new theories and philosophies appear as complete systems that interpret texts in a consistent manner. In addition, some ideas resist a too systematic or too "scientific" expression. This has led many a scholar to make aphoristic, poetic, or novelistic utterances. The new doctrine, which I call "existential semiotics," is precisely of this kind. Its fundamental theses start to take shape in my mind in an intuitive way, and as yet I can convey them only fragmentarily.

As a semiotician, I am faced with challenging tasks. Time passes—already decades ago, the first generation of semiotics gave place to the second generation of sign theory. Still, the classics of semiotics from Peirce to Greimas and Sebeok have not, of course, lost their pertinence and validity. Even the later works of Foucault, Barthes, and Kristeva can be considered a "second-generation semiotics," not to mention Eco's novels, Derrida's deconstruction, cognitive science, Baudrillard, Bourdieu, and so on. It is common to this second generation that the foundation of classical semiotics has been pushed into the background; yet in spite of all, that foundation still exists, and the texts of these later thinkers cannot be understood without this connection. The avoidance of new theories in the proper sense characterizes all of these second-generation semioticians. Their texts reflect the conditionality of all permanent values, unbelief, the inner conflicts of postmodern man, particularly the dangers of anything "social," "communal," chaos instead of structures. After the glorious days of structuralism, no one has dared to create a new theory of semiotics. Joseph Margolis has spoken about universes of flux, where everything is in motion. Nothing is stable, schematic, or fixed. The rigid models of classical semiotics are not suitable for analyzing such a universe. Is it possible to model the dynamically changing, temporal, flowing world?

Is it possible that by enriching first-generation semiotics, by adding there, perhaps, the Heideggerian "timefilter," we might construct a new approach? Or shall we completely reject the old sign theories and rebuild them on a radically new basis? If the answer to the last question is "yes," then why should we continue speak of "semiotics" at all? There are, naturally, schools that persist in believing that things are this or that because Peirce or Greimas said so, and not because things *are* so. Every now and then, the semiotician wandering around the world meets such sectarians who, like the Amish people in Lancaster, Pennsylvania, strive to maintain their doctrines untouched. I am afraid they have become the "arteriosclerosis" of semiotic circulation. Semiotics has to be renewed if it wants to preserve its position on the vanguard of thought.

The next question on the way to a new semiotics concerns how to portray, in an intellectually satisfactory way, certain intuitive, visionary aspects, to which the instinct may guide a scholar. One should not despise intuition; but the problem is, how can it be rendered into a communicable model, into a metalanguage? In this vein, one encounters entities such as the "existentials" of Heidegger or the "synthetic a priori judgments" of Kant. Consequently, I am encouraged to introduce some theses of my own:

1. Reality consists of "energy fields," in which prevail particular laws that can be described or conceptualized only with great difficulty. In such a field, similar situations or events effactually pull each other together. Correspondingly, energetically negative or positive events are connected and strengthen each other: Disasters call forth more disasters, successes bring about more successes. As it says in the Bible, the one who has much will be given more; whereas the one who has little, even that will be taken away. If something is in our minds, it soon happens. Everything that is immanent in the human mind strives for manifestation; the hidden or unconscious must be revealed—it must rise to the "surface" of reality.

Stop. Have we now sunk to the level of the psychology or telepathy of some weekly magazines? Good heavens, no!—since our modest endeavor is still strictly "scientific." Insofar as the aforementioned intuitive knowledge can be made explicit, one really would obtain a method for explaining the past as well as forecasting the future. This would involve an effort to render the time-bound "existential" intuition into something objective. We would resolve the dilemma of Karl Jaspers: "What is valid for all the times, is objective, whereas what is transitory in a moment, but still eternal, is existential."

In fact, however, one recognizes the above-mentioned connections of events only if he or she is *there,* not by external observation. Anthropologists realized this long ago, when they invented approaches such as "participating observation" or "observation making someone participate." The observer can perceive correctly the human, semiotic field of energy only by participating in it, while at the same time being aware that he/she also influences it. Georg Henrik von Wright lectured years ago about "the argument of a brain surgeon," a delusion that the objective description of the neural network would free us from interpretation and lead to universally valid knowledge about human action. The human world of *Dasein* is always based upon the presence of a subject therein, where even absence is a significant fact. Maybe the theory of Yuri Lotman was, on the level of culture, an attempt to model its "flux," as it were, from the inside.

2. The aforementioned thesis already touches closely the categories of 'being out' or 'being in' (*In-sein/Ausser-sein*), or simply external/internal. The said thesis includes the error that research would only be possible in the category of the external. Even about those phenomena of which a subject may have "inner" knowledge, he/she must first pretend to be ignorant, to be placed outside of them, thereby to "prove" or legitimize the correctness of what one knows. This is a phenomenon that endlessly recurs in arts studies, among other places. One imagines that the *Firstness* of phenomena would constitute such an objective zero-point for interpretation.

After all, the concepts inner/outer cannot be separated from the classical distinction objective/subjective, to which Kierkegaard dedicated so many pages in his philosophical output. The prevailing scientific paradigm determines the relationship between objective and subjective as follows: The objective conditions of physics and its laws set limits upon our subjective emotions and choices. However, the Kierkegaardian thesis is even more radical: The subjective and the objective never meet. They are not like separate spheres, such that where the "objective" finishes is where the subjective starts. Rather, they are two different approaches to the same world of *Dasein*.

In *Interpretation, Radical but Not Unruly* (1995: 52), Joseph Margolis thinks along the same lines when he argues: "There is no known procedure (rule, criterion, algorithm, law, or the like) by which, *from* a description of any physical events, we could infer in a reliable way any culturally significant events we spontaneously (normally) recognize; nor *for* any culturally significant events, could we infer any reasonably detailed and pertinent physical events in which they would be embodied and by reference to which they could then be indexed."

Nor does the so-called "supervenience theory" hold true in existential semiotics. This theory says: "If *x* and *y* have the same physical structure and *x* has the mental quality of *P*, then *y* must also have this quality *P*." One need only think of what happens in the novel *La luna e i falò* by the Italian author Cesare Pavese: The main protagonist returns from the United States to Italy, to a small village of his home region, Piemonte. He goes to the same house in which he spent his childhood; he encounters there the same signs as earlier. But at the same time everything has changed. The places *x* (the village before) and *y* (the village now) are physically quite the same, but spiritually they are entirely different from the viewpoint of the subject.

The structuralists wanted to show how individual interpretations were dependent on history, tradition, and surrounding culture. My subjective judgments only repeat the "automatisms" of a culture. In order to be able to estimate the degree of subjectivity and freedom of my existential choice, I have to know in which context and according to which norms it was done. I must be conscious of the limits of my choice and act, what I could and could not have done, departing from my own conditions. Especially if I am judging the individuality of an artist, his voice in the choir of texts and discourses, I must know to what extent he knew and followed the "grammar" or *langue* of his time. But am I right when I place myself, my own subjectivity, into his skin—by unscrupulously stepping into his place?

In any case, we must have an idea of how it was to be a subject in ancient Rome, in the court of the Sun King, or in the cafés of post-war Paris in order to understand Lucretius, Racine, or René Char.

The categories subject/object are, of course, contained as early as in the actantial model and narratology of Propp and Greimas. But what does it mean to be a subject or object in some position determined by the semiotic square? In the new existential semiotics, one must aim for seeing the signs from the *inside*, to recognize their inner microorganic life. The narratological model and the theory of psychoanalysis both start from the hypothesis that there is a subject and object. The situation is such that the subject wants to have the object. The catalyzing power, thus, is the Freudian *Trieb* or the Lacanian or Kristevian *désir*. But what does it mean? If the object of the desire is a value object, say the Ring of the Nibelungen and the power it represents in Wagner's work by the same name, the case is overtly a very simple one. Certain individual and collective values have been invested in the object; therefore, it has become desired in the *Dasein* world of the protagonists of the drama. (There are naturally even here, according to psychoanalysts, all kinds of fetishizing surrogate objects that shape the processes of one's mind.)

More difficult would be a situation in which the object is another subject, or in which the subject becomes an object. In human communication the existential law prevails: A subject who deals with another subject as his object is himself soon put in the same position; that is, he becomes treated as an object and thus is treated the same way he has treated others. On this principle of human dialogue, among other things, is based the ethics of altruism: Do to other people the same as you would have them do to you. Nevertheless, since human communication is never perfect, the subjects do not always understand that they are also objects to each other. The priest from the countryside in the novel *Journal d'un curé de campagne* by Georges Bernanos does not realize what kind of *sign* he functions in his parish, and is thus mistaken in his judgments and in his acts.

Another basic problem of human knowledge is whether a subject can experience himself as an object. Imagine a situation in which a subject must undergo a biopsy by a physician. The subject brings to the clinic a jar containing a small bloody piece of himself, which contains objective information about him that could determine his entire future. Is this not a situation in which a subject, in an embarrassing way, notices himself to be simultaneously subject and object?

On the other hand, one might imagine that to be a subject—at least that is something rather unambiguous. *Cogito, ergo.* . . . However, to Kierkegaard's mind nothing is more difficult for a subject than existing. It is so difficult that it is a lifelong task for the subject just to try every moment to become an existing subject. He can never entirely *be* it; he can only aim for it. Kierkegaard says: "An existing subject has to choose between two avenues. He can do all he can in order to forget that he exists, which causes him to become ridiculous, since existence has the peculiar property that the existing exists whether he wants it or not." (The pianist and musicologist, Charles Rosen, "the most versatile of living musicians," as he has been advertised, once said that he would like to become a learned man. "But you are already a learned man," I exclaimed. "No, one can only *become* a learned man, never *be* it," he answered. I remarked how this idea coincided with the thought of Kierkegaard. Rosen replied, "It is no wonder, since the idea is genuinely romantic, and Kierkegaard got everything from the German school of philosophy of Jena.") In addition, the idea of an existing subject appeared already in Augustinus, in his powerful vision about the time before it, the world of the pagans, and after it, the state of God (*De civitate Dei*).

A suspicious semiotician-reader may at this moment throw my essay into the corner and say, "What has all this to do with semiotics? It is of no interest." What I am searching for is perhaps the most important thing in semiotics; namely, the states *before* the formation of signs, accordingly "*pre-signs*" (in Finnish "*esi-merkkejä*"). When the sign has crystallized, there remains almost nothing to be done—on the level of signs themselves. Peirce tried to classify signs in relationship with themselves and made some interesting findings, like the relationships of legisign/sinsign/qualisign or type/token, etc. Nevertheless, the most interesting, existential moment of signs is in the moment before or after them, since the life of signs does not stop, of course, with their fixation into objects. In any case, if there are existential signs, they are always in a state of becoming. Therefore, only in exceptional cases can the analysis articulate the text or situation into clear-cut units. They can have moments, which constitute existential demarcations. There are situations in which the continuous becoming, flux, and streaming of signs—which hence imitates the inner movement of subjects carrying them—stops, stagnates for a while into a phase of *l'être en soi* (the sign is the same as its concept). There form and substance, matter and mind, communication and signification are united in oneness. However, the pause is always temporary.

3. Signs always appear in connection with a certain situation. For Sartre, a situation was something social, almost political. In this connection, it is yet to be understood in a broader, "philosophical" sense. The sign situation means a given and concrete temporal-local position in which the sign appears. The situation can be predictable or unpredictable. In the latter case, it is identified with a structure. In fact, then, one can no longer talk so much about a situation. Rather, the sign emerges from its union with the structure. The sign can be in any existential relations with its situation; it can either deny or affirm that situation.

In some cases, signs get all their power from their situations. In that case, they are actually weak signs; they do not have in themselves any inner force. Even signs that are a part of a structure are weak, but not so feeble as completely situational signs. Structures, out of which they grow, always have a greater permanence. Sometimes signs are in a relationship of negation to their structure. They seem to be strong when they set themselves in their position of opposition, but they are not strong intrinsically. Such signs are altogether dependent on their structure, against which they rebel. For instance, one may mention the behavior of some marginal social groups, which appear as negation of the prevailing establishment. Such marginal social groups bring about signs—language usage, dress or fashion, music—which *look* strong, but are in fact completely dependent on the object of their negation. Correspondingly, some externally modest, even entirely inner sign—like a sign seen in a dream—may form a decisive impulse to one's action. Very strong are signs that radiate the properties of their situations. For example, the leitmotifs of Wagner's operas are "strong signs," since they are situational but do not follow any system or structure; their significance grows from the situations in which they appear.

Are there particularly "semiotic" situations—in a sense other than the fact that even the illustrations chosen by semioticians reflect some traits of their world? It is hardly an accident that the model phrase of Chomsky's compelling generative grammar portrays a situation in which "John beats his sister," or that analytic philosophy favors absurd cases like "the bald-headed king of France," or that the favorite animal of logicians is a wombat.

In everyday life, *Dasein,* one may take as a sign that situation in which a subject has to seek a correct code for his action. If what is involved is an ethical situation, one has to use the ethical code, not the aesthetical code; if the situation is historical, one has to apply a historical code; if existential, then an existential code. But how can a subject find a correct code? By guessing? By reasoning? When can one know that he has adopted a wrong code, that he has acted erroneously? A theory of semiotic mistakes could be as interesting as the theory of lies (as noted by Umberto Eco, in his *Theory of Semiotics*).

In these cases, the situations are kinds of isotopies, which serve as criteria. Therefore, one has to describe various sign situations and the choices of different subjects within them. The essential thing is the openness or closedness of a situation. An open sign situation is not exhausted with the finding of a code, but constantly demands reinterpretations and changes of code. Only the one who can pursue them is able to act correctly in a semiotic sense.

What about situations in which there are many correct solutions? One may prepare a list of semiotic situations: (1) rules of society—the *politeness* code comes before the *truth* code; (2) historical situations, in which one has to be able to read and correctly interpret the signs of the past; (3) existential situations, in which the opposition life/death manifests (examples: the scene in the movie *La Grande Illusion,* in which a French soldier meets a German woman in her mountain cabin; the last composition of the young Jewish pianist, Gideon Klein, in Theresienstadt; etc.); (4) situations of communication, including self- or autocommunication; (5) situations of power—the relationships of individual and social groups, hierarchical social fields, decorations and humiliations; (6) religious situations or experiences in which the act of signification is transferred to some supra-individual entity, a leap, a thrownness, resorting to "grace" (When I saw the sacred mountain of Fuji in Japan, I thought: If there is a God, he sees everything; then one is free from the obligation to prove his or her existence to other human beings, through acts and signs.); (7) culinary situations—the symbolisms of food; (8) erotic situations—in principle, the projection of the human body onto signs—or the whole problematics of gender; (9) moral choice situations—contradictions between the principles of pleasure and reality.

The list could continue. Yet one must also take into account that a situation can quickly change into something else, or that the same situation may, from the viewpoint of one subject, belong to one genre; while for another subject, the situation may seem to belong to a different genre.

Situations are always concrete and particular, most often non-recurrent. In existential semiotics, one is simply looking for the individuality and particularity of phenomena, their "soul." Existential semiotics is opposed to a science that only strives for constants. What is the "semiotic" constitution of the world? Certainly it is different from Carnap's outline in his *Der logische Aufbau der Welt*. One may think of Finland. What are the particular situations, codes, and the "concrete logics" taking place in the Finnish culture or *Dasein*?

In fact, people, societies, places, moments, cultures, and acts are judged on a quite different level than one would expect. They are judged and must be approached in terms of their immediate *Firstness*. What remains in our minds of a person may be some striking gesture, perfume, expression, some quality beyond the "official" image of his personality. A town may be remembered because of its first impression, which can be some passing sign apparently without any context: Helsinki smells of the sea, Paris of the dust of the metro and Gaulois tobacco, Bahia of dendée oil, and Imatra of the wood industry. The way a person shakes one's hand, brushes back his hair, glances, and walks—all these are often more important, in this sense, than his rational, cognitive messages. These overtly marginal and momentary qualities have their own logic, which can be more determining than the manifest symbolic order. Are we then investigating a kind of hidden semiosis? Not insofar as the aforementioned qualities are there to be perceived by anyone, although most people pass by them. They cannot "read" the world surrounding them. (What keeps one in Finland? Nothing but these basic qualities of the Finnish identity—the perfume of the air, light, the intonation of language, gestures, the signs strewed here and there by memories, the deserted austerity of countryside and towns, which in its melancholy is as poetic as the landscape paintings about the village of Luveciennes by Sisley at the gallery of Le Musée d'Orsay in Paris.)

5. The dialectics between the enunciator and the enunciate, in a certain situation of enunciation. The starting point for a significant act is the desire of everyone to become significant, full of significations—to oneself and to others. To be understood. This pushes us to make science, arts and semiotics—but it is also the great theme of the "semiosis" of everyday life.

Thus, the sign itself is no longer in focus; instead, it is the dialogue, not only among people but between man and text (enunciate, utterance). The concepts of Roland Barthes, such as *lisible* (readable) and *scriptible* (writerly), contain this essential distinction. In a text that is only *lisible,* one aims to forget the aforementioned dialectics and to merge with the enunciator inside the text. We read holding our breath. We listen as if enchanted. We look with eyes staring. But when we consider the text to be "writerly" (*scriptible*), we move to another degree of reality into a more semiotical consciousness. We see the text through the "eyes" of another text. We hear in some musical passage a reminiscence of Debussy. We see in this and that painting an allusion to Picasso. We read in this and that phrase a tinge of the Proustian *mémoire involontaire,* etc. Even life can be experienced as a text. The autobiography of Stefan Zweig, *The World of the Past* (*Die Welt von Gestern*) is written in such a way that the phases of the writer are first depicted as written, *scriptible,* an orderly text. At the end, when one approaches the present time, the text glides into the Barthesian category of *lisible* (a similar effect takes place in a recent novel by the Finnish semiotician Henri Broms, *The Spirit of Place*). Zweig's book was written amidst the chaos of the Second World War, which, in a threatening way, comes closer and closer to the reader toward the end. Similarly, the degree of the existential presence of the enunciator increases toward the close of the biography.

The phenomena of an existential semiotical nature open themselves to a subject only through his/her presence. What does this mean? A critic writes a report about a theater performance or concert. He attended the occasion, but was not really *there.* He was perhaps physically present and described what happened objectively speaking. But he was absent in the existential sense. In that case, his portrayal is nothing but a reification of the phenomenon and proves to be of a more or less serious degree of alienation. He might be over-present or under-present; that is, he is either in an overexcited, over-participative state of mind, losing his ability to judge; or he might be absent-minded and unreceptive.

Finally, the interpretation is possible only in a certain moment. Can the utterance ever be detached from its specific time and place (or is the Greimasian disengagement, or *débrayage*)? Does the discourse have any stability? Yes, if it realizes the universal concealed in the moment. Then the text portraying the world is always present, actual, present at the same time in the "now" moment of the historical stream and at any time.

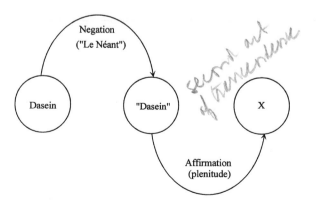

DIAGRAM 1. The Journey of an Existential Subject via the Acts of Negation and Affirmation

6. In the analysis, the principle of 'letting-things-be' (the Heideggerian *Gelassenheit*) is essential. How can we be sure that our interpretation, our analysis, does not violate the object? The analysis must not damage the phenomenon or change it by force. The interpretation is only possible by being inside the world of *Dasein*—but at the same time transcending it.

The new essential concept in semiotics is *transcendence*. It creates the dialectics between 'being' and 'not-being' (or Nothingness), which is so essential in everything existential.

A subject becomes an existential being that creates significations through two acts. First, he finds himself amidst the objective signs. Let it be simply called *Dasein*. There all the laws, grammars, and generative courses of the objective semiotics hold true. But then the subject recognizes the emptiness and Nothingness surrounding the existence from which he has come, that is, which precedes him and comes after him. The subject makes a leap into Nothingness, to the realm of *le Néant*, described by Sartre. In its light, the whole earlier *Dasein* seems to have lost its ground; it appears to be senseless. This constitutes the first act of transcendence, or the negation.

In the theories of existentialist philosophers, the movement of a subject stops here; Sartre remains in his *Nausée,* Camus in his *The Fall.* The experience of Nothingness is anguishing. But it can become a creative experience if the movement of a subject goes forth.

When the subject returns from his negation, the transcendence of his *Dasein,* he sees it from a new point of view. Many of its objects have lost their meaning and have proven to be only seemingly significant. However, those which preserve their meanings are provided with a new content enriched by the new existential experience. The subject is, as it were, reborn as a "semiotic self" (this self, a concept of Thomas A. Sebeok, is interpreted in such a way in our context).

Nevertheless, the movement of the subject continues further and now follows the second act of transcendence. He encounters the opposite pole of the Nothingness—the universe, which is meaningful but, in some supra-individual way, is independent of his own act of signification. This act can also be called "affirmation." As the consequence of this act, he finds what Peirce called the *Ground.* It is not the same as isotopy or semiosphere, notions used in classical semiotics and which are valid in the world of the primary *Dasein*. Rather, it radiates a new kind of signification also to the subject dwelling in it. The effort of Thomas Sebeok to prove that the whole universe is basically of a "semiotic" nature, at least for its living organisms, comes unexpectedly close to this philosophico-theological view (the question of the Lithuanian interviewer to Sebeok—Are you a pantheist?—may be justified in this respect).

In the dictionary by the Russian philosopher Vladimir Soloviev, one finds definitions describing the situation. When speaking about gnosticism Soloviev says: "Es genügt der Hinweis, dass der Buddhismus das absolute Sein nur in negativer Weise, als Nirwana, bestimmt, wohingegen das Sein im Gnostizismus positiv als *Fülle* (Pleroma) definiert wird" [It is enough to say that Buddhism determined the absolute being in a negative way, as Nirvana, whereas gnosticism defined it as a Fullness or Plenitude (pleroma)] (1965: 115).

Elsewhere in the dictionary, when speaking about *die Weltseele,* Soloviev states: "Weltseele ist die einheitliche innere natur der Welt, die als lebendiges, strebendes, vorstellendes und fühlendes Wesen gedacht wird. Viele philosophische Lehren, die die Einheit der Welt aus dem ewigen Bereich des idealen oder intelligiblen Seins ableiteten, erkannten doch auch die (Existenz einer) Weltseele an, die als untergeordnetes Prinzip in allen Erscheinungen lebt und die die höhere ideale Einheit, die ewig im absoluten Prinzip ruht, im sinnlichen Bereich und im zeitlichen Prozess wahrnimmt und verwirklicht" [The soul of the world—anima mundi—is the unitary, inner nature of the world, which is thought to be a living, willing, conceiving and feeling being. Many philosophical doctrines which derived the unity of the world from the eternal sphere of conceptual and ideal being, postulated also the existence of the world soul; it lives as the basic principle of all phenomena and is realized there as a higher ideal unity, both in the sensorial reality and in the temporal process] (348).

Surprisingly enough, the concepts of "world soul" and "Fullness" now have a place and a use in my existential semiotics when one is describing the field found by the act of affirmation—the second transcendence. Yet even thereafter, the subject returns into *Dasein* and its worldliness. Now he creates new signs and objects, which are purely existential, but whose essence is understood only by the subject, who has himself gone the same path via Nothingness and Fullness, of negation and affirmation.

Are these signs devoid of the codes of *Weltlichkeit*? Do they have a secret code system through which they function and open themselves? Do they appear exclusively to similar-minded subjects, to the *edle Geisterschaft,* which Goethe mentions in his famous poem *Vermächtnis*? Do we see a new type of esoteric group forming here, always a little suspect as a closed form of society? No, since the group of existing subjects is never closed. Nor can the existing signs constitute any ready-made system. What is involved is the society of "silent subjects," described by Kierkegaard, as a contrast to the noisy enunciators living in the sorrowlessness of the primary *Dasein*.

6. Accordingly, what are the existential signs? First of all, they are signs that are detached from the world of *Dasein,* and that start floating in the gravity-less space of Nothingness. This represents a kind of levitation of signs, as in the painting of Marc Chagall where things can hover in the air—or, rather, not things but their signs or signifiers. Or then they are signs that have been moved to the state of Fullness. The signs can be split into two: They can leave their signifieds in the objectal world of *Dasein,* that is to say, be emptied, and start moving as mere signifiers without any content. However, also the contrary can happen: The surface cover, the materiality of signs can stay in the world of *Dasein,* whereas the content is transferred to the environment of Nothingness.

Who puts signs in motion? The transcending subject, of course, in his act of existing. In both cases, the original modalities belonging to the original worldliness disappear. When shifting to the area of Nothingness, the willing, wanting, being able to, knowing—all these vanish gradually in their movement toward the core of the darkness of the 'not-being'. Correspondingly, when they return, they again start to be connected with these modalities, but now perhaps in an entirely new way. After the visit to Nothingness, the modalities are never the same as they used to be. In the sphere of Fullness again, the signs become immensely heavy, full with the *Ground* with which they are united.

The existential style in the arts reflects this transcendence, of either the world of Nothingness or of Fullness. Serial music imitates the act of negation: Its signs are tones that have lost their signifieds, or contents. But there is also music that may reflect the second act of transcendence, or affirmation. In such music, the old content is provided with a new signified, a manifest form, tonal expression by abandoning itself to the more profound musical laws. It is the music of utopia; it creates a new sonorous universe, which is not even the *Dasein* purified by the negation, but which offers a completely new, transcendental landscape and vision. Consequently, there are two kinds of existential style: the anguished or rebellious; and the transfigured one, which blends into the "harmony of the spheres," as in Richard Strauss's *Death and Transfiguration* (*Tod und Verklärung*).

In any case, the inner value of a sign must be pondered according to its degree of existentiality. In every artistic sign there must be an existential moment. In order to reach it, one first has to pursue the primary negation, to observe the signs against the Nothingness. Hence, the signs are liberated from their cover. In general, the first step toward becoming existential is a rebellion, a *"sakernas uppror"* (or "upheaval of things," as it was put once in a poem by Henry Parland). The second degree is the principle of *Gelassenheit*, throwing oneself into the care of Fullness, breathing in time with the world soul.

7. On the basis of what has been said above, one might think that we have here a very solipsist world view: What is involved is a subject who essentially moves alone in the universe, without the presence of other subjects. One might argue that this is not a better subject than the subject of any abstract philosophy—a disembodied subject, or *sujet desincarné*.

Nevertheless, both Heidegger and Jaspers are of the opinion that the "real manifests in the resistance." The subject is confined by something called "reality." Reality is to the subject that which he cannot change, which sets limits upon his activity, which forms opposition. But where is this resistance placed? In the sphere of transcendence, or in the world of *Dasein*?

Communication is possible only when there is some Other, which does not fuse together with the enunciating subject or agent. (Yuri Lotman gave an illustration of such a case in a lecture at Helsinki University in May 1987: Spouses who have been married for decades start to be like two similar entities, concentric circles that finally identify completely with each other.) Therefore, all forms of communication and media based on the principle of such a fusion or immersion are basically only destroying communication!

The real, the Other, which offers the resistance necessary for communication, can be anything against which one may prove and test his values, behaviors, and theories. The real does not need to be an empirical, physical sphere, where one would make tests or experiments that would, in effect, "resolve" objectively some problem. No, it can be anything that provides us with a resistance (*Widerstand*) to a subject in the world in which he is acting and functioning. For Kierkegaard, this resistance was God, a completely real being to him. To Sartre, it was *le Néant*, against which he mirrored his being, responsibility, and existence, the key terms of his philosophy. To Peirce, it was that part of the universe that he called the Object, and in relation to which one could ask questions. His way of distinguishing *First, Second,* and *Third* applied the principle of a curtain; that is, it started from a kind of artificially distinguished zero-point; it is a completely different view from the hermeneuticians who presume that man as early as in his *Firstness* lives in a certain understanding of his being. To Hegel, this resistance was the History, albeit a bad resistance.

According to the level, quality, and degree of the resistance, various discourses emerge—as in Northrop Frye's theory (*Anatomy of Criticism*), there are various modes of narration. If the resistance is on a higher level than the narrator—for instance a philosopher or semiotician—the result is a text with a theological or mythological character (Kierkegaard, Nietzsche). If the resistance is on the same level, pragmatic texts emerge, which move on the practical, empirical level (Peirce, Sartre as author). If the resistance is on a lower level, it brings about comical, grotesque or parodistic texts (like Pirsig's *Lila,* Nietzsche's *Fröhliche Wissenschaft,* Voltaire's *Zadig* or Diderot's *Le neveu de Rameau*).

However, scientific scholars can also have their own particular opponent-subject, on which they are completely dependent (I do not want to mention who they would be in semiotics; use your own imagination!). All the precursors of existential semiotics, Kierkegaard, Peirce, Heidegger and Sartre had their own spiritual opponent—Hegel—but in different ways than they believed.

Kierkegaard believed that he was resisting in Hegel the so-called objective science. But at the same time, he continued the Hegelian subjectivism, albeit in an unsystematic form. He likewise classified reality in ternary terms. Mozart's operatic figures Cherubino, Pamino, and Don Giovanni were various developmental phases of the same erotic subject (see Cecile Ortoli's recent dissertation at the University of Aix en Provence); but in the same way, we could form a typology of the existential heroes in the movies by Aki and Mika Kaurismäki, of protagonists who display the dignity of the life of fallen people, in the same line as The Liar—The Zombie—Rodolfo.

Peirce thought that he was opposing Hegel's nominalism. However, he still adopted as the foundation of his realist doctrine Hegel's ternary categories (of which one might accuse even our present model of existential semiotics: Why should the movement of transcending be necessarily restricted only to those three forms of *Dasein*?).

Heidegger pretended that he had transformed all the 'being' in the 'being-in-the-world', but introduced within it a dichotomy between authentic (*Sorge*) and inauthentic (*das Man*) existence; he saw 'being' (or existence) at the same time as his own possibility, as death, and as fallen; the Hegelian dialectics functioned in his philosophy like glasses of different colors, through which the world appeared either in a somber or a bright light. Moreover, Heidegger departed from Hegel on the level of discourse, which is the unhappiest form of blending together—non-communication. The consequences are seen in Derrida.

Sartre, in turn, transformed the Hegelian movement between 'being' and 'not-being' into a subjective psychological problem. Nothingness was the same as loss of sense, or meaningfulness.

Accordingly, in the same way as Peter Weiss spoke about the aesthetics of resistance (*Aesthetik des Widerstandes*), there exists the semiotics of resistance. It appears in the most varied ways and on many levels, in the processes of communication and signification.

REFERENCES

Bernanos, Georges. 1936. *Journal d'un curé de campagne.* Paris: Librairie Plon.
Broms, Henri. 1993. *Paikan henki* [The Spirit of Place: A Novel]. Helsinki: Arator.
Camus, Albert. 1963. *The Fall.* London: Penguin (in association with H. Hamilton).
Carnap, Rudolph. 1974. *Der logische Aufbau der Welt.* Hamburg: Meiner.
Eco, Umberto. 1979. *A Theory of Semiotics.* Bloomington: Indiana University Press.
Frye, Northrop. 1990. *The Anatomy of Criticism.* Harmondsworth: Penguin.
Heidegger, Martin. 1967. *Sein und Zeit.* Tübingen: Max Niemeyer Verlag.
Jaspers, Karl. 1962. *Die Philosophie.* Berlin, Göttingen, Heidelberg: Springer Verlag.
Kierkegaard, Søren. 1993. *Päättävä epätieteellinen jälkikirjoitus* [The Concluding Non-scientific Post-scriptum]. Finnish translation from the Danish. Juva: WSOY.
Margolis, Joseph. 1995. *Interpretation, Radical but Not Unruly.* Berkeley, Los Angeles, London: University of California Press.
Ortoli, Cecile. "L'Erotisme musical ou le sujet de la musique." Doctoral thesis submitted at the University of Nizza Sophia Antipolis, May 13, 1995.
Parland, Henry. 1970. *Sakernas uppror* [The Rebellion of the Things]. A novel in the collection *Säginteannat. Samlad prosa 2,* ed. Oscar Parland. Helsingfors: Söderström et Co.
Pavese, Cesare. 1950. *La luna e i falò.* Torino: Giulio Einaudi Editore.
Peirce, Charles Sanders. 1992. *The Essential Peirce: Selected Philosophical Writings.* Vol. 1 (1867–1893), ed. Nathan Houser and Christian Kloesel. Bloomington: Indiana University Press.
Sartre, Jean-Paul. 1943. *L' être et le néant. Essai d'ontologie phénoménologique.* Paris: Gallimard.
Sebeok, Thomas A. 1979. *The Sign and Its Masters.* Austin: University of Texas Press.
Soloviev, Vladimir. 1965. *Philosophie, Theologie, Mystik, Grundprobleme und Hauptgestalten.* Freiburg im Breisgaus: Erich Wevel Verlag.
———. "Die Weltseele." In *Deutsche Gesamtausgabe der Werke von Wladimir Solowjew,*

ed. Wladimir Szylkarski, Wilhelm Lettenbauer, and Ludolf Müller, vol. VI: *Philosophie, Theologie, Mystik*. München, Freiburg im Breisgaus: Erich Wewel Verlag.

Tarasti, Eero. 1994. *A Theory of Musical Semiotics*. Bloomington: Indiana University Press. (In French: *Sémiotique musicale,* trans. Bernard Dublanche. Collection Nouveaux Actes Sémiotiques. Limoges: Presses Universitaires de Limoges, 1996.)

———, ed. 1995. *Musical Signification: Essays in the Semiotic Theory and Analysis of Music*. Berlin: Mouton de Gruyter.

Weiss, Peter. 1988. *Ästhetik des Widerstandes*. Hinter jedem Wort die Gefahr des Verstummens: Sprachproblematik und literarische Tradition in der Ästhetik des Widerstands von Peter Weiss. Ed. Hans Höller with Peter Göllner. Stuttgart: Heinz.

Zweig, Stefan. 1992. *The World of the Past* [Die Welt von gestern: Erinnerungen eines Europäers]. Frankfurt am Main: S. Fischer.

2

Signs and Transcendence

Semiotics and structuralism, together with all their pre- and post-phenomena, will surely stand out in history as central paradigms of the sciences of meaning in our century. Semiotics has a long tradition, but it only solidified into a discipline during roughly the years 1880 to 1980. In those years, in both Europe and the United States, a certain integral whole of concepts and approaches took shape which I call "classical semiotics." In it one can distinguish two main streams: (1) A language-based semiotics that flows simultaneously from the structural linguistics of de Saussure and the Russian formalist school (among the latter is the Finnish school of folklore studies). One may aptly call this language-based paradigm "European semiotics." (2) The other main stream is "American semiotics," which focuses more on non-verbal communication than on language proper, and takes its inspiration from philosophy and from the behavioral and natural sciences. The father of American semiotics was, of course, Charles Sanders Peirce, a contemporary of de Saussure. These two schools have engaged in stormy battles against each other's views. Yet now, from the vantage point of the end of the century, the two schools seem to have become reconciled in a broader vision of semiotics. One might generalize further and say that most so-called classical semiotics now accepts the idea that semiosis is the same as communication plus signification. The central notions of semiotics—sign and meaning—are not exhausted by mere description of the process of communication as a chain going from sender to receiver. Nor is the entire truth of semiotics revealed only by the elucidation of the structure of the sign, without investigation of its context, isotopy, or semiosphere.

Even one of the most seminal representatives of the empirical line of semiotics, Thomas A. Sebeok, admits in his book *A Sign Is Just a Sign* that "semiotics is not about the 'real' world at all, but about complementary or alternative, actual models of it and—as Leibniz thought—about an infinite number of anthropologically conceivable or possible worlds. Thus, semiotics never reveals what the world is, but circumscribes what we can know about it; in other words, what a semiotic model depicts is not 'reality' as such, but nature as unveiled by our method of questioning" (1991: 12).

In any case, the great research findings of semioticians such as Lévi-Strauss, Greimas, Foucault, Lotman, and others remain pertinent even today. In relation to the masters of the turn of the century—de Saussure and Peirce—the semioticians just mentioned constitute a second-generation semiotics. And in the 1980s, still newer trends appeared which might be called a third-generation semiotics. This last generation includes various approaches in the cognitive sciences (which often cite semiotics as part of their makeup), in deconstruction and Derridean philosophy, post-structuralists like Bourdieu, Foucault, Baudrillard, Kristevan feminists, and so on. Common to all these recent trends in the "third generation," is the fact that they cannot be properly understood without knowledge of first- and second-generation classical semiotics.

In my own thinking, I have started to abandon "structuralist semiotics" in its Greimasian forms, and have been looking for a new basis on which to construct a theory of semiosis. In this new direction, I have sketched a theory that I call "existential semiotics," whose inspiration has come from existentialist philosophers such as Kierkegaard, Heidegger, Jaspers, Jean Wahl, and Sartre. In a broader sense, my sources have also included Kant, Hegel, Schelling, and other German philosophers. Let me stress that my new theoretical construction is still semiotics and not just a return to existentialism—as fashionable as the thinkers of the 1940s and 1950s may currently be in Paris.

Nevertheless, my own undertaking is not untimely, insofar as it reevaluates the notion of the subject, which has become a central issue in many post-structuralist theories. In these theories, meaning is not situated in any particular place—for instance, in a message, sign, or text—as little as one can say that the subject lives at a particular "address." Meaning is instead present—in fact, omnipresent—in a *dialogue* between the subjects of enunciation and enunciate. Such a dialogue contains very little that is object-oriented. Moreover, an essential aspect of my model is that it connects meaning to *temporal* processes; meaning emerges via a kind of "journey" made by the subject (the Romantic episteme of "wandering," as in Liszt's *"pélérinages,"* is not far from such an idea). Finally, one must bear in mind that scientific theories are usually rationalizations and universalizations of certain empirical experiences. In this sense, my new theory of semiotics, while aiming for a more general status, has certainly been influenced by the fact that I am a music scholar.

I have outlined a model that is based upon the concept of *Dasein*—existence—which constitutes the world in which our "semiotic subject" lives, acts and reacts. In this model, all the operations elucidated by classical semiotics hold true within the limits of the primary *Dasein*. In other words, Greimas's "generative course" and other concepts are still valid and useful in the context of *Dasein.* They represent what philosopher Karl Jaspers tries to capture by his concept of *Weltorientierung* (orientation to the world). My model is based upon the idea that the subject living in this world glimpses and strives for transcendence, since he or she experiences the world of mere *Dasein* as being insufficient. Thus, the subject performs a transcendental act, which is of two kinds: negation and affirmation. In my model, these acts have been placed so as to occur consecutively on the temporal axis. (Lately, however, I am more inclined to think that they should instead be described by vectors leading in various directions from the *Dasein.* Also, I have realized that there might be several transcendental acts—in principle, an endless amount of them.)

Nevertheless, in my present model there are two basic types of such acts, the first of which is negation. This is the leap into emptiness often eloquently described by the existentialists, the Sartrean experience of Nothingness (*le Néant*). After this leap, the subject returns to his/her world, only to experience its objects as having lost some of their previous significations. Nevertheless, the subject does not linger in the existentialist anguish caused by its encounter with emptiness. Rather, he/she goes forth with another experience, which is of a contrary nature to the first. In this experience, the subject senses that the universe is full of meanings, what the gnostics called *pleroma,* or what Schelling (as well as the Russian philosopher Soloviev) termed "world soul" (*Weltseele*). The French philosopher Jean Wahl used the designation *trans-descendence* for the act of negation, and *trans-ascendence* for affirmation, or the experience of the universe as a plenitude. When the subject for a second time returns to his/her world of *Dasein* and creates signs, these are existential, in the sense that they reflect the subject's journey through transcendence (see Diagram 1 on p. 10).

It is essential that a theory of semiotics brings to light entirely new types of signs for investigation. Among them, one can conceive of signs that detach themselves from the world of *Dasein* and float in a gravity less, transcendental space, only so as to become reconnected with it. It is precisely in such a process of departing and returning that signs come into continuous motion; they are no longer fixed, ready-made objects, but are free to take shape in many completely new ways (as in Sartre's philosophy one is not satisfied with the mere principle of *'being-in-oneself'*, but is constantly changing, choosing oneself). On this view, what is interesting in semiotics are the states that both *precede* and *follow* the formation of signs.

On this basis, I have thus far been able to distinguish six new species of signs: (1) *pre-signs,* signs in the process of forming and shaping themselves; (2) *trans-signs,* which are signs in transcendence; (3) *act-signs,* those signs actualized in the world of *Dasein*; (4) *endo-* and *exo-signs,* which are signs in the dialectics of presence/absence; (5) *internal/external* signs; (6), and finally, *as-if-signs*—in German, *als ob Zeichen* (as Vaihinger calls them)—these are signs that should be read *as if* they were true.

In what follows, I shall ponder more closely what is intended here by the concept of *transcendence.* I first approach my topic by way of some criticisms that one may encounter in taking on such a task. Then I shall see what consequences the notion of transcendence might have for a new sign-theory.

CRITICAL ARGUMENTS

Each individual, society, and culture forms its own conception of transcendence, according to its unique spatial, temporal, and actorial situation. Such a conception of transcendence occurs inside the world, and is nothing but a kind of idealization or "virtualization" of the "subject" of *Dasein.* As such, it should not be confused with transcendence in the proper philosophical sense. We may further state that orientation to the world, the enlightening of existence, and, finally, metaphysics (the three essential moments of Karl Jaspers's philosophy) constitute steps along the way to actual transcendence. These categories of what Kant called "transcendental analytics" come into play such that the reality of *Dasein* is compared to a transcendental idea; for instance, that of truth, goodness, or beauty. This involves the desire to attain a more stable fulcrum for one's existence, since in *Dasein* everything is evanescent, ambiguous, all its pertinence mere appearance. Some sociologists, particularly Peter Berger and Thomas Luckmann (1994), tend to think that "transcendental" ideas are nothing but absolutizations, idealizations, and conceptualizations—what they call "reifications" of the social reality. A completely solitary person, for example, who each morning repeats a certain series of actions and behaviors, might say something like, "Well, here we are." Gradually, such a phrase becomes a sign or symbol of his activity. According to Berger and Luckmann, when one starts to believe that such a phrase has an independent existence without the action really taking place, then a kind of "transcendentalization" occurs. They think that "transcendence" is nothing but an abstraction that has become detached from the social reality.

In the same way, on the level of the individual, feminist semiotics has arrived at a theory of *corporeality.* According to Kristeva and other psychoanalytically-oriented semioticians, corporeality is the main site of human semiosis. It is the *khora,* which according to them is an autonomous realm of desires, gestures, and rhythms; and upon the *khora* is overlaid the symbolic order as a kind of repressive network. Viewed in relation to this symbolic network, we might conclude that the corporeal world of *Dasein* appears as the negation of transcendent semiosis. Transcendence would be something that comes from the "outside" or from "above," as an intrusion of the patriarchal order or the male-principle. Such a view—that is, the identification with the symbolic phallic principle—would provide our concept of transcendence with a negative content. In that case, the whole of transcendence—the most constant ideas that are external to the body—would appear as only a kind of projection of the body onto a more superior level, and in this manner, such ideational constants could be reasoned away.

The sociological and feminist models both reject transcendence as being an autonomous reality. Hence, those models belong to the category of "nothing-but" theories. One would think, however, that yet another conception of transcendence could emerge; namely, one might assume that the body takes on, as it were, a symbolic, virtual shape as the continuation of "real," physical communication (as Merleau-Ponty has shown). For instance, one may imagine buildings being constructed as a kind of virtual body. And in music, one could postulate that the performers form a sort of musico-imaginary "body" of the music they play. In a sense, the music becomes part of the musician, and he or she conveys precisely this musico-imaginary body to listeners via tonal signs. When the listener encounters the music, he/she hears the tones in relationship to his/her own body, and senses on this virtual somatic level whether the interpretation is pleasing or not. In such a case, the musical communication would be literally a transmission between two musico-imaginary bodies, from their "touching" of each other to a complete union. Is then such an imaginary body a kind of "transcendental being," which has greater universality and stability than a physical body? Undoubtedly, yes, since on this level we can communicate with temporally and spatially distant, "transcendental" musical bodies.

The process I have just detailed may well describe the formation of transcendence in a psychologically convincing way. Still, the concept of transcendence is not exhausted by it. Nor is my view of transcendence quite the same as that in Plato's doctrine of ideas; i.e., that the individual, society, and culture of *Dasein* are only reflections of some universal "form" of a unique individual, society and culture. What is crucial, in my view, is that such a transcendental idea has always emerged from the acts of negation and affirmation in relationship to its appearances in the world of *Dasein*. Negation and affirmation are semiotic operations by which the connection to transcendence is realized.

Another argument against the concept of transcendence concerns the question of how it can be investigated. A semiotician would no doubt think that it can be examined only by special, transcendental signs; that is, only insofar as it appears as a text. Naturally, a transcendental experience that a subject may have can manifest as a particular sign after negation and affirmation, but it can also appear as a particular illumination or special "flavor" of pre-existing signs or of those in the process of formation. Husserl's *noema* included expressly the whole intentional sense of a sign with all its nuances and overtones. In the same way, Peirce's *Firstness* encompassed reality in all its emotional, chaotic, and rich entirety.

Therefore, transcendence is not a concept of the "upstairs," so to speak, which graciously deigns to visit the more worldly moments of the "downstairs." Rather, transcendence occurs amidst the world of *Dasein* as its unexpected illumination. Even the most common everyday experience can suddenly (or even gradually) change into a transcendental one when it is compared to a transcendental idea. It occurs as a new illumination of a sign, object, or text of *Dasein*. Through negation or affirmation, such an experience is either reduced to the essentials, while behind it shimmers the transcendental essence, or a more profound meaning is added to it, which the everyday sign unexpectedly starts to convey.

Literature contains many portrayals of such a transcendental experience. In *The Brothers Karamazov,* for instance, Alyosha has such an experience when, under the starry night sky, he recognizes that the universe is filled with a transcendental meaning via affirmation. Something similar happens at the very end of Tolstoy's short story "The Death of Ivan Ilych." In the novel *Borderliners,* by the Danish writer Peter Høeg, a delinquent youngster in the boarding school for boys finally feels himself to be at "home," thus ending his restless searching with an affirmation. As another example, the narrator-hero of Proust's novel *Remembrance of Things Past* suddenly realizes the emptiness of sign systems and the practices of society, and conceives of what Henri Bergson understood by his concept of *le moi profond,* which was only disturbed by external communication. Transcendence is attained at the moment of autocommunication; although apparently when one enters a dialogue, one has already taken a step toward transcendence by moving toward the Other. According to Emmanuel Levinas, transcendence is the same as Otherness, *l'autre,* which one experiences as the negation of the Same—which psychologically can be something positive or "euphoric"—or as the affirmation of the Other, by the complete acceptance of Otherness (Levinas 1971: 24–27). In music, too, we often encounter transcendental moments, in the sense of affirmation, of negation, or of both consecutively:

Transcendence as affirmation: Beethoven, Op. 111 (Arietta, bar 118) or Liszt, Sonata in B minor, the perfect triads at the end.

Transcendence as negation: Sibelius, Fourth Symphony, Movement IV: O–R, the "chaotic" moment.

Transcendence as negation/affirmation: Ernst Chausson, String Quartet, the section before the return of the Adagio theme at the end of the Finale (score nos. 60–61).

Transcendence as a "sought-for object of value": Bartók (to whom folklore represented a transcendental sphere, which he tried to attain but without ever finding it completely); parlando rubato.

Transcendence as a "lost object," the longing for transcendence: Bohuslav Martinů (the string cantilenas in the upper register: "show me the heavens").

I want to emphasize that my view on transcendence is a semiotic and philosophical one; although in order to illustrate it, I use psychological, literary, musical, aesthetic, and anthropological cases. Nothing would be more misleading than to identify semiotic "transcendence" with, for instance, "transcendental meditation," shamanistic practices, astral projection, or psychedelic experiences. My theory has nothing to do with such things.

TRANSITIONAL SIGNS

Some time ago I became familiar with the work of Danish semiotician Jørgen Dines Johansen, who has started to develop further Peirce's sign-theory. Johansen begins with the concepts of dynamic and immediate objects. Then he deviates from the semiotics of signification in a strict sense, in the direction of a semiotics of communication. He does this by taking into account the human subject behind the signs—that is, the utterer as well as the interpreter. I find in his efforts something analogous to my own processive sign-theory. Also similar to my thinking is the new research by an American semiotician, Floyd Merrell, especially in his book *Peirce's Semiotics Now*. There he announces that he will study the life of signs: "I highlight *processes* in order to suggest the idea of ongoing change, the incessant movement, and even the growth, of signs" (1995: vii). Encouraged by these ideas, I have continued my elucidation of the concept of transcendence.

A situation in which transcendence would appear as a kind of transference of signs, as a transition, a shift between two *Dasein*s, could be described as in diagram 2. Its fictive, intuitive counterpart could be the sharing of signs, for instance, between two style-periods of art, or between two historical phases of the same society, or between two temporal moments in the life of an individual. In any case, what is involved is the infiltration of signs from *Dasein* 1 into *Dasein* 2:

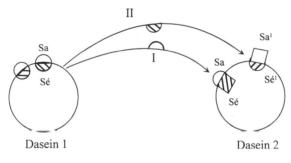

DIAGRAM 2

In this diagram, the roman numeral I means that the same motif (as signifier) is provided with a new signified in the course of history, when a shift takes place from one phase or style period (1) to a new phase or period (2); for instance, from Viennese classicism to Biedermeyer, or from realism to symbolism, or from modernism to postmodernism. On the level of society and culture, this occurs when one is transferred from organic to mechanical solidarity, from a monological communication to a dialogical one, from an ethnosemiotic state to a sociosemiotic one.

Roman numeral II on the diagram indicates that the same signified, or idea, yields a new "concretization" over time. Then, from the point of view of *Dasein* 2, the situation may be as if these signifieds had leapt forth from Nothingness as kinds of Platonic ideas or their token manifestations. Basically, of course, they constitute "ideas" and "signifieds" a posteriori.

With respect to *Dasein* 2, the signifieds are conceived as detached from their original world, particularly as stripped of their *das Man* surface (this last expression describes signs that adapt themselves to prevailing conditions of communication at the cost of their contents, their signification). They may be interpreted in *Dasein* 2 in a completely different way, such that their original connections are forgotten; they may even appear as entirely transcendental ideas.

Yet the essential thing is what happens in between, that is, during the shift from *Dasein* 1 to *Dasein* 2. Can the distance from the original signifier/signified to the transferred sign be described with Peircean categories such as similarity, contiguity, conventionality, or symbolicity? This would be the emergence of *inner* iconicity, indexicality, and so on as a function of history or time.

My hypothesis is that the so-called modalities (as defined semiotically by Greimas) carry and support the transcendental "journey" of signs to Otherness and then back to Sameness. In such cases, one has to distinguish between two kinds of modalities: (1) *sending modalities,* which force or propel the signs toward transcendence, and (2) *receiving modalities.* Yet it must be noted that *Dasein* can resist the detachment of signs from its *Ground.* This occurs as a particular modal situation in which the overtaking or possessing modalities are dominant. Furthermore, *Dasein* can, by means of certain repelling modalities, later block or resist the return of signs that have left their *Dasein.* Such modalities prevent the re-attachment to *Dasein* of these signs, which once were floating in transcendence. Or the rejecting modalities may distort and transform those signs according to their own worldly situation. This happens, for instance, when a philosophical, scientific, or artistic invention that has been elaborated outside the unifying *das Man* principle of *Dasein* is not accepted, and thus cannot influence the *Dasein* except in a falsified form (for instance, by being "mediatized" or ideologized):

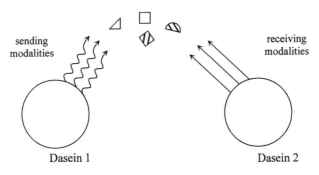

DIAGRAM 3

This situation comes rather close to Greimas's model, which distinguishes competence on the sender side, performance on the receiver side, and thereafter, interpretative competence in the recoding of the message by the receiver.

My own model goes further by positing an intermediate state in which the sending modalities no longer operate and the receiving modalities do not yet function. In that state, the signs operate on the basis of the principle of "modalized modalization," i.e., of modalities embedded in the signs themselves. Once set on its way, a sign does not arrive unless compatible modalities are waiting for it, modalities that attract and pull the sign back to the world of *Dasein*.

(At this point one may ask, Is the carrier of modalities a collective agent, or are the modalities of an individual and a collection the same? Is some agent supporting signs during the transcendence? Here we recall that the travel of signs in transcendence has been described in philosophy by, among others, Schopenhauer with his modality of the 'will', as well as by Jean-Claude Coquet with his concept of *meta-vouloir*.)

In any case, the lifespan of signs in transcendence probably depends not only on the strength of the sending modalities, but also on the functioning of modalities embedded in the signs themselves. The appeal of signs makes them return to the sphere of *Dasein*.

Let us take an example from music history: the various phases in the reception of Bach's *St. Matthew Passion*:

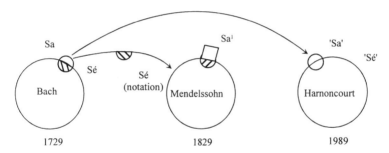

DIAGRAM 4. *St. Matthew Passion*

In this diagram *Sa* = *St. Matthew Passion* in the time of Bach; *Sa1* = *St. Matthew Passion* as "found" by Mendelssohn and performed by him; and *'Sa'* = the effort to reconstruct the original *Sa* as authentically as possible.

In the time intervals between its concretizations, the *St. Matthew Passion* exists as notation, as a score, in a latent form, as it were, without complete semiosis or connection of *Sa* (signifier) and *Sé* (signified). (The abbreviations of the French terms are used here: *Sa* = *signifiant*, signifier; and *Sé* = *signifié*, signified).

METAMODALITIES AND TRANSCENDENTAL IDEAS

Is transcendence, then, a kind of social and conceptual vacuum? In a sense, yes. For signs can exist as physical objects yet not exist semiotically. For instance, physical landscapes have always existed, but landscape poetry did not appear until the beginning of the nineteenth century—when such poetry prompted what Ruskin would later censure as the "pathetic fallacy"; that is, landscapes were seen as being "modalized" by human subjects. Therefore, the journey of a sign is an invisible event, not the physical removal of a sign from place A (*Dasein* 1) to place B (*Dasein* 2).

Yet analytic philosophy operates with just such an empty transcendence; the examples by Peirce, for example, prove the ahistorical nature of pragmaticism as regards both the individual and society. By contrast, in existential semiotics one supposes transcendence to be in motion and inhabited by metamodalities.

If modalities do exist in transcendence, then what kinds are they, and how do they function in relation to the modalities of *Dasein*?

One may speak of so-called metaphysical modalities, i.e., modalities that are valid outside the world of *Dasein*. As I mentioned before, these are of two kinds: sending modalities—which push, launch, thrust out signs from the world of *Dasein* to its surrounding infinity—and those which tempt, attract, or call signs back into the world of *Dasein*. Clearly all communication over long distances constitutes this kind of transcendental transmission, in which the sender of a message cannot know its receiver. Yet is it not true that all communication is like that? Even the briefest interval of time can change the postulated destinatee into a completely different person from what was assumed by the destinator. It seems that all communication, all sending of signs, presents a risk, a leap into the unknown.

The task of the modalities is to carry this leap from the Fichtean entity of *ich* ('I') to that of *nicht-ich* ('not-I'). Greimas spoke about endo- and exotactic modalities. This could now be interpreted in a more philosophical way as a metaphysical distinction between those two species of modalities.

Likewise some distinctions in Kantian philosophy come close to my own, but there is a difference between the "transcendence" of Kant and that of my existential semiotics. Kant ponders whether there are synthetic, a priori concepts. In contrast, the starting point of existential semiotics is the dissolution of a posteriori notions and principles to such a level of generality and abstraction that they seem to assume the role of a priori entities.

What is an existential moment like in the world of *Dasein*? It is such that existence *simulates* transcendence. But if transcendence is the same as Levinas's "infinity," then one may ask, Are there any modalities? And what are the signs in this state of infinity and negation?

Signs are seldom totally empty, 'not-being', and just as rarely are they full, completely affirmative. Most often they are only partially transcendent. A completely transcendental sign would no doubt be identified with some idea. Let us presume that three "ideas" obtain in transcendence: the True, the Beautiful, and the Good (that is to say, the epistemic, aesthetic, and moral principles). When they are realized in existence, or when existence starts to simulate them, it is quite possible that only in such a way are these ideas modalized in the world of *Dasein*. Do the ideas themselves have any modalities? Yes—as kinds of metamodalities, which have been emptied of the desire that once launched them. There-fore, there is 'will', 'can', 'know', 'must'—all these modalities *an sich,* in them-selves—as kinds of meta-'will', meta-'know', meta-'can', and so on.

These metamodalities correspond to the Kantian transcendental analytic: They are freed from *Sinnlichkeit* or sensuality, and become categories of under-standing (*Verstehen*). Metamodalities can be connected with each other and with signs in a different way than are the more "psychological" modalities of *Dasein,* which are closer to man's social and corporeal needs and inseparably bound to them.

When the Good, the Beautiful, and the True appear in an existential situa-tion, something occurs that we experience as though it were necessary, as though "it must be"—not from any "outer" necessity, however, but as if from some "in-ner" obligation. At the same time, however, we sense that such a phenomenon is at every moment free to take shape as it does. In other words, we encounter si-multaneously 'must' and unlimited 'will'. In an existential situation, one 'knows', 'can', 'will', and 'must do'/'be' in a Good, Beautiful, and True manner.

In negative transcendence, the previous sign-complex dissipates or dissolves. It is necessary that we investigate all possible kinds of negation—when a sign detaches and distances itself from its connections to *Dasein*—on both the indi-vidual and social levels. Correspondingly, one has to ask, What is affirmation? How does it happen that, from universal meaningfulness, something oozes or leaks, as it were, into the signs in its proximity? As a sign comes closer to the core of affirmation, it gradually is filled with meaning.

Why do we have a temporal articulation in our model? That is to say, why is the experience of plenitude possible only *after* the experiencing of Nothingness? Are they not rather like two lines leading in different directions from *Dasein,* or like two alternative states of consciousness, which tinge the world with two dif-ferent colors, one with shades of sinister despair, and the other with hues of bright hopefulness?

FROM GENERATION TO TRANSILLUMINATION

As mentioned earlier, Karl Jaspers speaks about three phases of philosophizing, which he calls *world-orientation, existence-illumination,* and *metaphysics.* Philoso-phizing concerns itself with *Dasein;* illumination—with existence; and metaphys-ics—with transcendence. In Jaspers's view, man is led to postulate the concept of transcendence because of his dissatisfaction with mere *Dasein.* In the world of *Dasein,* everything is incomplete and perishable. Narrative models reflect pre-cisely this property. For in narrative, the action is catalyzed by an "initial lack" (as Vladimir Propp describes it)—the fact that the subject is "disjuncted" from an object, which it desires and searches for (as Greimas puts it). Applying Jas-pers, one could state that most so-called classical semiotics investigates the world of *Dasein* as such, while existence appears as a kind of marginal semiotics, and nothing is said of transcendence. Therefore, the analysis of *Dasein* could be identified with the explanation of phenomena, and existence-illumination correlated with understanding them (in the sense of Lucien Goldmann and von Wright).

Classical semiotics could be articulated in a similar way. "Semiotics with a world-orientation" is constituted by all those semiotic fields that study objects and texts, including those which construe subjects and thoughts and behaviors as texts and "signs." In this sense, even Peirce and Saussure belong to this category, as do those researchers who generally identify semiotics with communication. Yet there are still other combinations, such as shifts from world-orientation and *Dasein* analysis to existence-illumination, as we find in the work of Kristeva and Barthes. Leaving aside Jaspers's middle phase, Lévi-Strauss's model in *Mythologiques* combines world-orientation and metaphysics: Mythical systems are "transcendent" in the sense that they are not meaningful in the consciousness of an individual (a typically structuralist attitude). Greimas dwells completely on the level of world-orientation, but his modalities open the gate to existence-illumination. (Greimas did not explore this himself, but it remains an open possibility for expansion of his theory.) Lotman's analysis, in turn (see Uspenskij et al. 1975), is a kind of existence-illumination of cultures in relation to their world-orientation.

In any case, semiotic transcendence is not the same as the "possible worlds" posited by logical-analytic philosophy, where in an actorless, spaceless, and time-less state one scrutinizes all possible variations of phenomena. Transcending is not the same as playing with "possible worlds" or with von Wright's counterfactual arguments in *Norm and Action*—in the sense of speculating about that which might have happened. According to von Wright, one can imagine what might have happened only on the basis of what has already happened. To para-phrase Jaspers, we can anticipate something—that is, we can see the possible choices in a given situation—only if we can remember what has already hap-pened. With this argument one could defend the necessity of a historical dimen-sion: Without history there is no freedom, since there can be freedom only if we know how things *could be,* and we know that only on the basis of recalling how they *have been.* Nevertheless, in addition to Jaspers's two kinds of transcend-ing—remembering and anticipating—there is, in my view, a purely imagina-tive consciousness of the "now" moment that is transcendent, creative thinking. Man's creativity cannot be restricted to only that which has already been. Other-wise, nothing new could ever emerge.

Moreover, semiotic transcendence always remains connected to *Dasein* and existence. In fact, existence is situated on the borderline between *Dasein* and transcendence: Existence is the transcendence that has become present in *Dasein,* that "place" where subjects live. According to Jaspers, a philosophical method requires that each level be "traversed" (*Überschreiten*). Why should the same not be required of a semiotic method? Among other ways, in the form of a generative model?

In fact, the traditional semiotic notion of a generative grammar—in which some sign-complex is generated, level by level, from a deep structure—such a notion appears in a new light in our existential semiotics. I am thinking here of constructs such as Lotman's top-down model: symbols–semantics–syntax–metrics–morphemes–phonemes (see Uspenskij et al.); Greimas's generative course; Chomsky's tree structures; and the like.

For instance, if our task is to research artistic sign complexes, the parsing and explication of their style constitutes *Dasein* analysis. In turn, when one examines the message of an individual artist or work, one is engaged in existence-illumination. What is a semiotic "existence-illumination," in which an individual subject expresses him or herself? A classical semiotician would immediately reject such a possibility and argue that an individual, say an artist, is always possessed by the code systems that he or she employs, and thus always speaks according to their automatisms.

Yet it is essential that there always remains a difference or gap between the existing subject and the "sign" or means of expression that he or she uses. In other words, existence-illumination can take place, but the expression of one's existence can succeed in a more or less complete way. Sometimes it fails; not all signs perform their existential task. (In fact, a paradigm of its own is formed by the existentially unsuccessful signs, which can be read sometimes from the signs themselves, and sometimes from other auxiliary signs, the surrounding intertexts.)

Following the linguistic model, the levels of generation in painting are those of iconography, representation, composition, metonymy relations (e.g., repetitions), figures, color (grades of darkness and lightness). But in our new, existential model those levels are not consecutive but *superimposed* phases, ways of looking at the painting. The four lowest levels are *khora* relationships, that is, pre-linguistic, "semiotic" in the Kristevan sense.

From this nucleus one might develop a new type of method that would be at the same time semiotic-generative and existential-transcendental. That is to say, the aforementioned levels can be distinguished in all sign-complexes, starting with their strong *Firstness* impression, and then becoming more rarefied and sublimated toward semantics and symbolisms. This process involves something like the five superimposed codes applied by Roland Barthes in his famous study *S/Z* (which have already been taken from literature and applied to music by Robert Samuels in his study of Mahler's Sixth Symphony). What is essential is that these levels or codes be like transparencies, laid one upon the other, through which an art work or text appears. Here we must ask, Is there something like a text, as such, which would constitute the kernel, the invariable substance that carries all these codes and interpretations? Is not the text itself the same as all these interpretations, and nothing else?

What is involved here is a kind of transillumination method that proceeds in the opposite direction from a scientific, microscopic examination. In that case, one gradually enlarges an object by microscope, and this brings into sight ever new "endo-semiotic" levels, which are not "conscious" of each other. In the present case, however, one starts from the minimal unit—the surface of a sign—and proceeds toward *macroscopic* levels, eventually reaching the most spiritual, non-material levels. In the language of my new semiotics: The starting point is the surface of the text, as a part of the world of *Dasein* where a strong sense of existentiality prevails (described by Peirce with his concept of *Firstness*). The trans-illumination method means a shift toward higher levels until one finally reaches transcendence, with its ideas and metamodalities. On the highest level—after those of representation, iconography, ideological connections, aesthetic allegories, and symbolics—there looms transcendence detached from *Dasein*. On this level, a sign complex is seen as part of a broader unity, which is not the same as the semiosphere, pictosphere, tonosphere, or gestosphere of *Dasein,* but is rather a kind of transcendental continuum.

NEGATION AND AFFIRMATION

The transfer from one level to another takes place by means of two logical operations. The first is that of negation, in which the present level (where one is) is perceived as being insufficient, incomplete. Next comes affirmation, where one reaches toward a new level and its possibilities by affirming them, by seeing their distant outlines through the deficiencies of the previous level, as if they were a promise held out by another, deeper frame of reference. It is this act of comparison that yields the operation of "reduction" or negation, and that of affirmation, which consists of "supplementing," of investing signs with a new meaning. The sign of the old level is "filled" with the meaning of the new level. One shifts gradually from the world-orientation of *Dasein* toward the inner transcendence of *Dasein* (here there are parallels with Freud's id/superego, Lotman's culture/non-culture, Greimas's topos/heterotopos, Kristeva's *khora*/symbolic order, Chomsky's deep level/surface). Inner transcendence can be realized in two directions: in the direction of either the surface or the depths, either close or far, toward presence or absence. But this inner transcendence is not the same as genuine transcendence; although, as a particular operation of negation, it can help us in our movement toward transcendence proper. Transcendence in the true sense is absolute, denoting absolute negation and absolute affirmation.

Thus, from the point of view of a transcendental subject, negation/affirmation appears either as a movement "away from" or "toward." Yet what is most pertinent is the "toward" which one reaches for, or from which one recedes. In such a process we obtain the following cases:

1. the movement away from, or negation of, *Dasein*; but at the same time comes—

2. the acceptance of Nothingness, affirmation;

3. the return from Nothingness to *Dasein;* this is the abandoning of Nothingness, i.e., its negation; but at the same time—

4. it is the (partial) affirmation of *Dasein;*

5. the movement away from *Dasein,* or its negation (and this is already in a
   sense the negation of the once-negated), and toward affirmation; this involves the affirmation of affirmation;

6. the return from affirmation, when it represents the negation, i.e., the rejection of plenitude; but at the same time this is a new affirmation of
   Dasein (or possibly the creation of a new *Dasein*).

Altogether we have six logical phases, in which signs either change their shape,
form, color, atmosphere, *noema;* or entirely new signs are created to convey precisely these operations or transcendental acts. Thus, we have here two parallel
processes: (1) the metamorphoses of pre-existing, already-fixed signs, in the six-
phase process just described; and (2) the creation of new signs that reflect and
follow the aforementioned movement.

The first-mentioned signs are *existentialized* signs, whereas the latter ones
are properly existential signs. How do these two species of sign relate to each
other? How do the old but existentialized signs relate to the new signs, which are
existential from the moment of their birth? Can one also imagine that some
signs, in the historic process and tumult of the world of *Dasein,* lose their existentiality? In other words, does *Dasein* 3 no longer experience the existential
signs of *Dasein* 1 as existentials in the proper sense; is *Dasein* 3 no longer able to
"existentialize" them?

The situation is made more complex by the fact that existential and existentialized signs must live side by side with non-existential signs, which do not possess this quality at all, and which do not participate in the process described earlier (that of going from existence toward transcendence).

In fact, one can speak about existence only in the cases of those double operations; i.e., negation of negation and affirmation of affirmation, as well as negation of affirmation and affirmation of negation, in which our transcendental
subject returns to his original world of *Dasein* after his/her "journey."

In any case, the movement from existence to transcendence is prompted and
sustained by the dissatisfaction of the subject, by his/her aspiration toward in-
variance. In life one is dissatisfied with the fact that everything perishes. Therefore, one seeks a more stable ground for one's existence. The same holds true for
the systems of symbols he/she has created. Texts open themselves to unlimited
interpretation, proceeding from their concrete existence toward transcendence.

One can easily see how existential semiotics, which underlines the role of a
subject, is a counter-reaction to positivist semiotics, wherein the structuralist
world view reflects the fusion of a subject to the external cosmic order. The problem of freedom and determination is also central in semiotics. The subject can

affirm and negate, but it is also subordinated to unavoidable and absolute transcendence in the temporal process of *Dasein*. The subject has to undergo the experiences of absolute negation and affirmation whether it wants to or not. Absolute negation and affirmation can be conceived only by abandoning oneself to their power. They can be either accepted or rejected. It is here where the determinism or freedom of existence lies, for the temporal process is deterministic. In this context, we should recall that Diderot and d'Alembert pondered the freedom of the 'will', and their questioning is still pertinent today with regard to existential semiotics.

A SEMIOTIC ACT AND EVENT

To conclude, I want to examine the operations of affirmation and negation, particularly in the light of Hegel's *Science of Logic*. Hegel can be interpreted in the "modern" semiotic context in the following way:

The course of logic—which is that of 'being' and its negation—describes the transformation of man's symbolic world. Or rather, it describes the semiotic subject itself in such a way that one phase, *Dasein*, dissolves into the following one, which, so to speak, "negates" the previous phase. In this way, these phases "peel off" one from the other like a series of endless transformations or "hatchings." *Dasein* 1 negates *Dasein* 2, which looms behind it and which the subject "affirms" or accepts; but it also carries in itself the outburst of *Dasein* 3, or its "dissolution" (*Aufhebung*). What is involved is, of course, not a change of the objective universe of signs. But as a part of the semiosis, signs undergo a continuous process of negation and affirmation, which moves and pushes them forward. Hence, in this model one is always on the way to Otherness, since the series of metamorphoses has no end, and the *Dasein*s blend into each other.

Hegel writes this about his notion of essence:

> The truth of being is essence. Being is immediate. Since knowledge wants to reach the truth about what being is, as such and for itself, it does not stop, but penetrates through it, presuming that there is still something else behind this being, which is not being itself, and presuming that this background constitutes the truth of being. . . . Essence lies between being and concept, and forms their middle ground. Essence is being in itself and for itself, since its general attribute is to emerge from being and to function as the first negation of being. . . . Being is nothingness in the essence.

Hegel's concept of essence can first be construed in the Peircean way, as a kind of interpretant, which shimmers as a kind of "post-sign" reflecting the "act-sign." In such a construal, we take into account only the situation in which a subject observes the already-fixed sign—such that in comparison to its "interpretant" it appears to be transparent, since behind it one can perceive the interpretant as a kind of "transcendental idea."

However, what about the situation before the sign is fixed into an act-sign? In this phase, the subject has within itself the "essence," which it wants to actualize or concretize into the act-sign. In other words, the subject conceives of a certain transcendental idea—the True, the Good, or the Beautiful—and this idea serves him/her as a kind of pre-interpretant, or "pre-sign," as I call it. Such a pre-sign is likewise something transcendental, i.e., not-existing before it is brought into being as a recognizable object of *Dasein*. In fact, in that case, the term "interpretant" should be replaced by another more active appellation, since what is involved is not the interpretation of anything already determined and clear-cut, but rather the production of some new sign. We should instead call it an *enunciant* or *utterant,* that is to say, a sign by which the utterance or enunciate is created:

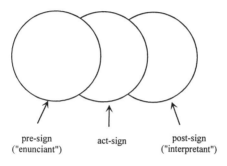

pre-sign   act-sign   post-sign
("enunciant")   ("interpretant")

DIAGRAM 5

A semiotic act occurs as the production of an act-sign by means of the help of a pre-sign or enunciant/utterant; or the act takes place as the interpretation of the act-sign by means of the help of the post-sign or interpretant. After all, the sign itself proves to be a rather ephemeral entity lying between these two "transcendences." If one thinks that pre-signs are somehow indefinite, unformed or shapeless signs, then one is mistaken: As transcendental ideas, pre-signs are in some cases completely determined and absolute. Only their concretization is approximate—which is to say that the semiotic act cannot always reach this transcendental idea. Proust's "lost fatherland" is not always found in a musician's performance; in moral action, the idea of the Good is not always fulfilled in an ethical act; the idea of Truth does not always manifest in an utterance, but may become a lie or a secret.

In this light, negation and affirmation can be reinterpreted in many ways. Absolute negation and affirmation do determine, a priori, the course of the semiosis—a subject cannot do anything about it. The semiosis unfolds according to a certain logic, in which 'being' creates a 'not-being' that is dissolved into the subsequent 'being'. This occurs along with the temporal process, almost like an objective phenomenon (and we recall here that Peirce believed his sign catego-

ries were an objective reality). Nevertheless, as a Fichtean, self-determining subject, one can decide to oppose this process or to accept it, situating oneself as a
part of it, riding atop its dialectical waves. In his treatise *Die Grundlagen der ge-
samten Wissenschaftslehre,* Fichte says this:

> *Das Ich setzt sich selbst, und es ist, vermöge dieses blossen Setzens durch sich*
> *selbst; und umgekehrt: Das Ich ist, und setzt sein Sein, vermöge seines blossen Se-*
> *ins. Es ist zugleich das Handelnde, und das Produkt der Handlung.* (Fichte 1996:
> 218)

> [The 'I' establishes itself, and, due to mere self-determination, it is; and contrar-
> ily: The 'I' is and establishes its 'being' only on the basis of its own 'being'. It is
> simultaneously an active person and the product of this activity.]

Fichte's definition also aptly describes the existential-semiotic subject. According to von Wright (in his treatise *Norm and Action*), we might say that the course
of semiosis which Hegelian logic depicts represents the occurrence of an event;
whereas, the latter activity—an individual perspective or view on this occurrence—would constitute the semiotic act in the proper sense. The myths of antiquity provide us with many illustrations of semiotic acts in which a subject retains for him/herself the power of self-determination. When Orpheus turns back
and perishes, this can be interpreted as the denial of temporal processes, as their
negation, and, in this sense, as a "semiotic act."

Likewise, the comparison of a sign to the transcendental idea in front of or
behind it yields either negation or affirmation. In a sense, the change of the pre-
sign into an act-sign means the abandoning of the pre-sign, its negation in favor
of the act-sign. Correspondingly, the comparison of the act-sign to the post-sign
means that the act-sign is negated in favor of a more complete idea looming behind it. On the other hand, the concretization of the pre-sign into an act-sign can
also be seen as its affirmation in the perceptual world of *Dasein*. Through such
concretization, the bare and empty world of "Object-ness," or *Gegenständlich-
keit,* becomes something existential—it receives a motivation, a ground for its
semiotic 'being'; in a word, it becomes significant. In the same way, when we compare an act-sign—the deficient, unsatisfactory object—to the transcendental
idea of its "essence," then this act-sign is, so to say, filled by the more profound,
essential meaning, a transcendental idea. Thus, when receiving an act-sign, we in
fact affirm the post-sign standing behind it.

The generation of signs, in relation to transcendence and existentiality, is
thus a bi-directional process. Jasperian existence-illumination means precisely
that an act-sign is understood as a mediate state between two transcendences
and is viewed in their light. Actually, Peirce's three categories describe the movement from an act-sign to a post-sign. (In this case, the act-sign would be a *First*,
which, following Peirce, could be strongly existential, like a melody, notwith-
standing the fact that we would not yet be able in any way to analyze it.) Yet the
movement also takes place in the other direction. By this we mean the process

before the *Firstness,* where departing from a kind of "quasi-*Thirdness*" and "quasi-*Secondness,*" we arrive at the *First.*

After studying Hegel, Peirce realized the movement of semiosis between existence and transcendence. He understood how the 'beings' of various degrees dissolve into each other when one is shifted from *First* to *Second,* and from *Second* to *Third.* Yet for the pragmatic Peirce, everything was a posteriori, after experience and practice. Kant, too, started from experience; but in his transcendental analytics, he came to examine those categories that enable such an experience. Structuralists have followed in the steps of Kant, when by means of their generative grammars they have searched only for those mechanisms or rules by which pre-signs become act-signs (that is, how they are transferred from a deep structure to the surface). Even the semiotic square of Greimas can be "Hegelianized"—it can be used to portray the processes of sign negations and affirmations as the function of time. In my work in musical semiotics, I have tried to show how a composer can utilize the semiotic square in order to create an individual message. The next step would be to study how situations—musical or otherwise—function as arenas of sign negations and affirmations.

REFERENCES

Barthes, Roland. 1970. *S/Z.* Paris: Editions du Seuil.
Berger, Peter L., and Thomas Luckmann. 1994. *Todellisuuden sosiaalinen rakentuminen* [The Construction of Social Reality]. Finnish translation by Vesa Raiskila. Helsinki: Gaudeamus.
Fichte, J. G. 1996. *Fichte.* Ausgewählt und vorgestellt von Günter Schulte. Hrsg. von Peter Sloterdijk. München: Diederichs.
Greimas, A. J. 1982. *Pariisin semioottisen koulukunnan esseitä.* Ed. Eero Tarasti. Jyväskylä: Jyväskylän yliopisto. Taidekasvatus, julkaisu 6 (moniste).
Hegel, G. F. 1989. "Logiikan tiede I ja II." Finnish translation by Eero Tarasti. *Synteesi* 1–2/89 and 3/89: 2–11 and 103–122.
Heinämaa, Sara. 1996. *Ele, tyyli ja sukupuoli. Merleau-Pontyn ja Beauvoirin ruumiinfenomenologia ja sen merkitys sukupuolikysymykselle* [Gesture, Style and Gender: The Phenomenology of the Body in Merleau-Ponty and Beauvoir and Its Meaning to the Gender Problematics]. Helsinki: Gaudeamus.
Høeg, Peter. 1957. *Borderliners.* Trans. Barbara Haveland. New York: Farrar, Straus and Giroux, 1994.
———. 1993. *Smilla's Sense of Snow.* Trans. Tina Nunnally. New York: Farrar Straus and Giroux.
Jaspers, Karl. 1948. *Philosophie.* Berlin, Göttingen, Heidelberg: Springer Verlag.
Johansen, Jørgen Dines. 1993. *Dialogic Semiosis: An Essay on Signs and Meaning.* Bloomington: Indiana University Press.
Kant, Immanuel. 1968. *Kritik der reinen Vernunft.* Stuttgart: Philipp Reclam Jun.
Lévi-Strauss, Claude. 1964–1971. *Mythologiques I-IV.* Paris: Plon.
Levinas, Emmanuel. 1971. *Totalité et infini: Essai sur l'extériorité.* Paris: Kluwer Academic.

Merrell, Floyd. 1995. *Peirce's Semiotics Now: A Primer.* Toronto: Canadian Scholar's Press.
Proust, Marcel. 1934. *Remembrance of Things Past.* 2 vols. Trans. C. K. Scott Moncreiff. New York: Random House.
Samuels, Robert. 1995. *Mahler's Sixth Symphony: A Study in Musical Semiotics.* Cambridge and New York: Cambridge University Press.
Sebeok, Thomas A. 1991. *A Sign Is Just a Sign.* Bloomington: Indiana University Press.
Tarasti, Eero. 1979. *Myth and Music.* Approaches to Semiotics 51. Berlin: Mouton de Gruyter.
———. 1994. *A Theory of Musical Semiotics.* Bloomington: Indiana University Press. (In French: *Sémiotique musicale,* trans. Bernard Dublanche. Collection Nouveaux Actes Sémiotiques. Limoges: Presses Universitaires de Limoges, 1996.)
———. 1996. *Heitor Villa-Lobos.* Jefferson, N.C.: McFarland Publishers.
Taylor, Charles. 1975. *Hegel.* Cambridge: Cambridge University Press.
Tolstoi, Leo. 1981. *The Death of Ivan Iliych.* Trans. Lynn Solotaroff, with an introduction by Ronald Blythe. Toronto, New York: Bantam Books, 1981.
Uspenskij, Boris, Vjaceslav Ivanov, V. N. Toporov, and A. M. Pjatigorskij. 1975. *Theses on the Semiotic Study of Culture.* Lisse: Peter de Ridder.
Vaihinger, Hans. 1920. *Die Philosophie des Als ob. System der theoretischen, praktischen und religiösen Fiktionen der Menschheit auf Grund eines idealistischen Positivismus.* Leipzig: Felix Meiner.
von Wright, Georg Henrik. 1963. *Norm and Action: A Logical Enquiry.* London: Routledge & Kegan Paul.

3

Endo-/Exogenic Signs, Fields, and Worlds

In my career as a semiotician, I have reached the conclusion that probably one of the most essential philosophical issues concerning all sign functions and activities is the following: Are the signs in the reality around us and in us created by ourselves, or do they come to us from outside, as objective entities, independent of ourselves and our activities? Of course, this is also the perpetual problem of the subjective and objective.

When this question was taking shape in my mind, some reflections on knowledge and intelligence in general led me to the following axiom: The more we invest our intelligence outside ourselves, "objectivize" it into various semiotic products, machines, computers, media, and the like, the less intelligence there remains for oneself. Correspondingly, the less "intelligence" there is in our surroundings, the more there is within ourselves. This explains why, for example, the meditations of a church father who has spent his whole life in the desert still have pertinence and actuality even to contemporary man. It also explains why we are still fascinated by certain mythological texts: They were created under conditions in which the human mind was left to "communicate with itself," to use the well-known phrase by Claude Lévi-Strauss. In light of this hypothesis, we can understand why people of the media age, bound to their computers and internets, can reason more stupidly than, say, German speculative philosophers of the nineteenth century, who created powerful systems of being, vision, and prophecy. Reading such philosophers remains rewarding, although their knowledge was much more limited than that of the contemporary European high school student.

It took some time, however, before I realized that these problems were also connected with a new theory of mine called "existential semiotics." More particularly, the issues I was pondering resonated with concepts on which Thomas A. Sebeok had lectured, and whose precise formulation is found in an article by Thure von Uexküll, Werner Geigges, and Jörg M. Herrmman on "Endosemiosis." In that essay, endosemiosis is defined simply as the transmission of signs within a living organism. At the same time, claim the authors, endosemiotic sign processes are directly linked with the environment of the living organism. As early as the turn of century, Jakob von Uexküll, an Estonian biologist and physician, coined two crucial notions: the *Umwelt,* which refers to the subjective, phenomenal world of an organism, the world of the 'self', in contrast to the *Umgebung,* the organism's actual physical surroundings. The semiotic consequences of this distinction are twofold: (1) Animals and humans are woven into a network of sign processes that connect them with their environment while protecting them by transposing this environment, according to its subjective meaning, into the Umwelt. This last is ultimately the same as what Greimas understood as *le monde natural,* which is anything other than a "natural" world, but is rather an already-semiotized, living world. (2) These signs are of a private nature; that is, they can be perceived only by the encoding subject—they are mere "noise" to all others.

Thure von Uexküll goes on to state that "exosemiotic sign processes which transform the objective environment into subjective universes or individual realities require endosemiotic processes which build up the immunologic and neural 'counterworlds' or 'inner worlds' in the animal or human body." With this he introduces another concept, that of "exosemiosis." From here on von Uexküll develops a theory of the meaning that emerges from interaction between the endogenic and exogenic. For instance, if there is a mouth (an endogenic unit) there must be food (exogenic); if there is a foot, there has to be ground; etc. Consequently, what is called the *signified* of a sign does not exist as such without this constant interaction (here we have the pragmatic principle analyzed by American semioticians from George Herbert Mead to Charles Morris).

Next von Uexküll ponders the problem of the "somebody," to whom, in Peirce's formulation, "a sign stands for something in some respect or capacity." From this he arrives at the principles of the semiotic 'self' and 'not-self'. As early as the level of cells, there prevails a principle of 'self', upon which is based man's immunological system, that is, his ability to eliminate harmful viruses from the organism. Altogether, his principle of the 'self' passes through four levels of integration in the endosemiotic process, starting from the lowest level of genes and enzymes and their "dialogue," up to communication among cells (second level), to the combination of cells via electric signals to organs in the nerve systems (third level), and from there to the process of translation (fourth level), in which one shifts from endosemiotics to a conscious level, that of psychosemiotics, the experienced or phenomenal world. In von Uexküll's system, it is somewhat paradoxical that although the endosemiotic process in humans takes place inside us, our relationship to it is completely exosemiotic; that is to say, we are not at all conscious of the endosemiosis: "For paradoxically we are 'outsiders' to all our 'inner' (endosemiotic) sign processes whether they occur in the nervous system or in the immune system . . . whereas we are 'insiders' of all sign processes by which the outside world and our body are presented to us as conscious realities. . . . That is, all consciously experienced outside realities are translations of inner sign processes which occur in our brain and are inaccessible to our experience and understanding."

I have not trotted out Thure von Uexküll's theory in order to demand that semioticians should immediately apply his biosemiotic terminology to processes that take place at the level of the psyche, on the borderlines of the endo- and exoworld. Instead, I shall employ the dichotomy of endogenic and exogenic in order to reinterpret some earlier semiotic theories, aspects of which are relevant to my existential semiotics. The Finnish philosopher Georg Henrik von Wright once warned about the metaphorical usage of linguistic concepts in the biosciences: Cell-to-cell communication cannot be similar to that between human "senders" and "receivers." Aware of this fact, and that the von Uexkülls have built a complete generative system, from a microsemiotic level to the phenomenal one, let us suppose that the transmission of signs follows the Peircean scheme: living organism, sign, interpretant, and a denoted object.

I shall be satisfied with using the distinction of endosemiotic and exosemiotic mainly as a heuristic device that opens avenues for the development of new sign concepts, and thus enriches our semiotic theory. Moreover, at the start of the present essay I did not dive into biology and medicine in order to find "objective" justification for my subsequent speculations. Rather, I sought to open a kind of horizon of understanding so as to "actualize" some classical semiotic and philosophical concepts. I might also have interpreted the concepts of endogenic and exogenic in a completely different way than they were intended, maybe even erroneously. Yet I consider myself entitled to make these "mistakes," if by doing so I succeed in creating a new model of interpretation and in elaborating new semiotic concepts, the pragmatics of which I can judge, naturally, strictly in the sphere of my own competence. In fact, my theory of musical semiotics already uses notions such as "inner/outer"—an essential category that transforms the Kantian-Greimasian schemes of time, place, and actors—in a way not far afield from what endo- and exosemiotic originally meant. Many musical processes consist of internalizing the external, of transforming exogenic signs into endogenic ones. Thus, a musical composition forms, in a metaphoric sense, a kind of living organism (the same idea can be applied to any text).

Modern biology holds that the basic condition for the functioning of an organism, on all of its levels, is the distinction between 'self' and 'non-self'. Is it not astounding that the same argument begins, among others, Schelling's transcendental, idealistic philosophy, when he advances the principles of *das Ich* and *das nicht-Ich*? And the same with Hegel, who presents his dialectical model at the beginning of his science of logic. Or going further in that stream of thought, take the English Hegelian, McTaggart, who in his *The Nature of Existence* says, "We have come to the conclusion that all that exists is spiritual, that the primary parts in the system of determining correspondence are selves, and that the secondary parts of all grades are perceptions. The selves, then, occupy a unique position in the universe. They, and they alone, are primary parts. And they, and they alone, are percipients."

In this light, what I wrote at the start—that intelligence is at its greatest when it is endosemiotic, and that the fundamental problem of the reality of signs and semiosis is to what extent that reality is endogenic and to what extent exogenic—is provided with a new interpretation, which was in fact already accomplished by my reformulating it in these new terms. On the other hand, as early as in Thure von Uexküll's observations, it is revealed that the distinction endo/exo is always relative and depends on what level the focus of examination is put.

Next I choose, as the "fulcrum" so to speak, the semiotic, conscious subject, or 'I', and define as endogenic what the 'I' experiences when he or she conceptualizes himself and the world. In this way I connect my reflection to other semiotic theories of the subject (Kristeva, the Greimasian modalities, etc.), and at the same time, to certain existentialist philosophers (Heidegger, Sartre) referred to in my thesis on existential semiotics. I believe that the distinction between endo- and exogenic, between the inner and outer aspect of sign processes, reorganizes the knowledge offered by classical semiotics. And with it we can weave moral-philosophical and axiological aspects even more tightly into our semiotic pondering.

It is not a central issue in morality whether the moral principles are endogenic categories—like the Kantian one—or whether they are exogenic, that is, principles internalized from the external world and nature (as in hedonism) or from society. In his classic *The Origin and Development of Moral Ideas* (1906), Edward Westermarck, the Finnish anthropologist, states the following, which may be taken to support our thesis: "that moral concepts are ultimately based on emotions either of indignation or approval is a fact which a certain school of thinkers have in vain attempted to deny." Or to put it in our semiotic terms, moral concepts are endogenic. That is, they are based on certain emotional reactions by which we conceive certain phenomena (denoted objects) either as good or bad—i.e., moral—*signs*. A certain emotional sanction in one's mind serves in this way as an interpretant, which, for instance, may adjudge lying to be a morally reprehensible sign. At the same time, Westermarck notices that moral judgments also assume an objective character. He takes an illustration from music:

> The aesthetic judgements, which indisputably have an emotional origin, also lay claim to a certain amount of "objectivity." By saying of a piece of music that it is beautiful, we do not merely mean that it gives ourselves aesthetic enjoyment, but we make a latent assumption that it must have a similar effect upon every-

body who is sufficiently musical to appreciate it. This objectivity ascribed to judgements which have a merely subjective origin springs in the first place from the similarity of mental constitution of men.

As a sociologist, Westermarck eventually concludes that "Society is the school in which men learn to distinguish between right and wrong." To put it in our own language, good and bad are learned in exogenic, not endogenic, communication. Accordingly, Westermarck considers the origin of morality to be objectively exogenic: "There was, in early society, practically no difference of opinion; hence a character of universality, or objectivity, was from the very beginning attached to moral judgements." These reflections could naturally be extended, to the presumption that a given society forms an endogenic world, which has its own endosemiosis and organization in relation to other societies and groups, which that society experiences as exogenic. This way leads to cultural semiotics, specifically to those articulations, which Yuri Lotman has theorized for cultures and Julia Kristeva for subjects, when strangers are analyzed as an exosemiotic element in the dominant culture.

I have raised all of this only to show that the dichotomy endo/exo fits well with the various levels of reality, as von Uexküll also demonstrated when he spoke about four levels of integration: The process runs from the phenomenal world of the psyche to the area of the alien-psychic, on up to society and culture.

In our definition, a major part of classical semiotics belongs to the area of the exogenic. It is the analysis of things (*Dinge*) existing objectively outside of our consciousness, a research of texts in the broadest semiotic sense of the term. But if we desire to look into the functioning of the signs, what happens therein, what it is to be a sign, and even inquire into the "soul" of a sign, then we have leave to take the path on which Floyd Merrell further develops Peirce's semiotics, asking: "What is it like to be a sign?" or "How do we interact with signs and those signs interact with us?"

Let us assume that signs can be divided into two classes—endogenic and exogenic (inner and outer)—and that this classification coincides with other principles such as Schelling's *Ich* and *nicht-Ich*, Kierkegaard's subject and object, Lotman's culture and non-culture, Sartre's *être-pour-soi* (the world of freely chosen shaping signs) vs. *être-en-soi* (the world of already fixed, determined, objectivized signs), and the like: How do these two fields relate to the basic concepts of our existential semiotics, *Dasein* and transcendence? Existence does not consist only of endo-signs; rather, its essential ingredient is formed by the field of exo-signs, which lies beyond that of endo-signs. *Dasein* can be defined as a perpetual interaction between those two spheres. Is, then, the shift from one's own sphere, the field of the endo-sign, to that of exo-signs a kind of transcendence? Not in the sense that one moves completely beyond temporal-spatial-actorial correlates; in that area, one should instead speak of particular *trans-signs,* which are by nature metagenic or metasemiotic entities.

Existential Semiotics

Endogenic or endo-signs   Exogenic or exo-signs

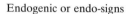

DIAGRAM 6

The aforementioned dichotomy also corresponds to a fundamental split in philosophy between the two orientations of idealism and realism. Idealistic doctrine argues that the endosemiotic subject can conceive the whole universe, that is, the entire area that lies beyond it. In such a theory, the exogenic is basically endogenic. Idealism is based upon the belief that endogenic concepts elaborated by a philosopher can sufficiently explain the whole exogenic world. In turn, the realistic attitude would hold that all endogenic phenomena in the mind of a subject are reducible to exogenic realities, that those phenomena get their objective legitimation only when they are shown a reason and ground in the exogenic domain. Thus, here we encounter two epistemological positions, which situate the ground of one or the other field.

Do these two basic classes of signs have any relevance for classical definitions of the sign definitions? Could one say that Peirce's *Firsts* were close to the endogenic, whereas *Thirds* were far from it? The indexical sign itself serves as an exogenic unit: Smoke is the external manifestation of fire. Doubtless, an essential difference is that endogenic signs are perceived inwardly by a subject; they belong to the subject's inner reality. In McTaggart's system, for instance, volition and emotion are exogenic insofar as they are directed toward something, but are nevertheless independent of cogitation (notice here the resonance with Greimas's concepts of "interoceptive" and "exteroceptive"): "Can we define the quality of 'being' as a desire? It seems to me that it is simple and ultimate and therefore cannot be defined. . . . " But elsewhere, "All desire is for something. . . . Whatever is desired, then, must be given in a state of cogitation" ([1927] 1988: 132–133).

In turn, exogenic signs belong to empirical reality, observable by anyone. For instance, in the semiotics of medicine one searches for exogenic signs—objective indicators—of endogenic states. In universities and academic life, exogenic signs (or "results") are sought by the endogenic work of scientists and departments. All criticism and evaluation of people is based on the exo-signs that they convey of themselves. Particularly at issue is the following question: By what rules of inference can we make correct reasonings, on the basis of external facts, about what is internal? The extreme behaviorists reverse the problem, saying that everything is in outer behavior and should be read therein; all is encoded "out there." In fact, the "inner" does not exist; the area of endo-signs is reduced to indefinite "effects of meaning," even in Greimasian semiotics. Only that which is visible counts—a maxim of media society.

The situation would be simple if all signs could be encoded by these two rules. However, there exist endo-signs that claim to be exogenic and have to be read as such. Correspondingly, some exo-signs must be interpreted in the endogenic field. Both areas have been penetrated by signs from a field that is alien to their own:

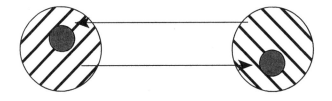

Exo-signs in the endofield   Endo-signs in the exofield

DIAGRAM 7

What do all these cases mean in practice? I take one example from an area familiar to many of us. Usually when awaiting our turn in the barber's chair or at the doctor's office, we absent-mindedly look at weekly magazines. Among them, at least in Finland, may be some publications that promote the so-called "natural" or "holistic" life. In one such magazine (*Voi hyvin,* June 1995), there appears an article written by Denise Linn that sports a quite semiotic title: "The Signs Indicate the Way." The caption below the title reads: "The universe whispers to us everything. It is sending signs by which we can make decisions at the important phases of our lives. Therefore listen to them, look around, anticipate and understand!" The article starts off like an introduction to semiotics: "You are always surrounded by signs which appear in various forms, whether you are conscious of them or not. . . . Although most signs can be seen they can also appear via a perfume, sound, touch, foreboding, or instinct. . . . Signs can help you to understand yourself, to find direction and deep meaning for your life. They can also reveal what your subconscious wants to communicate to you."

The continuation gives advice on how to attract signs to oneself; for instance, one can unthinkingly page through a book, letting a finger "find" the right place. The article argues that people create the conditions in which a sign can appear. Often signs can be found in the conversations of others, at times when you accidentally overhear them. For instance: "Mrs. X, standing in a queue for the cashier, hears the lady in front of her talk about the bursting of an automobile tire. She then goes to her own car and notices that one of its tires has a potentially dangerous weakness; thus alerted, she has the tire repaired and avoids having an accident." Another case: "Antti saw a man who reminded him of his classmate, Lasse, from 30 years back. Antti immediately felt the need to speak to Lasse, though they had had no contact after their school years. Lasse was delighted to hear from Antti: 'How nice to hear from you! I've been trying to reach you—we want to organize a reunion of all our old classmates!' "

These stories illustrate situations in which an exogenic sign is interpreted as endogenic and then back to exogenic. An invented sign is understood as an "objective sign," though it is not so in reality. Yet how to approach such writing and semiotics of everyday life? The purpose of such texts is to show, in a therapeutic sense, that the exogenic field can be mastered by endogenic signs, thus creating the sense that we are masters of our own destiny.

No one takes this magazine article very seriously. It is read *as if* it were true, although the reasonable reader knows that the article conveys scant vital information. In fact, most signs around us are precisely signs of an "in-between" status—endo-signs that aspire to be taken as exo-signs, and exo-signs meant to be interpreted as endo-signs. Together they constitute what Vaihinger, in his theory of fictional entities, calls *als-ob* signs (as-if-signs). Actually, many of the signs employed by a culture must be read non-literally, non-seriously. An important area of such as-if-signs are, of course, aesthetic signs. The latter must not be understood as "real," even in realist narratives and other forms of true-to-life art, but only as symbolic representations. For instance, when someone says that music is a language of emotions, that statement must be understood in precisely this sense: Music is as-if it were the language of emotions; music is, as Susanne Langer says, a logical expression of emotions but not their symptomatic arousal.[1]

Therefore, although the article in our health magazine is laden with logical mistakes—propositions that are not true in the proper sense—we enjoy reading such a text, for it gives us the illusion that we can control reality. All play, games, rituals—all social life is, to a great extent, based on the functioning of such as-if-signs, that is, the reading of "normal" signs only as if they were true. In Italy, if a road sign announces a speed limit of 50 miles per hour, the driver may continue to barrel ahead. But then comes the sign "Danger! Reduce speed to 10 miles per hour." Then the driver slows down a little bit. This is an example of the opposite attitude: A serious sign (50 mph) is interpreted as an as-if-sign. It tells us that a strong stimulus is necessary for one to take a sign seriously.

Of course, the adopted epistemology and world view determines whether endo-signs visiting the exofield are experienced as elevations or degradations from their "normal" status, or whether, contrarily, exo-signs in the endoworld are treated as part of a higher reality. Jean Wahl, a French existentialist philosopher, has coined terms to describe such ascending or descending "transcendence." The former is called "trans-ascendance," the latter "trans-descendence." If one's frame of reference is realistic, such that reality is perceived as fundamentally external, measurable and physical, then endo-signs get their raison d'être only when they "rise" into the exofield, where they can receive objective verification: A doctor believes the patient's complaints only when objective signs of disease appear, such as too high a temperature, runny nose, low blood pressure, and so on. There is mold in the air only if the machine that measures such things indicates it. Correspondingly, if our world view is idealistic, such that endogenic, phenomenal, and spiritual reality is the only one that is relevant, then exo-signs perform effectively only if some human purpose raises them to a meaningful level: Without belief, prayer is an empty gesture; without real content, artistic virtuosity fails to move us; a statesman's acts are legitimate only when supported by right ideas; and so forth.

The foregoing illustrations of the endo/exo division are, however, only the first we have encountered when applying these notions to semiosis. Other fundamental issues remain:

How Can One Investigate Endosemiosis or the Endoworld?

To the extent that the endoworld is the same as the meaning-horizon of the inner mind, all issues related to such a study are topical. Of course, everything is but a variant of one basic problem: How can a person be, at one and the same time, both the subject and the object of his cogitation? Many solutions have been found. For Husserl, the answer lay in phenomenological "reduction," which "means that everything transcendental, what is not given to me immanently, must be nullified." Endogenic semiosis, therefore, operates in such a way that anything contextual, lying outside the endogenic field, means nothing—endogenic signs manifest strictly noema or sense (*Sinn*). Sense also includes the entire experience and its state, its atmosphere or mood. These states must be taken as *pre-signs,* which come into play before the mind becomes fixed on a perceptible sign-object.

The Finnish psychiatrist and philosopher Lauri Rauhala has pointed out that "the linguistic analysis of meaning is not generally interested in these phases [of pre-sign], because its starting point is the already-manifested mind and the already-conveyed intention" (1993: 16). Nevertheless, one may suppose that endogenic signs are, to a great extent, just such pre-signs, that is, sign processes that are not yet established in our consciousness. In that case, they would naturally include fictive signs. In *The Idea of Phenomenology,* Husserl gives an example of fictive as compared to perceived color. The imagined color does not belong to the now-moment of cogitation, but yet it is given in some respect. It appears merely as sensation, as sensory content.

From this point of view, such fictive color is essentially a signified of a sign without a signifier. Elsewhere I have discussed how signs can be detached from the world of *Dasein,* float beyond it, and then reconnect to it. In this process, the element in motion may be the signified alone. Such is the case with Husserl's imagined or fictive color, which in the new *Dasein* receives a new signifier; this may happen, for instance, in the work of an artist who, with his painting, redefines the color "red." This endogenic functioning of signs also accounts for the temporal aspect of the semiosis. What is involved is the inner transcendence of the endogenic field, according to this diagram:

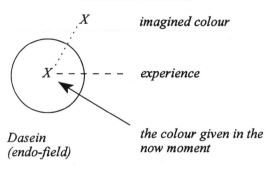

imagined colour

experience

*Dasein
(endo-field)*

*the colour given in the
now moment*

DIAGRAM 8

Sometimes, in turn, an exogenic sign is immediately perceived as representing something endogenic. In his book *Sources of the Self,* Charles Taylor gives the example of a person who enters a room: Everything in that person's outer appearance refers to his or her inner dignity. Stance, walk, gaze, general demeanor—all are a sign of something endogenic, the inner value.

Of course, one way to analyze endogenic signs is to take the approach endorsed by some anthropologists. This is the so-called "emicist" attitude: For instance, the investigator of a certain tribe permits the informants to define the signs by which they can be approached. The researcher walks awhile in the "other person's shoes," so to speak. Unfortunately, this approach only takes a step further from the problem, since even the tribe members, when telling about their behavior, must exceed or transcend it. They have to take some distance from their original endo-signs in order to transform them into verbal exo-signs. If we take the Malinowskian approach, relying on the native's viewpoint or ability to reveal his unique world view, then even in this early phase, we may be diverted from the core issue.

Von Uexküll's early essay speaks of a kind of system theory and the ways it might help us to grasp the so-called "black box" that is man's endosemiotic reality. In cybernetics, the black box method is used "when a system is given, about which one knows first or can define first which input and output values it has, and whose inner structure for some reason cannot be directly investigated (by 'opening the black box')." This method has two phases: (1) One first scrutinizes the variations of input values, while at the same time registering the changes of output values, such that the relationship between the two kinds of value can be graphed. (2) On this basis, and utilizing earlier experiences, one can hypothesize about the inner structure of the black box. One may presume that, like cybernetic systems, the endofield is a "dynamic self-regulative system which aims for balance."

Some modern cognitive scientists are trying to model endosemiosis in terms of neural networks. As with cellular endosemiosis, of which the subject that carries it cannot be conscious, so it is with neural activity at the level of endo-signs. Thus, some scientists speak about *sub-symbolisms,* which precede the formation of signification and even of sense. To speak in such a way, however, calls upon exosemiotic, reductionist ideas; for example, that the mind can be reduced to a kind of sub-symbolic combinatory or bundle of "rules." In this model, it is hard to see how the level operating with subsymbolic, non-significant units can finally produce phenomenally perceivable units. Although the model should represent a pure analysis of the endogenic, it is basically an attempt to reduce the endogenic to exosemiosis, which is taken to be a kind of objective reality (on the basis of neural connections, used to explain endophenomena). This leads us to our next problem:

How Does the Transition from Endoworld to Exoworld Take Place?

Often, endo- and exo-signs are supposed to complete each other in such a way that the understanding of a phenomenon means the interpretation of its endo-signs, and explaining it is the same as the reduction of endo-signs to exo-signs. A classical illustration is provided by Lucien Goldmann in his *Le dieu caché,* written during the heyday of genetic structuralism. The image is that of circles enclosing each other. As the innermost circle we have Pascal's "pensées" and the plays of Racine; in the next circle, the Jansenist religious sect; and as the outermost circle, the social classes of seventeenth-century French society. Explanation involves reducing and moving the inner circle toward the outer ones and the language they represent. Understanding also moves in the opposite direction: The outermost exofield, that of French society, is understood by the examination of Jansenism, which is in turn explained by the study of Pascal and Racine. Goldmann's approach finds some resonance in hermeneutics.

The hermeneutic method distinguishes two levels of understanding: actual or "real" understanding (*das eigentliche Verstehen*), and pre-understanding (*Vorverständnis*). The former appears as signs that are enacted, realized in one's conscious mind. They are kinds of *act-signs.* Yet they come only after the *pre-signs,* of the level of *Vorverständnis,* which in turn are dependent on man's situation. Man has a huge store of various existential alternatives, paradigms of which some are irreducible, necessary, irrefutable: Man has been thrown into certain situations whether he wanted to be there or not. Some of these situations man can influence by his choices. Yet according to Heidegger, man can never completely "pre-understand" himself or articulate the whole field of his existence. Actual understanding always presupposes taking some distance from pre-understanding, since knowing is always knowing from some point of view, in some light, as something (*als etwas*). What is involved, then, is necessarily a transition from endosemiosis to exosemiosis, because that "something," to which the unique endo-sign is related, is an exo-sign or exofield. How this transition takes place depends on the ability of the pre-sign to be transformed into an act-sign. The as-if-signs constitute in this movement a kind of virtual space or terrain of mediation. According to Rauhala, man is predetermined to inauthentic knowing. Thus, hermeneutics presents the exofield's relationship to the endofield as something inauthentic, the fallen state of 'being' of *das Man*. On the other hand, Rauhala states that both approaches are required—empathic or endogenic interpretation and understanding, and quasi-naturalistic explanation of relationships among exogenic signs (in passing one may ask whether this equals Peirce's view on the alternation between *First, Second,* and *Third*).

When we investigate the transitions between these two fields, we first have to solve the problem of whether endo- and exo-signs are basically of the same nature, or whether they pertain to completely different phenomenal fields. Are endo-signs phenomenal, experienced φ entities, whereas exo-signs are only physical, phy-phenomena? Here we encounter the old positivist issue of conversion; that is, whether phy-phenomena can be completely converted into φ-phenomena. The problem of transition from the endoworld to the exoworld is transformed into the problem of how to reduce one to the other. On the other hand, even if one construes endo- and exofields as being of the same nature, this does not eliminate the problem of reductionism. One may suppose either of the fields to be more fundamental. So it is, for example, in psychoanalytic theory, which sometimes has been accused not only of reductionism but also of normativism and determinism. The analyst inducts the patient into an expressly psychoanalytic self-understanding, by using such concepts as the unconscious, becoming conscious, repression, resistance, transference, motif, id, ego, superego, and the like. However, if the patient fails to conceptualize his life and his experiences in terms of these notions, then one would obviously come to the conclusion that the analysis has not advanced, and would probably interrupt it at that point. If not in "pure psychoanalysis," which according to specialists is an illusion (see Rauhala), then the patient may gain self-understanding by other frames of reference, say that of *Dasein,* or in Jungian or Frommian concepts—or perhaps in semiotic terms; otherwise, the patient continues to understand him/herself neurotically. In the terminology of the present essay, what is involved is the reduction of endogenic signs into exogenic ones. In Husserlian phenomenology, for example, one might speak of what I refer to as "pure endogenic knowing." This would come about when, as the result of phenomenological reduction, everything fortuitous and accidental has, in a transcendental act, been eliminated, and there remains only the "thing," or endophenomenon, itself. This would constitute pure endogenic knowledge.

To speak about "pure psychoanalysis" is also contradictory in the sense (as Lauri Rauhala states) that it is always connected with an emancipatory function, an effort to heal the patient, to improve his situation. In the terms of existential semiotics, such an analysis is transcendent in Wahl's sense of "trans-ascendance." The neurotic endo-signs are reduced to "objectively existing" exo-signs, which elevates their status and renders them into a more universal mode of 'being'. Needless to say, the major part of so-called structuralist analysis is like this. When a phenomenon has been reduced to the language and symbolism of a formal semiotic terminology, it should also reveal its general, intersubjective, and often intertextual substance. At the same time, however, some original qualities also disappear in the process. The question is: How far can we permit the original phenomenal qualities to be reduced without the analysis losing its sense and without causing our understanding of the phenomenon to vanish?

Yet if one starts with the hypothesis that endo- and exoworlds are different in nature, then there are also theories that proceed in an opposite direction; that is, they return from the "objective" exoworld to the principles of the endoworld. Friedrich Wilhelm Schelling's *System des transzendentalen Idealismus* (1800) is such an effort, opening with these words: *"Alles Wissen beruht auf der Übereinstimmung eines Objektiven mit einem Subjektiven . . . wir können den Inbegriff alles bloss Objektiven in unserm Wissen Natur nennen: der Inbegriff alles Subjektiven dagegegn heisse das Ich, oder die Intelligenz."* There is no better way of saying what we have been looking for with our dichotomy of endo/exo. According to Schelling, either one emphasizes the objective (exoworld) and asks how it is possible that in it something subjective (endo-signs) appears, or one thinks first of the subjective and asks how it is related to the objective. Schelling's own position is clear: *"Die höchste Vervollkommnung der Naturwissenschaft wäre die vollkommene Vergeistigung aller Naturgesetze zu gesetzen des Anschauens und des Denkens"* [The highest perfection of the natural science would be the complete spiritualization of natural laws into rules of intuition and thought]. His own transcendental philosophy starts from the subjective as the first and absolute, then lets the objective emanate from it.

Next Schelling asks how such endogenic knowing is possible. In his mind it is possible in two ways: Either the endo-signs correspond fully to exo-signs, things as such (*Dinge an sich*), which exist in an unchanging state; or the endo-signs emerge in our consciousness freely and without force—having no "iconic" similarity with things—and then move from the world of thought to the real world, thereby attaining objective reality. In the latter case, the things, or exo-signs, are changing and depending on the endo-signs. Schelling's solution to this problem is that there must prevail between endo- and exo-signs a kind of pre-established harmony that originates from a productive activity (*produktive Tätigkeit*). Accordingly, he sets the pragmatic criterion as the highest when deciding about the truth value of signs, since this is precisely what the correspondence of endo- and exo-signs means.

In the end, Schelling comes to a surprising conclusion: Schelling's productive activity is artistic by nature; thus, both the ideal world of art and the real world of objects are products of the same activity. He says: *Die objektive Welt is nur die ursprüngliche, noch bewusstlose Poesie des Geistes.* With this statement, Schelling situates art in a privileged position, as an avenue for all philosophy. The goal of transcendental philosophy was to reach *der innere Sinn,* the inner sense—the Husserlian *noema*—and this appears only by inner revelation (*Anschauung*), which in turn is realized in production (*Produktion*).

Schelling's articulation of the endo- and exoworld is one of the most fascinating and, after reinterpretation, most useful in the context of existential semiotics. 'I' becomes an object via the act of becoming self-conscious. According to Schelling, 'I' is, in general, an object only to himself, but never to anyone else nor to any external. But if the 'I' is subordinated to external influence, then it has to be an object to someone who is "outside." From this outer point of view, 'I' does not mean anything. Thus 'I', as an 'I', cannot be influenced from outside. On the other hand, 'I' becomes an object, which means that unless the 'I' is not originally an object, then it is the antipode of an object. But since anything objective is something tranquil, fixed, unable to act, it can only be the object of action. So 'I' is originally only action. And since 'I' is action—and as Schelling stresses, *endless* action—then it is also the basis of everything real. The fact that this endless and limitless action becomes an object to itself and therefore is given its boundaries, is the precondition of self-consciousness ([1800] 1971: 567).

Later Schelling connects the 'being' as an object—or as an exo-sign, as we would say—with the distinction between the inner and outer sense. There is a limit between 'I' and object, which is established in such a way that: *"Ich und Ding sind sich so entgegengesetzt dass was Passivität im einen, Aktivität im andern ist."* (Recall here what I said about intelligence at the very beginning of this essay: Intelligence becomes passivity when it is moved from the 'I' to the sphere of 'non-I', from endo- to exoworld!)

One possible interpretation for this would be to identify the arch of human life with the growth of the endo- and the reduction of the exo-. First, the situation is that man is only exo-, with input and sensation coming to him from outside, he is *geworfen* (thrown), as it is said. But by the time the relevance of these external stimuli diminishes, man's character, his endo-aspect, shoots forth; the external is more and more transformed into the internal, until at the end of his life man has, in the best case, become completely himself; he is entirely of the endosemiosis and completely independent from the impact of the exoworld.

In my earlier existential semiotic analyses, I quoted Kierkegaard. Now, after reading Schelling, one can see not only his indebtedness to the German philosopher, but also how Kierkegaard adopts an even more radical standpoint than Schelling with regard to the problem of endo- and exo- which we have formulated here. Kierkegaard opposes the idea of situating knowing outside existence, but at the same time, he admits, like Schelling, that existing is movement and therefore, action. It is a kind of *First*, as we could put it, since, as Kierkegaard says: "If I think of existence, I finish it, and no longer think of it."

For Kierkegaard, to become subjective is the supreme challenge to any thinker—in a sense, an endless task to anyone, like Schelling's *unendliche Tätigkeit!*—of which Kierkegaard warns that one might fulfill it too fast ([1846] 1993: 171). He rejects objective, abstract thinking, or in our terminology, the exoworld. He states: "The way of objective thinking renders the subjective accidental and at the same time [it renders] existence indifferent and evanescent. The way to an objective truth leads away from the subject, and when subject and subjectivity become indifferent, the truth also becomes indifferent. . . . Therefore the way of objective thinking leads to abstract reflection, mathematics, and many kinds of historical knowledge" (200–201). Kierkegaard believes that such objective thinking does not have any relationship with an existing subject. Accordingly, he abruptly denies the possibility of reducing endo-signs into exo-signs. System—by which he doubtless thought not only of Schelling but also of Hegel—strives for the unity of subject and object, thinking and being. Existence, in turn, is based on the separation of these two (134).

Of course, man may forget his existing; however, by doing so, he does not get rid of it, but merely becomes ridiculous. He can live without any reflection on the world of primary *Dasein,* but the subject becomes semiotic in the proper sense only when it has transcended *Dasein* in an act of negation, and after having returned thereafter to his *Dasein,* now changed (see my previous model on p. 10, diagram 1). Therefore, exogenic and endogenic never meet each other in Kierkegaard's model.

Can Endo- and Exoworld Be Described with the Same Metalanguage?

In the above, it was confirmed that in various epistemologies and philosophies endo- and exofield could be constituted by using each other. This results in the fact that, after reduction, they can be described with the same language. Another view considered above was that only the description of the endoworld is valuable and reasonable, as Kierkegaard argued, and so it is sufficient for a philosopher to decipher only that description.

Nevertheless, there are cases in which one has attempted to create a language that would cover both and endo- and exoworld. Such a system is Rudolph Carnap's monumental *Der logische Aufbau der Welt,* in which he elaborates his "constitution" model on the basis of so-called elementary experiences or phenomenology. He distinguishes three kinds of relationships between physical and psychic things. The first is a psychophysical relationship, which prevails between a psychic state and its equivalent state in the central nervous system. Second, an expressive relationship *(Ausdrucksbeziehung)*: From sounds, expressions, gestures, and other corporeal movements, we can reason about what is "moving inside him." In that case, physical movements or almost all bodily expressions, especially involuntary ones, would belong to the area of exo-signs, whereas, the latter would include such things as emotions, or endo-signs. Third, there are also sign relations that prevail between physical entities that mean something and that which they mean (for instance, the word "Imatra" and the physical place where we are). Thus, it seems that the first two relationships would exist between endo- and exofield; whereas, the latter would be excluded. But as Carnap says, often the same physical entity is at the same time in both an expressive and a sign relationship to something psychic.

Moreover, Carnap accepts the existence of spiritual entities that transcend the endogenic and exogenic spheres. They need not always exist in actuality; that is, they need not be physically manifest. Instead, they may appear at certain moments as psychic manifestations. For instance, a man decides to take off his hat. By doing so, he manifests a habit, which exists as a spiritual entity. A musical work by Mozart also constitutes a spiritual entity, which may be actualized via performance. The documents of such spiritual entities we call lasting, physical images, in which the spiritual life has somehow "crystallized." In the moments of its manifestation—for instance, the performance of a musical work—the spiritual life actualizes both the above-mentioned expressive relation (what the musical piece means for the performers and listeners) and the sign relationship (what Mozart meant by his work, its musical and spiritual topography). Therefore, spiritual entities can appear after having been documented in both the endo- and the exofield. Altogether, Carnap distinguishes among four various species of entities: spiritual, alien-psychic, physical, and auto-psychic entities. Of these four species, the last is the basis of his whole system, which gives the impression that his metalanguage is endogenic in nature. However, Carnap emphasizes that the "given" is subjectless; that is, if the starting point or basic element is the so-called elementary experience, an indivisible whole, it can be called 'I' or psychic only after the areas of 'non-I' and non-psychic have first been distinguished. Before this, the basis of the system is neutral. The experience belongs to some 'I'—and is in the existential sense endogenic—only when we speak about other's experiences. The 'I'-form is not any quality of the original, basic elements.

Though Carnap's system is based on elementary experiences, which are indivisible, they can nevertheless be scrutinized by means of "quasi-analysis," which constitutes a kind of relational description. For instance, the triad c-e-g is an indivisible unity, but it belongs to three paradigms or chord classes with which it has as a common note (c, e, and g). So each of these tones forms a possible direction from which one may proceed to other possible chords. Such an analysis means that we situate the elementary experience in question—here, the chord—on the basis of its family resemblance to various paradigms, such that it is not dissolved into its parts but only "embedded" in different fields. (This is often a method of biographical research: A person is studied, as an organic unit, as being embedded on the basis of certain features that he/she shares with others, with various contacts and networks, relations with other people, and so on. For an example, see Shostakovich's "Confession," in which he performs a "quasi-analysis," by not speaking of himself, but by focusing on his friends.) In addition to elementary experiences, the system needs a basic relationship, which is constituted by so-called *Ähnlichkeitserinnerung,* or the remembrance of a likeness.

The Carnapian system is like a huge semiotic construct of endo- and exo-signs, but it is certainly not an existential semiotic theory, though it deals with basic semiotic elements as well. Carnap specifically says: "The constitution [of the system] does not present the process of perception in its concrete form, but constructs it rationally afterwards in its formal state." For instance, we may say that when someone learns a language to understand the meaning of its words and phrases, this learning does not take place by reasoning thought but instead it occurs in an associative, intuitive way, especially when one learns one's mother tongue. Otherwise it would be true that all Chinese and Finns are monumentally intelligent by nature because they can master such difficult languages. The constitution model makes explicit the interdependence of expressive and sign relationships; this interdependence holds true in the understanding under all conditions, whether it happens intuitively or rationally. Yet the essential point in existential semiotics is precisely the "how" of signs, not their abstract, timeless, spaceless, and actor-less structure.

An interesting aspect of Carnap's system is the difference between the autopsychic (or endogenic) and alien-psychic (exogenic) worlds. The world of other persons is built semiotically from others' elementary experiences, which in turn have been inferred via expressive and informative relationships (*Angabe*). *Angabe,* in Carnap's view, is a phrase that means a certain state of affairs. For instance, the sentence "Karl beats Fritz" is a proposition whose meaning is the state that has the greatest total weight in relation to this piece of information. In this moment, we may see Carnap coming a little closer to the field of existential analysis, although by a somewhat comical example. In his analysis, the state of affairs in the phrase consists of two beings, Karl and Fritz, and the relation between them. The weights of meaning are distributed so that the three first are given to the units Karl, Fritz, and "beat," while the fourth one is the most important in the existential sense; namely, it is at its greatest when the state really prevails, that is, when Karl really beats Fritz. It is smaller if this state does not prevail. In semiotic terms, the weight of meaning is the greater the more *deicticity* there is in the phrase. The more deictic, the more existential, we could say.

Finally, Carnap comes to the intersubjective world. It consists of the "intersubjectively convertible" properties of subjects S1 and S2. Some believe that only this world is the semiotic world in the proper sense, since it is the universe of general order, commonly accepted identities, signs established by certain societies. The European tradition of Saussurian semiotics starts from this world. Also Carnap states that the intersubjective world constitutes the proper domain of scientific entities. To him the world of one subject, the *ego,* is of less value. For existentialists, it is, of course, the primary world and *l'enfer sont les autres* (Sartre). It does not follow from *cogito* that "I am"; from the fact that "I experience" does not follow the fact that "I am," but rather that "this experience" *is*. For Carnap, a more appropriate expression than "I experience" would be "this experience." In another context, this could be a form of alienation, as well. In any case, Carnap attempts to step out of the distinction endo/exo via the Husserlian way.

There is a strongly positivist feature in Carnap, namely, the effort to understand philosophico-semiotic problems as problems of language use. It may be astounding, but from a semiotic point of view, there is a similar feature in Hegel's entire system of logics. The latter, too, is based on the belief that only one metalanguage would be sufficient to describe both endo- and exoworld; this is the dialectical model. Hegel's definition then migrated to Sartre's *"l'être et le néant,"* but there dealing with 'being-for-oneself', 'being-in-oneself', and their unity. In Sartre, the endoworld is clearly the world of free 'being'; whereas, the exoworld represents "others," 'being' as an object, fixed and determined, almost dead. His reasoning and logic stem from Hegel.

CONCLUSION

Our distinction has proved to be a principle that traverses many philosophical systems, which take various standpoints on the matter of endo/exo. It could also be investigated in relation to the Kantian categories of time, space, and subject. Yet it seems to me that the domain of endo/exo has already shown itself to be of sufficient complexity that I need no further documentation. In some interpretations, endo-signs are connected to the existential ego-feeling and to self-determination. In that case, the exo-signs are external to 'I'; they address the 'I' from the external world, be it social or natural. In other theories, the distinction of endo/exo is placed wholly inside the subject.

As yet, I have not been able to demonstrate the utility of these notions in the existential-semiotic analyses of cultures. Probably this dichotomy is connected with other dichotomies, such as the issue of present and absent signs, the ability of the endo- and exo-signs to detach from their sphere of *Dasein,* to be transported from their historical time into transcendent, cosmological time. Then they can return and be actualized in the world of *Dasein,* but at the same time be connected in a new way to their *Ground.*

For instance, from art history we know that the same sculptural motif can "wander" for long periods, for centuries, finally to be connected to the endo-sign field of another culture and there assume a new content. An example is the giant carrying a globe. In antiquity this was a sign for the mythological figure of Atlas. Two hundred years later it became the exo-sign of an angel, thus taking on a Christian content.[2] In music we have another setting for the wandering of the same topos (e.g., "march style") from one period to another, assuming various contents. This is called *iconography* when individual exo-signs are taken into account, and *iconology* when whole periods of endogenic sign fields are investigated.

When we distinguish the two sides of a sign, signifier and signified, we should complete our model, extending into four dimensions by adding these two new aspects: the endo- and exo-side of a sign. Any signifier can be seen from both inside and outside, and the same for signifieds. When we encounter signs that are unfamiliar (e.g., when we approach a culture that is foreign to us) and when we generate new sign complexes (as the arts sometimes do), we always first experience them as exo-signs. Only gradually, via closer acquaintance, can they be transformed into endo-signs. Sometimes the signifier can be familiar, while its signified would in some contexts be strange, exogenic to us. And vice versa. In any case, all these aspects joined to the definitions of the classical semiotics, bring us closer to a genuinely existential semiotic analysis. But without the concept of transcendence, we can make no progress in our observations.

In brief, the results of these reflections are: The distinction between endo/exo-signs, -field, and -world can mean various things. At least three basic meanings can be made explicit: (1) it means a division, into the world of psyche and the physical world outside it; (2) it means the separation of autopsychic or solipsist ego world from the alien-psychic, and ultimately social worlds and their signs; (3) it means the distinction of 'being-for-itself' and 'being-in-itself', which in turn designates an opposition between the world of choice and freedom, existence, and that of a fixed, ready, established, and conceptualized world.

Altogether, endo/exo-signs take place in the sphere of *Dasein*. Beyond them remains the world of transcendence in the proper sense, which represents cosmological time in contrast to the historical time of the endo/exo-signs. Signs in the state of transcendence I shall henceforth call *trans-signs*. Correspondingly, signs preceding the endo/exo fields, that is, prior to their state as endo/exo units, I call *pre-signs*. Therefore, both endo- and exo-signs belong to the species of *act-signs*.

NOTES

1. I am indebted for these observations on the *als-ob* character of music to the American philosopher Cynthia Grund.
2. See the dissertation by Altti Kuusamo: *Tyylistä tapaan. Semiotiikka, tyylii ikonografia* (Semiotics in the Service of Iconography and the Study of Style). Tampere: Gaudeamus, 1996.

REFERENCES

Carnap, Rudolph. 1974. *Der logische Aufbau der Welt.* Hamburg: Meiner.
Goldmann, Lucien. 1994. *Le dieu caché* (étude sur la vision tragique dans les Pensées de Pascal et dans le théâtre de Racine). New ed. Paris: Gallimard.
Grund, Cynthia. 1996. "How Philosophical Characterizations of a Musical Work Lose Sight of the 'Music' and How It Might Be Put Back." In *Musical Signification,* ed. Eero Tarasti, pp. 64–79. Berlin, New York: Mouton de Gruyter.
Husserl, Edmund. 1964. *The Idea of Phenomenology.* Trans. William P. Alston and George Nakhnikian. The Hague : Martinus Nijhoff.
Kierkegaard, Søren. [1846] 1993. *Päättävä epätieteellinen jälkikirjoitus,* suom. tanskasta Torsti Lehtinen. Juva: WSOY.
Linn, Denise. 1995. "Merkit viitoittavat oikean tien." *Voi hyvin* 6: 7–12.
McTaggart, J. McT. E. [1927] 1988. *The Nature of Existence.* Ed. C. D. Broad. Vol. II. Cambridge: Cambridge University Press.
Merrell, Floyd. 1995. *Peirce's Semiotics Now: A Primer.* Toronto: Canadian Scholar's Press.

Rauhala, Lauri. 1993. *Eksistentiaalinen fenomenologia hermeneuttisen tieteenfilosofian menetelmänä.* Vol. 41. Tampere: Tampereen yliopisto. Filosofisia tutkimuksia Tampereen yliopistosta.

Schelling, Friedrich Wilhelm Josef. [1800] 1971. *System des transzendentalen Idealismus.* Frühschriften. Eine Auswahl in zwei Bänden. Zweiter Band. Berlin: Akademie Verlag.

Taylor, Charles. 1989. *Sources of the Self: The Making of the Modern Identity.* Cambridge, Mass.: Harvard University Press.

von Uexküll, Thure, Werner Geigges, and Jörgen Herrmann. 1993. "Endosemiosis." *Semiotica* 96 (1/2), 5–51.

Vaihinger, Hans. 1920. *Die Philosophie des Als Ob. System der theoretischen, praktischen und religiösen Fiktionen der Menschheit auf Grund eines idealistischen Positivismus.* Leipzig: Verlag von Felix Meiner.

Wahl, Jean. 1944. *Existence humaine et transcendance.* Être et penser, Cahiers de Philosophie. Neuchatel: Editions de la Baconnière.

Westermarck, Edward. 1906. *The Origin and Development of the Moral Ideas.* London: Macmillan and Co.

4

Understanding, Misunderstanding, and Self-Understanding

For the most part, semiotics has investigated only the conditions of understanding, as Umberto Eco observes in his *La struttura assente,* and not the moment of understanding itself. Eco defines his own semiotic program as follows: "All communication functions by sending messages, which are based upon codes; every act of communication, performance, is based on a preexisting competence; all *parole* presupposes *langue.*" Indeed, semiotics considered it a big step forward to withdraw from the study of meaning and the experience of meaning in structures. But by demonstrating that meaning as an experience was something vague and illusory, one also abandoned the crucial phenomenological starting point for any formation of signification.

Now many seek to "erase" the structuralist phase of semiotics altogether and return to the event of understanding signs, to catching the idea of the message. Without such an act of understanding, meaning does not exist. For isn't understanding the most essential moment in our lives, that which distinguishes us from other beings—even though on the biosemiotic level we are connected to the semiosis of all living nature? The moments when humankind has understood something central about itself, society, and history are the moments that are remembered and that leave those traces called signs. According to some theories, to understand means to return to the conditions of understanding, to those structures that yield the phenomenon or behavior in question. One understands oneself, for instance, when it is said a person *is* such and such, *did* this or that; because they *belonged* to such and such family; because their father or mother was such and such; or because they belonged to a certain social class; or had such and such an education; was Finnish, Russian, French, Brazilian, because the citizens of these nations behave in a certain way; or because one suffered this or that illness, and on and on. In all of these cases, the subject's degree of existence decreases due to the fact that one becomes only a sinsign from some legisign, a token of some type, whether it be class, race, nation, age, gender, education, culture, and the like. In this kind of understanding, the subject is, in a manner, reduced to something; and when the amount of one's existence is reduced, one takes less responsibility for what one is and instead becomes merely an emanation from a structure or a system that conditions and determines our being. Even if one takes Lucien Goldmann's view of understanding and explanation, such an understanding is rather an explanation: A person is always moving from one circle to another.[1] In Goldmann's model, which appears in all of its splendor in his study on Racine and Pascal, *Le dieu caché* (1994), real understanding is represented by movement inwards: Society, class, family, people are understood through a single and unique case of a certain individual, which shifts one from the abstract to the concrete. It seems to me that this is also the direction in which existential semiotics operates. It aspires to be a science of real events, of what really happens. Behind people's "official" biographies loom the streams of daily emotions and inner experiences that guide their choices.

But understanding does not limit one to only the linear reading process of a text, whether the latter be a form of conduct, an object, or whatever; rather, it takes into account the alternation and plurality of the levels of communication. Why is Nietzsche so modern? Because he took into consideration not only the enunciate but also the enunciation itself. This is clearly foregrounded in paragraph 247 of *Beyond Good and Evil,* where he says the following:

> How little the German style has to do with the sound and the ears is proved by the fact that precisely our good musicians write so badly. A German does not read aloud, not for the ear, but only with his eyes. . . . The man of antiquity when reading for himself read with a loud voice. With a loud voice, that is to say, conveying all the crescendos, inclinations, changes of tempo, in which the Ancient world rejoiced. . . . A phrase was to the people of former times a physiological whole, insofar as it is united by one breath. . . . Only a preacher in Germany knew what a syllable, a word weighs, on which conditions a phrase beats, jumps, rushes, runs and reaches its goal.

In this passage Nietzsche foregrounds understanding on quite a new level: To understand a phrase is not only to catch its syntactical-semantic content but also to weigh its enunciation.

The semiotician says that understanding is to find and apply the right code. But how does the application of a code take place? A structuralist argues that understanding means to see the system as whole. To his mind understanding is possible only by means of complex operations of de-structuring and re-structuring. He denies the possibility of an immediate understanding. The scientist states that to understand is to see invariances, to interpret the particular as a part of the general, to locate singular instances within their proper paradigms. But in these cases, we remain distanced from the meaning process that really takes place. For meaning does not become functional without an act of understanding.

Understanding is a kind of cognitive event within one's mind; its consequences may vary, but the event itself is always internal and thus difficult to investigate experimentally. Understanding cannot be merely a reduction of one level to another. For instance, the phenomena of cultural and psycho-semiotics do not become more comprehensible if they are reduced to biosemiotic processes. In the act of understanding, man can conceive otherwise linear events as simultaneous; he can exceed the disengagements of time and place; and he can experience, so to speak, the moments *t1* and *t2* as simultaneous and the places *p1* and *p2* as coinciding.

One way to understand the world is to view it as a text.[2] But how does the world become understandable when it is conceived that way? It is possible that the world, as such, is not a text, but that we project text-likeness on it. Of course, a consequence of this projection is that people start to behave as if they were in a "text"—they understand their own behavior as part of a text, manuscript, scenario, libretto, and the like, and this conception of self forces them into certain actantial roles. Yet most probably, these roles, as complex as they may appear in contemporary society, do not attain the status of what Bergson called *le moi profond.*

When man behaves according to tradition, he feels himself to be in the right. It is much more difficult to behave according to one's inner categorical imperative—which may go against tradition and environment—and still feel oneself to be in the right. In such a case, one is oriented directly away from transcendental categories.

Jorge Luis Borges (1988) speaks of the world as a text, when he quotes Mallarmé, who claimed that the world exists in order to be written.[3] Borges notes, however, that for the Greeks, the world existed primarily as spoken, not as written. Pythagoras did not write. It was not until the fourth century B.C.E. that there emerged the idea of a silent, mute reading of a book. According to Borges, it is from this moment that the written word began to take dominance over the spoken word. In semiotic terms, this moment marked the rise to power of the enunciate over the enunciation. Therefore, the age of the enunciate sometimes feels a nostalgia for the age of enunciation or speech and invents what is called *énonciation énoncée,* that is, the way the enunciate imitates the enunciation (this distinction is also important in music, as is seen in the shift from oral tradition to written notation). According to Borges, Scott Carlyle said that the universal history is Holy Script, "something which we interpret, read and also write and in which we are also written" (1988: 120). Borges also reports that Mallarmé thought that the world existed as a book—thus, as a text—and in Leon Bloy's mind, we are letters or words in a magical volume, and this endless book is the only thing in the world. Or rather, it *is* the world.

Borges's view anticipated structuralist theories, among them, the theories of Lévi-Strauss, who believed that the myths of Indians really existed only when written in his *Mythologiques.* One may say that our desire to be written reflects our other, deeper aspiration to understand ourselves. Signs and semiotics are to function as an objective and objectifying mirror in which the world is reflected and in which our desire is consummated. Thus, the idea of the world as a text is perhaps a kind of expansion of the Lacanian mirror phase to cover everything semiotic. We experience the world as a text that we are writing and that we have written, and it becomes comprehensible because it ceases to be alien to us. As a text or a book, the world becomes a mirror for us, a mirror in which we recognize ourselves; and in this way, the threat of the Other is abolished, much like the Proustian *double*. In the end, this involves a form of self-understanding and of understanding others. Here we are not necessarily any closer to solving the enigma of the Other: the problem of how two worlds alien to each other, how two separate semiospheres or individuals can understand each other. By changing that which is alien to us into a text, we only shift the problem of encountering the Other further away. We conquer the world and take it into our possession; but at the same time, we bind it under our will. We do not come closer to, but rather we distance ourselves from the modalities and the will of the Other.

Therefore, and paradoxically, it is in misunderstanding where a possibility of understanding the Other lies, and even more than in apparent understanding. In misunderstanding there occurs a meeting with the other reality, although in a negative sense. But because misunderstanding often develops into a conflict, it makes the latent situation manifest and thus enables one to correct the misunderstanding. It opens the possibility for a dialogue, since ego has to listen to alter-ego (in the ideal case).

To see the world as a text may also be a terrible mistake, because how can the Other, who has become textualized, resist the actantial role into which he or she has been positioned in the text of the ego? Perhaps by creating its own text in which this situation is corrected—by behaving in a way other than that which the previous text would presuppose.

The textualization of the world, the idea of seeing it as a book, is therefore only a form of solipsistic self-understanding. By contrast, the de-textualization of the world opens the possibility of seeing and understanding the Other. The structuralists, particularly Roland Barthes, believed that one first "de-structures" the world before "re-structuring" it, that is, before transforming it into a text.

UNDERSTANDING AS A SEMIOTIC PROBLEM

subject $s1 \rightarrow$ sign $\rightarrow$ subject $s2$

Subject $s1$ produces a sign that is received by subject $s2$. We do not say that subject $s1$ "understands" the sign but that he or she expresses something by sign when engaged in the act of producing it. Correspondingly, we may well say that subject $s2$ either understands or misunderstands the sign. There are two sorts of misunderstanding: either subject $s2$ misunderstands the sign because he or she does not use the same code or sign system as that of the sender, or as Husserl would say, the same *Bedeutungszeichen* as $s1$. Or $s2$ misunderstands the sign by mastering its basic meaning as a *Bedeutungszeichen* but not as an *Ausdruckszeichen*. Then the misunderstanding is an existentially significant event. The misunderstanding may also be due to the fact that *s2* applies to the sent sign a different "idea" as an interpretant than that of *s1*.[4] Or it could be that *s2* connects the sign to a different *habitus,* or semiosphere, from that of *s1*, in which case we come to what Walburga von Raffler-Engel understood by her idea of "crosscultural misunderstandings." In sum, one can say that in such a misunderstanding, subject *s2* does not reach the intentional world of subject *s1*. Subject *s2* is not able to enter into the sign activities of *s1* (his *Ausdruckshandeln,* in Alfred Schütz's terminology), and therefore subject *s1* remains something *fremdseelig,* alien-spirited to subject *s2*. Understanding does not obtain in such a communication, and this can bring on many kinds of practical, often fateful consequences.

One may go on to ask, What, then, is *self*-understanding? To this one may answer: It is precisely existential understanding. I understand myself via objectified signs; that is to say, my aspirations are crystallized into something objective. For instance, I read letters I wrote thirty years ago, which are the signs and traces I have left behind. I could then ask, Is the one who now tries to understand himself still the same person as the one who once objectified his intentions into the signs in question? Whatever the answer, in this sense subject *s1* has produced a sign, an objectivization of his will, in order to express something with it. When he later sees this realized expression as objectified in a sign, he returns back to himself by means of it—he reconstructs his earlier ego at moment *t1*, and in this reflexive movement understands himself. He returns in his present stream of experiences (which Schütz calls *Erlebnisstrom*) to his earlier experiential flow, and tries to see those signs as a part of it. In this case, we are confronting *le fait accompli*, so to speak. In understanding, the mind moves backwards. A society understands itself via its history, by means of its pre-world (*Vorwelt*).[5]

Yet understanding is something that takes place now. When it concerns the solitary ego and its understanding, it may be opened to a whole universe of some signs, for instance, artistic signs, by the process in which it suddenly realizes an isomorphism between a sign or sign complex or sign continuum *and* the continuum of its own stream of experiences. Understanding is a kind of correspondence between two levels. A verbal text, for example, unexpectedly opens to us as we read it, in such a way as to touch or speak to us. What then happens is in fact very fundamental in the philosophical sense, because then knowing (*Wissen* or *savoir*) becomes feeling or experience (*Kennen, connaissance*). Precisely this shift is important in the philosophies of the Lithuanian-Finnish scholar Wilhelm Sesemann and the Frenchman, Vladimir Jankélévitch (discussed below), who both moved on a phenomenological basis.

Edmund Husserl, in his *Logische Untersuchungen. Untersuchung zur Phänomenologie und Theorie der Erkenntnis* (1913), distinguished between the notions of *Ausdruck* (expression) and *Bedeutung* (meaning). The latter refers to the meanings of verbal terms that exist—as Alfred Schütz emphasizes—prior to the act of speaking or expressing oneself. In turn, "expression" means that such a sign—which constitutes an objective semiotic entity with a structure (signifier/signified, semes, isotopies, etc.)—is used in a certain situation in order to convey something. The subject uses it in order to express his intentions and modalities to another person who is living in his *Mitwelt,* "with-world," in the same *Dasein.* Husserl says this:

> An articulated sound complex expresses something only insofar as a speaker uses it in order to express something, i.e., if he in a certain psychic act provides it with a sense, which he wants to transmit to a listener. This transmission, however, is only possible when the listener understands the speaker's intention. And he is able to do this only if he conceives the speaker as a person who does not only produce mere sounds, but is *speaking* to him—accordingly issuing with sounds a certain signifying act, whose sense he is conveying to him. What makes this spiritual communication possible in general, and what turns speech into speaking, is based on the correlation between the physical and psychic experiences of the communicating persons, whichsaid experiences are transmitted by the physical aspect of the speech. They, so to say, hold together. Speaking and listening, the announcement of psychic experiences in a speech, and their reception are mutually interlinked.

Here Husserl reverses the initial situation of our investigation. We started from the hypothesis that there is subject *s1,* to whom *s2* is essentially "alien" (*fremdseelig*). The question then becomes, How can the same, or subject *s1*—whose standpoint we for a moment adopt—understand the Other, or subject *s2*? According to Husserl, however, the existence of speech is already premised upon a certain togetherness of subjects *s1* and *s2.* The problem of understanding or misunderstanding is thus not a problem of a solitary ego, but a problem of a certain community to which ego and alter ego, 'I' and the Other, already belong.

A speech in which subject *s1* tells something of himself to subject *s2* Husserl calls *announcing* (*Kundgabe*), about which he makes this remark:

> To understand an announcement is not only its conceptual comprehension but it is based upon the fact that the listener takes into account the speaker as a concrete person, who expresses this or that. When I listen to someone I consider him as a speaker, I hear him to tell, prove, doubt, wish, etc.

If I have understood Husserl correctly, in his reasoning we see two essential points regarding the problematics of understanding. First, the starting point of understanding is that the subjects belong to the same "with-world," *Mitwelt;* second, their mutual understanding takes place via two-leveled signs: *objective* signs, which follow certain grammar and code systems, and *expression* signs, which are used in certain situations.

Let us try to put this situation into familiar concepts of classical semiotics. In lectures at the University of Helsinki in 1973 (see also *Bevezetés a Szemiotikába*), Vilmos Voigt has said that the difference between semiotics and semantics lies in the fact that if we go to the marketplace in our own town in order to buy a kilogram of potatoes, the problem is purely a semantic one; but if we go to the marketplace of another, distant culture (say, African or Persian), then the problem is semiotic. In Husserlian terms, Voigt's semiotic problem is the problem of *Bedeutungszeichen,* whereas the semantic problem is the problem of the *Ausdrucks* function of signs. In fact, the latter can be subdivided into two aspects, namely, the given content of the signs that take place in the action and whose truth criterion is pragmatic: If the seller starts to measure apples for us instead of potatoes, the sign has not functioned. Moreover, the expression "I would like to have one kilo of potatoes" can be expressed in many ways. It can be colored (or "modalized," as Greimas would say) in many ways, thereby conveying the psychic state of the subject. For example, it can be uttered as an order, disdainfully, helpfully, boastingly, indifferently, or in a thousand other ways, which also can depend on the social situation and/or the pragmatic consequences.

To summarize the preceding discussion, there are two kinds of understanding—that of expression and that of meaning—and they are interconnected such that the expression cannot be understood unless one first catches the meanings. There is no *Ausdruck* without *Bedeutung.*

However, the situation is more complicated than that. For example, if we shift to the psychoanalytic terminology of Julia Kristeva, we can say that Husserl's *Bedeutungsfunktion* (the objective "grammatical" meaning of the signs) corresponds to her symbolic level. Yet in Kristeva it is preceded by the semiotic level in the proper sense, i.e., the level of *khora,* which is that of desires, rhythms, gestures, kinetic energy, and pre-verbal activities that form the primal, archaic stage of our existence. Take, for instance, the situation in which we follow a conversation in a foreign language that is unknown to us. The conversation is not completely misunderstood nor incomprehensible, since we can receive the speech on the semiotic level by inferring its affective content from intonations, stresses, gestures, tempo, rhythm, accelerations, retardations, and the like. This involves the archaic, "naive" level of communication that is always present in every communication; we need not return to this level nor reduce our normal discourse to it, but it is nevertheless always present in the exchange. This level is somehow trivially referred to as an "emotional" logic. Just as trivial is the notion that men better understand the *Bedeutung* level of communication, whereas women better grasp its *khora* level, its *Ausdruck,* in the sense of applying so-called vital affects and amodal abilities.[6]

In other words, for Kristeva, understanding is primarily an event of the *khora*; it is the core of the iceberg whose top is only formed by the manifest verbal signs. Husserl also has a term for this aspect of communication:

> . . . on the other hand, there are acts which are indifferent to the expression but which are however in a logical connection to them in the sense that they fulfill the meaningful intention to a greater or smaller extent (strengthen, increase, il-

lustrate, etc.) and thus create or actualize their own objective relationship. These acts which blend together with the sense-creating acts, we call meaning-fulfilling [*Bedeutungserfüllung*] acts. This expression we can use only when there will be no confusion with the entire experience in which meaning-intention is realized in the equivalent act . . . But in reality the significant expression is united with the meaning-fulfilling acts. The sound complex is identified with its significant intention and it again is identified with the fulfilling of the meaning in question. By an expression-form here one understands nearest only the case in which it is no longer mere "expression," but a meaningful, *Sinnbelebte,* or experiential expression.

In other words, in Husserl the concept of *Ausdruck* covers both the Kristevan, pre-verbal *khora* meaning and the Greimasian meaning carried by modalities. They are both, of course, bound to a certain situation in which the subject *s1* exists. Through this situation, what is involved is also an existential semiotic distinction; that is to say, via a situation, the expression reflects the position of a subject in his *Dasein,* his transcendental acts, temporality, and so on.

We notice now that understanding starts to receive more content, but at the same time, more complexity. If understanding is so difficult, how is it even possible? One might classify theories according to the distinction between whether they set themselves in favor of mutual understanding or of misunderstanding. Is understanding the basis of everything, in relation to which misunderstanding is an exception? Or is misunderstanding the norm, due to the isolation of subject *s1* from subject *s2*? Or does subject *s1* appear to *s2* principally as an alien entity in the world of his lonely ego, such that the experience stream of *s1* can reach the stream of *s2* only momentarily and by means of some signs? This distinction is closely connected to a general problem of two different types of philosophizing which Peirce called *tychism* and *synechism.*

Tychism begins with the argument that the world is an accidental place where subjects live in a kind of initial, primitive state without any rules. This is the world of British empiricism from Locke to Russell, and it is reflected in all Anglo-analytic philosophy. For instance, Rawls's classic work *A Theory of Justice* starts from the idea that "justice" and the "social" are something that can be added, step by step, to this primal situation. Locke, Hume, and Russell all deny "necessary connections" and believe that the world is without any sense and logic other than that which we place there ourselves.

Another standpoint is represented by *synechism*, to which Peirce came in his essay "Evolutionary Love." In such a world, everything is interlinked, *tout se tient;* everything is based on continuity, and the interconnectedness of concepts only reflects the meaningful contiguity of reality itself. I have characterized the latter standpoint as "romantic semiotics."

These two standpoints also have an impact on the problem of understanding. Understanding is not only the privilege of the latter point of view, since even the title of Locke's book was *An Essay concerning Human Understanding.* Now I have started to imagine that there might be some perspective from which both of these views might be possible. Would a semiotic philosophy be possible in which even such different theories would be only kaleidoscopic, manifold, polylogical variants of some higher level theory?

SOME CASES OF UNDERSTANDING

Against this background I would like to present, as an hypothesis and testing ground, some of the main categories of understanding. I present them as a series of theses with accompanying remarks.

1. "Understanding is to see the general through the particular." As a rule, in scientific explanation one aims to generalize concepts from particular instances. For example, one attempts to view some idea, behavior, person, or work as a variant of a broader paradigm and to locate that variant within its proper model. Often this case takes place in practice as the conceptualization of the object in question. Understanding is to name something with a notion; for instance, medical diagnoses. But do we better understand an artist when viewing him or her as part of a narrative of illness? Wagner was a narcissist who had attacks of *pavor nocturnus*. When this has been said, do we understand better his music? Nietzsche's spiritual collapse was due to such and such sickness. Knowing this, do we now better understand *Zarathustra*? This species of understanding is clearly only one kind of *argumentum ad hominem,* especially when one tries to understand the signs left by this person. To relate them to an individual psychology closes the horizon of understanding and obstructs the process of interpretation. What is involved basically is that the type is seen via the token, legisign via sinsign, and sinsign via qualisign. This is therefore the movement from *Thirdness* toward *Firstness*.

2. "Understanding is a shift from knowing (*Wissen*) to feeling (*Kennen*)." This is to say that the knowledge becomes personal, subjectively felt. To a great extent, so-called learning is precisely this activity. Although in the postmodern society of electronic mass communication, the scope of feeling is continually expanding, it still has its limits. What is involved is the old distinction between theory and practice. It is said that some knowledge is mere theory, whereas there are things which can only be felt. Usually the existential things are such.

3. "Understanding is to see something as an intertext, as a part of a network of other texts or signs." The ending of the last chapter of Nietzsche's *Gay Science* may be analyzed as an intertext. There the musicality of the text is foregrounded, and it also imitates the enunciation by the gradual acceleration of its rhythm. Its intertextual counterpart is not difficult to guess—it is the Finale of Beethoven's Ninth Symphony. This is even more obvious due to an indexical sign Nietzsche has embedded in the text: ... *Nicht diese Töne* ... which is a direct quotation from Schiller's *Ode an die Freude*. Nietzsche's text becomes an iconic-indexical imitation of Beethoven/Schiller. Consequently, the understanding of a text

means to connect it to the continuum of signs, to the chain of interpretants. To misunderstand is to relate the phenomenon to the wrong interpretants.

4. "Understanding is to see the enunciate in relation to enunciation, to reduce the *énoncé* into *énonciation.*" It is believed that the uncovering of the process of communication leads to the understanding of a phenomenon or message. This is also called nowadays the "contextualization" of a phenomenon. Misunderstanding is, among other things, the reification of the enunciate, taking it as given, and a blindness to the conditions of its production.

5. "Understanding is to reduce performance to competence, to see some conduct as a consequence of something which precedes it." In order for semantics to be possible, one must first master the semiotic level; in order to speak, one must know the grammar. Misunderstanding is the lack of competence, which can perhaps be corrected.

6. "Understanding is simply the disappearance or abolition of misunderstanding." For instance, subject *s1* has always believed that subject *s2* thinks of him in a particular way, and this has prevented them from communicating with each other. Then suddenly, for some reason, the wall of misunderstanding crumbles and *s1* and *s2* see each other in a new light. Misunderstanding is a state in which things continue as they are, with the two subjects remaining alien to each other.

7. "Understanding is more an event of *parole* than of *langue.*" Misunderstanding is due to the fact that *langue* forces us to act according to certain automatisms, although we do not wish to do so. One can express oneself only through the dominant *langue.*

8. "Understanding is to move from phenotext to genotext, or in general to reduce something from the 'surface' to something 'deeper'." This is the dream of the structuralists. One variant of this idea is that 'being' is more basic than 'appearing'. Because something can be made to look other than what it really is, thus creating misunderstanding as to its "essence" or real nature, understanding is to uncover the 'being' that looms behind the 'appearance'. To understand an "ideology" is to see "through" it to the person or group that tries to legitimize its power with the ideological discourse.

The same problem appears as early as on the individual level. Consider these lines from André Gide's *Journal:*

> My mind was once occupied by the question whether one first has to be and then appear, or first appear and then be what one appears (like those who pay a debt on account and only thereafter get worried about the amount of money to be charged them; to appear before being is the same as to become indebted to the outer world). Perhaps man exists only to the extent that he appears as something. Consequently we get two wrong arguments: (1) We are in order to appear; (2) because we are, therefore we appear. These concepts must be bound to a mutual dependence. Thus we get the wanted imperative: one has to be in

order to appear. The appearance must not be distinguished from the being; the being is affirmed by appearing; appearing is the direct manifestation of being.

According to Gide's reflections, we can no longer be so sure whether the understanding of something means that the phenomenon of manifestation is reduced to mere 'being' or immanence. On this view, misunderstanding would be to take the appearance as something that really exists.

9. "Understanding is to reorganize the elements of a certain field." This is another structuralist argument. (In music, for instance, there is Jean-Jacques Nattiez's paradigmatic method of melodic analysis.) The idea comes close to that of a game. To understand a game one has to know the rules, as in playing cards, which determine the right choices. This idea applies to society viewed as a game.

10. "Understanding is based on a morphology tied with time, it is to see how things unfold from each other." This is a Goethean or evolutionary view. To understand the behavior of someone is to show the phase-by-phase development which led to that person; that is, it is to go through the history of an individual or of a society. Misunderstanding, in turn, is to falsify this history or to ignore it.

11. "Understanding is a paradigmatic event, in which one sees the alternatives." Georg Henrik von Wright, in his theories of logic, speaks about so-called counterfactual statements—what might have happened. To understand is to see all the alternatives presented to an individual before one chooses to act. Understanding is therefore the same as to see the possibilities of choice. In the words of Robert Musil: *"Wenn es Wirklichkeitssinn giebt muss es auch Möglichkeitssinn geben."*

12. "Understanding is to see the real nature of things, to reduce the phenomenon to statistical facts, to confirm it by scientific experiment." This argument is very contradictory and quite anti-(or non-) semiotical. Semiotics generally claims to do nothing other than elaborate models and hypotheses concerning reality. To infer a phenomenon as from natural laws is for a semiotician a mystification, when we are dealing with some human cultural or social behavior. For instance, it would be impossible to claim that the differences among cultures stem from the symmetry of brain hemispheres, according to the dominance of either the right or left side (Vladimir Petrov's thesis); and it would be equally impossible to believe that there are inevitable natural bases for historical events. It would be just as illogical to state that cultural products emerge from race, climate, or landscape. These are all mystifications, and to resort to such "natural" principles is nothing but the pseudo-understanding of a phenomenon. Biosemiotics has already taught us that the *Umwelt* of an organism is in fact chosen by it (von Uexküll's thesis). Our senses only receive information and stimuli typical of it; all other inputs are mere noise.

13. "Understanding is to see the subject in some actantial role." This species of argument belongs to case number 1, above, in which the general is seen via the

particular or vice versa. For instance, the actantial role of a generality becomes understandable when an individual enacts that role with all its mannerisms and peculiarities; for example, Napoleon as seen by Tolstoy in *War and Peace;* or Marechal Mannerheim becoming understandable when he is provided with vignettes and with anecdotes of his table manners. Even the actantial role of a "Marechal" can be broken down into individual characteristics.

14. "Understanding is basically an internal, cognitive or 'auto-communicative' event. Thus, we speak of the subject understanding him/herself." The varieties of self-understanding are many. People do not understand themselves before mirroring themselves before others; thus, self-understanding may be basically an entirely social event. This was supposed by Mikhail Bakhtin in his principle of dialogue, and it has been also noticed by George Herbert Mead in his social psychology.

Mead distinguishes between the concepts of 'I' and 'me'. The 'I' signifies an ego who acts as a kind of spontaneous, unpredictable agent—but only insofar as his acts have not yet been projected to others and back to his own ego, whereupon it becomes 'me'. According to Mead, this difference becomes clear when we think of the following situation: I talk to myself and remember what I said and what I perhaps felt at that moment. In that case, my earlier ego is the same as 'me'; it is the ego which serves as an object to itself. The same occurs in relationship to others: 'Me' is the ego seen by others. Mead says: "The 'I' is the response of the organism to the attitudes of the others; the 'me' is the organized set of attitudes of the other which one himself assumes" ([1934] 1967: 175).

This model also explains the emergence of the social. Man's self-understanding is that one sees the 'I' as a kind of "sign"; it is the 'I' that has turned into a sign either to itself or to others. After this experience of 'me', one may suppose that the ego functions in a different way, such that he is supposed to respond to the expectations of others, and for this reason:

> The 'me' represents a definite organization of the community there in our own attitudes . . . there is no certainty in regard to it. . . . There is a moral necessity, but no mechanical necessity for the act. (178)

Thus, in Mead's view, a certain amount of "existentiality" enters the scene when he says that the distinction between 'I' and 'me' is not fictitious, that they are not identical, and that the 'I' is always something unpredictable. From this model, Mead also deduces his own definition of semiotics, since symbols are signs in this constant discussion wherein the 'I' is reflected to the Other and back. In such interaction, gestures are a "significant symbolism and by symbols we do not mean something that lies outside of the field of conduct. A symbol is nothing but a stimulus whose response is given in advance" (181).

In other words, a symbol is a tool by which subject *s1* guarantees that subject *s2* behaves in a certain way, since he can assume that the latter knows in advance the symbol's meaning. Therefore, if in a conversation there prevails a mutual understanding, it is a sign of the fact that the interpretation of subject *s1* of a symbol was correct. This is in turn known by subject *s1* on the basis of the reaction of subject *s2*. If *s1* says, "Open the door" and *s2* responds by closing the window or turning on the radio, then *s1* knows that the sign used by him is not a symbol in the ordinary sense of the word. Thus, misunderstanding is the same as the failure of a symbol or sign.

Hence, in Mead's theory the self-understanding of a subject, as conceived in the dialectic between 'I' and 'me', is fundamentally social. A typical case of misunderstanding is a patient who fails to realize that he is ill; he lacks the sense of illness.[7] Such a person does not understand himself as 'me'.

15. "Understanding is a shift from 'I' to 'not-I', which is the basis of all morality and ethics." Solidarity and compassion are based on the ability of a subject to put himself in another's shoes, to adopt the position of another subject. This is the mystical event in many a moral philosophy (e.g., that of Soloviev).

All the cases of understanding listed above are essentially different semiotic operations. Does this mean that in semiotics we have basically been studying the understanding of signs, without our even being aware of doing so? Not necessarily, since in semiotics little attention has been paid to this aspect of sign processes, and more given to that which can be quantified and objectified. There is no doubt that understanding provides another way to approach semiotic processes. This should become clear as we next scrutinize examples of work by two scholars who have investigated understanding.

ALFRED SCHÜTZ AND VLADIMIR JANKÉLÉVITCH ON UNDERSTANDING

Alfred Schütz's theory of signs has been almost categorically neglected by mainstream semiotics, although it constitutes an ambitious effort to lay the foundation for a sign theory starting from Husserl's phenomenology and sociology. When Schütz, in his 1932 work *Der sinnliche Aufbau der sozialen Welt* (whose title may be a reference to Rudolph Carnap's *Der logische Aufbau der Welt*), finally comes to the definition of sign, it may at first sight unsettle the reader by its complexity:

> Wir können also 'Zeichen' wie folgt definieren: Zeichen sind Handlungsgegen-
> ständlichkeiten oder Artefakte, welche nicht nach jenen Deutungsschemata
> ausgelet werden, die sich aus Erlebnissen von ihnen als selbständigen Gegen-
> ständlichkeiten der Aussenwelt konstituieren oder für derlei Erlebnisse von
> Gegenständlichkeiten der psychischen Welt in jeweiligen Erfahrungszusam-
> menhang vorrätig sind (adäquate Deutungsschemata) sondern welche kraft be-
> sonderer vorangegangener, erfahrender Erlebnisse in andere (inadäquate) Deu-

tungsschemata eingeordnet werden, deren Konstitution sich aus polythetischen
Setzungen erfahrener Akte in anderen physischen oder idealen Gegenständ-
lichkeiten vollzog. . . . Unter einem Zeichensystem verstehen wir einen Sinn-
zusammenhang zwischen Deutungsschemata, in den das betreffende Zeichen
für denjenigen, der deutend oder setzend gebraucht, eingestellt ist. (1932: 168)

Schütz emphasizes that by "meaningful connection" he understands the
link between the meanings of signs, *"wofür die Zeichen Zeichen sind,"* i.e., the
experiences of a thinking ego, who forms the signs or indicates by them. Taken
directly from Husserl is the distinction between expressive schemes and indicative schemes (*Ausdrucksschemata, Deutungsschemata*). The former are signs that
I have used at least once when spontaneously expressing some experience. The
latter are signs that have been frequently used previously as signifiers of the experience in question. The indicative schemes thus represent so-called natural
language, which must already be well known to the speaker (here Schütz refers
to the idea of competence).

Behind Schütz's complex definition lies the effort to understand that which
is alien, a process he calls *"Fremdverstehen."* His central theme is to understand
the alien in a social world. By "understanding" Schütz means to catch the sense
(*Sinn*) of something: "since all understanding is directed to the meaningful and
only that which is understood is with a sense" (1932: 140). The problem then becomes how the 'I' understands his fellow human beings, whom he first notices as
bodies in his world, i.e., as things, but whom he later assumes to follow a similar
stream of experiences as his own. Schütz distinguishes three aspects of the social
world: *Umwelt,* the world surrounding man, *Mitwelt,* the world a little further
away, and *Vorwelt.*

According to Schütz, the path of the ego's experiences corresponds to the
experiential stream of another person, which we suppose to be somewhat similar
to our own. This supposition allows us to somehow take the position of this
Other. Yet the difference between *eigenseelig* (own psyche) and *fremdseelig*
(alien psyche) lies in the fact that although the two psyches live in a kind of coexistence (i.e., they exist side by side), the 'I' only recognizes fragments of this
coexistence. When we observe a body alien to us, we do not only consider it a
body, a thing in the outer world, but we understand that its gestures are signs of
the other person's experiences. Still, my experiences of experiences alien to myself still remain my experiences. Thus, the only thing we can be sure about is our
own intentional stream of experiences, whose duration is continuous and complete, whereas we understand the alien incompletely and fragmentarily. Therefore, the alien psyche is always something doubtful in relation to the certainty of
our own experiences and their doubtlessness. That is why in the construction of
the 'you' sphere of the social world, the 'we' signs play a crucial role. They are for
Schütz, as for Mead, social functional units, which bridge the way from a lonely
ego to the social universe. But they always include a certain uncertainty. They are

a kind of hypotheses concerning the alien psyche, which we try to understand but which we can also misunderstand.

Another philosopher of our century who focuses on the problem of understanding is Vladimir Jankélévitch. He also starts from a phenomenological basis, but is more fascinated with misunderstanding than with understanding. He goes even further and distinguishes between the concepts of *le malentendu* and *le méconnu*. In his *Le-je-ne-sais-quoi et le presque-rien,* in the chapter "Appearance and Time," he says that if consciousnesses had fewer secrets, if they were less ironic, less impassioned, less shy, less nervous, they would be either understood (*comprises*) or not understood (*incomprises*) but not misunderstood (*mécomprises*), i.e., understood wrongly. One could say of some geniuses that they are misunderstood, even though their fame rests upon such factors as those which make them geniuses. Therefore, the mistake is not to admire Liszt in general, but to admire him only as a great pianist even though he was just as great a composer. Similarly, Chopin is well-known but misunderstood if he is taken as the composer of waltzes and *polonaises* when his real essence appears in his *scherzi* and *ballades.* To this one might add that Sibelius is a well-known composer in Central Europe; namely, as the writer of *Valse triste.* He is misunderstood there, however, since he is not appreciated as a symphonist.

Jankélévitch has concentrated particularly on showing the dissimilarities of similarities, and on how difficult it is, in the age of positivist progress, with its unifying appearance (in fact his idea comes close to Heidegger's *das Man* principle), to distinguish the counterfeit from the genuine in the area of morality. The ostentative man (*l'homme ostentatif*) imagines that pretending to have an intention is the same as having one. Acts which only *seem* to be done because of duty (although in reality stemming from selfish roots) are taken as acts that have *really* been done because of duty (Kant).

According to Jankélévitch, all intentionality is something that is easily misunderstood (*méconnu).* Two positions (attitudes, gestures, etc.), identical in shape, structure, mass, and the like, can correspond to two completely different intentions. The same amount of light may shine forth at sunrise and at twilight, but whether the sun is rising or setting greatly alters the situation in which the light appears.

This brings us very close to the core issue of semiotics, specifically, the question of how to study unquantifiable or unobservable meanings. Greimas admitted their existence, and even dared to establish, as the deep level of his whole positivist system, the notion of isotopy, which cannot be observed experimentally, but which can be recognized only by persons having the required competencies. Or, as a teacher crystallized his experiences of many years: "Some realize—some do not." Isotopy is a category of understanding, though the Paris school never stated it quite so explicitly.

We are also rather close to the problem of fakes, as studied by Umberto Eco.

A fake is of course a deliberate *méconnaissance,* a misunderstanding that is concealed. According to Jankélévitch misunderstanding starts with the possibility of two interpretations. Allegories, for example, are such intentional misunderstandings. The denoted matter somehow "reminds" us of a sign, but it is not that sign at all. Jankélévitch particularly studies the thesis that the world keeps going only on the basis of a tacit and accepted misunderstanding. He sees basically two kinds of forgery: Either it takes place in good faith without one becoming conscious of it, or the forgery is recognized and is simply permitted to continue.

From these two kinds of forgery we may derive the following sub-genres for each case, according to which subjects *s1* and *s2* do or do not participate in the misunderstanding:

1. Two subjects in communication both wrongly understand each other. This is a double misunderstanding, which is the most lamentable since perhaps no one will ever know the truth. The listener has misunderstood although his partner in dialogue thinks he has understood. We see this situation when someone loves another without ever having the courage to tell the person, since he or she believes that the other does not love them. In this mutual ignorance, both wait for a decisive step from the other, a word that would change everything. In the end, the lovers die without ever knowing that they cared about each other.

2. One of the subjects misunderstands, but the other understands that this is a misunderstanding, or he believes himself to have been misunderstood. In this case, the circle is broken if the one who is aware informs the one who is unaware. If he does not do so, then the misunderstanding is merely a sham. Misunderstanding is not that the one who understands consciously lets himself remain misunderstood. The swindler continues the misunderstanding, and he does not hurry to correct his mistake. Or perhaps he or she just lacks the courage to do so. In that case, the issue is not so much that of fraud as of sluggishness.

3. Completely understood misunderstanding involves a false fraud. Both partners communicate with a kind of ghost, who is someone other than their real interlocutor. Here we are in a kind of false situation, of whose falsehood both are conscious. This kind of dialogue is experienced as collusive and yet wary. It is as if we belong to a secret society, in which we suspect each other of something. I understand you, I know that you understand me, and you understand that I understand. In other words, I am conscious of your consciousness. Operas and plays are based upon this kind of deliberate "misunderstanding," which in those cases is called performance. Another case is seen in the lawyer who defends a person even though he knows him to be guilty. Society, with its many practices, is based on this kind of voluntary and double misunderstanding.

In French sociology there recurs the idea of a "plural" person, which indicates the fact that a single subject assumes various roles. Roles are kinds of social formations, ways in which people represent themselves to each other, i.e., a process which is to a great extent based on deliberate and continued misunderstanding, and even sought-for, acceptable, and favored mechanisms of misunderstanding. The misunderstandings may arise from the fact that we are not received and observed as we really are but as what we represent. We are placed into some actantial role, often against our will, and even without our knowing it. Subject *s1* can, however, always either accept or reject the actantial role offered to him by subject *s2*. Thus, there always prevails a tension between what Bergson calls the deep ego and the actorial roles offered to us.

Among other scholars, Bernard Lahier, in his new book *L'homme pluriel: Les ressorts de l'action* (1998), ponders the roles and habituses of postmodern society. Does the idea of *l'homme pluriel* help one to understand oneself and others? The fact that man changes his roles helps him/her to view the world from various viewpoints. But what logic or supra-reasoning tells him which roles are compatible and which incompatible? The roles also carry their own modalities. All the modalities are not compatible. This may cause in an individual new forms of self-misunderstanding (or "self-deceptions," as Thomas A. Sebeok puts it). One may not understand why he behaves in ways both A and non-A. Yet one can make such behavior understandable: that one does so because when doing act A he was playing role X, and when doing act non-A he was in actantial role Y. It is typical of postmodern society that there is no longer any super-logic, conscience, master narrative, and the like, which would guide our various roles and modalities. This lack, as we know, leads to the disappearance of man's inner coherence. So one is forced to live in a continuously complex isotopy.

NOTES

1. On this process, see also von Wright, in his *Explanation and Understanding* (1971).
2. The textualization of the world is one of the great epistemes of European philosophy. Marek Kwiek speaks of two directions in philosophy, one emphasizing the communality, the other textuality:

> The opposition is between "community" and "text." It is worth noting that "community" (*communauté*) has recently become one of the most important terms on which some interesting philosophical discussions focus. . . . I take Barthes's attempt to describe the situation in Authors and Writers to be paradigmatic. Who is the writer and who is the author—who is our textualist and who is our communitarian (or a "Hegelian" and a "Nietzschean")?

According to Kwiek the first-mentioned acts in words; the word itself is not a tool, but he/she asks how to write and considers literature the goal. Literature is for him unrealistic, but it is that unreality by which he can pose questions to the world (like the Kantian unsocial sociality or Hegel's cunningness of reason) (Kwiek 1998: 165).

Instead the writer takes the word as a means. He proves, indicates, gives lessons. Language supports a certain praxis but does not constitute one of its own; language is a communicative tool. The author is like a priest, the writer like a functionary. Textual Authors and Communitarian Writers form their own typology.

This distinction is interesting since it seems to refer to the two essential paradigms in semiotics: signification and communication. The one for whom the sign is only a means for action, to maintain the communality, sees the situation differently from the one who views the sign essentially as a means of signification. But does the textualization of the world at the same time provide it with a meaning, and especially under the conditions of the Barthesian *auteur*? Its antithesis would be to make the world communicable, when the world is seen as a praxis. In it, are the signs as such secondary, and in it, do we presuppose that we continually act in reality?

Then the solution to the problem of understanding would be that we abandon the textualization of the world, which, as stated above, only leads to solipsism, to the rejection of the Other and the alien. The solution would be to join oneself to the world as a praxis, as a communicative unity, in which the Other is met directly, as such. But is this not just an illusion, as the structuralist and textualist authors have claimed? The world as mere communication does not exist for them. Or perhaps it exists, but rather as a fallen world, into which we are "thrown" in Heidegger's sense; it is mere *Schein,* mere communication, an enormous network of inputs and outputs in which one never asks what the message means, what meaning the sign is carrying, in which one participates in the communication scheme of sender-message-receiver but stops short of understanding.

In existential semiotics it is essential to see signs and communication as expression or *Ausdruck.* As Husserl said, the mere *Bedeutungs* function leads only to the study of the Saussurean *langue,* to the same kind of objectivization of meaning of which Barthes spoke in his text on Writers. We do not get into the sense of the process, which can be grasped only via understanding.

3. I am indebted to Lisa Block de Behar for pointing out Borges in connection with this context.

4. It is probable that Peirce, in his concept of the interpretant, was influenced by Locke's notion of "idea."

5. It is interesting that von Wright (1971) contrarily sees understanding as something teleological and forward-oriented.

6. I am grateful to Susanna Välimäki for introducing these notions into our discussion.

7. According to Dr. Heikki Majava, the patient who fails to see himself as being ill is an essential problem in psychiatry.

REFERENCES

Borges, Jorge Luis. 1988. "On the Cult of Books." In Borges, *Other Inquisitions 1937–52,* trans. Ruth L. C. Simms. Austin: University of Texas Press.
Eco, Umberto. 1968, 1983. *La struttura assente.* Milano: Bompiani.
Gide, André. 1953. *Journal.* Paris: Pleiades.
Goldmann, Lucien. 1994. *Le dieu caché* (étude sur la vision tragique dans les Pensées de Pascal et dans le théâtre de Racine). New ed. Paris: Gallimard.
Husserl, Edmund. 1913. *Logische Untersuchungen. Untersuchung zur Phänomenologie und Theorie der Erkenntnis.* Tübingen: Max Niemeyer.
Jankélévitch, Vladimir. 1957. *Le Je-ne-sais-quoi et le Presque-rien.* Paris: Presses Universitaires de France.
Kwiek, Marek. 1998. "Between the Community and the Text." *Trames: A Journal of the*

Humanities and Social Sciences 2, no. 2: 47–52 [Estonian Academy of Sciences and Tartu University].

Lahier, Bernard. 1998. *L'homme pluriel: Les ressorts de l'action.* Paris: Nathan.

Mead, George Herbert. [1934] 1967. *Mind, Self, and Society from the Standpoint of a Social Behaviourist.* Edited and with an Introduction by Charles W. Morris. Chicago and London: University of Chicago Press.

Nietzsche, Friedrich Wilhelm. 1974. *The Gay Science.* New York: Vintage.

———. 1997. *Beyond Good and Evil.* Mineola, N.Y. : Dover Publications.

Peirce, Charles Sanders. 1955. "Evolutionary Love." In *Philosophical Writings of Peirce*, selected and edited by Justus Buchler, pp. 361–374. New York: Dover Publications.

Rawls, John. 1973. *A Theory of Justice.* Oxford: Oxford University Press.

Schütz, Alfred. [1932] 1974. *Der sinnhafte Aufbau der sozialen Welt. Eine Eineleitung in die verstehende Soziologie.* Frankfurt am Main: Suhrkamp.

Voigt, Vilmos. 1977. *Bevezetés a Szemiotikába.* Budapest: Gondolat.

von Wright, Georg Henrik. 1971. *Explanation and Understanding.* Ithaca: Cornell University Press.

5

Signs of Anxiety; or,
The Problem of the Semiotic Subject

As a student about thirty years ago, I started to translate Martin Heidegger's work *Sein und Zeit.* I managed to translate a third of the book before I noticed that hardly anyone was interested in it. I soon became involved in French structuralism and rejected German philosophy in favor of Lévi-Straussian anthropology. I could not then have imagined that Heidegger would come back to poststructuralist semiotics in the 1980s with Derrida's deconstructionist doctrine by Derrida, as a philosopher justified by deconstructionism.

In any case, in the tradition of classical semiotics—by which I understand the theoretical whole (though not a system) formed by Peirce, Greimas, Lotman, and some other scholars—a new kind of application of semiotics has emerged. Greimas's death in 1992 left the Paris school of semiotics in a state of uncertainty and anguish, since the epistemic situation at the beginning of the 1990s does not seem to favor such rigorously axiomatic systems as Greimas's generative trajectory. Nevertheless, although the Paris school may vanish, Greimas lives, in that concepts and approaches created by him can be used even in a changed context. Greimasian semiotics can be "deconstructed," and it can still be applied even if one does not believe in the idea of a generative course.

In what follows, I return to Heidegger, whom I try to link with a concise semiotic analysis of anxiety.

WHAT IS ANXIETY?

Does not the concept of anxiety itself seem somehow like a German invention? In a world in which Cartesian categories have conquered, with the artificial intelligence and cognitive approaches, how can there be any place for "anxiety" other than as a subjective meaning experience?

Do signs have another life apart from the rules of play which determine their conduct? More particularly, do signs have inner life, a soul? The existence of anxiety is a sign for something, namely the existence of a subject.

But can we semiotically imagine a universe that would consist of only one anguished subject? Probably not, since insofar as this subject is joined to any significations, those significations emerge from the fact that the subject is in some kind of relation to the universe surrounding it. This subject dwells in the universe, in the semiosphere which belongs to it, in the field of signs, whereas a subject is itself a sign to some other. A subject that only "is," is hardly an anguished subject in the Greimasian sense. According to Greimas, a subject is euphoric when it possesses an object, when it is conjuncted with it: $S \wedge O$. A subject is dysphoric when it has been disjuncted from an object: $S \vee O$. Would, then, anxiety be reducible to a modal, pathemic state because a subject is disjuncted from the euphoric object which pertains to it? Is this not too unequivocal? Perhaps, but it still undeniably suffices for the analysis of simple narrative situations like operatic scenes, advertisement videos, or mythical stories.

Nevertheless, if we think of our semiotic self and of the situations into which it enters in the universe of signs, do we not need another kind of metalanguage, a method to portray things from the inside? We need to describe what happens to a subject when it loses an object, becomes disjuncted from it, when it approaches and encounters it, or when it finally decides to leave the object as such—or finally, what Heidegger depicted by his concept of *Gelassenheit*. In fact, this Heideggerian notion can be taken as a criticism of Greimas's narrative grammar, that the latter remains too rough a "representation." In *Gelassenheit,* Heidegger has a "teacher" say: "It (*Gelassenheit*) is not at all thinkable, as long as we have to represent it and bring it in front of us objectively and violently as a present interrelation of objects, one of which being called man and the other the encountered one."

If the concepts of "subject" and "object" are too crude for a Heideggerian approach, then so is the alternative of describing their relationship as a simple dichotomy—conjunction and disjunction. In Heidegger's view, the relation of subject to object—to "the encountered"—should be portrayed by Heraclitus's term "approach": "I think this term would be splendid for the relationship of the essence of knowledge: it very clearly expresses the character of going toward something and of getting closer to objects".

If we then attempt to make our semiotic concepts more subtle, such a viewpoint may be found in the philosophy of Heidegger. On the other hand, what is involved is the same "method" that great artists have used in their novels, compositions and paintings. If we adopt this viewpoint, our attitude to the outer, physical reality of signs radically changes.

Signs are no more than a surface, cover, *Schein,* inside which the subject, the soul, moves.

In fact, it is precisely the concept of anxiety as a particular "passion" that has led us to this observation.

Angst is perhaps a passion met particularly in the German culture. It is a state of being that does not lead to a resolving action; it is a virtuality of narration, which, according to Claude Brémond's narrative theory (see *Logique du récit*), does not bring us to a "passage to an act" and its achievement. As soon as it shifts to these states, it ceases to be a passion called *Angst*.

Therefore, anxiety as such is a sign of the existence of a subject. However, it has its own proper temporal structure. The modal situation is quite different if anxiety concerns either the past or future. To put it in a Greimasian way, anxiety is a state in which a subject has been disjuncted from its value object.

If we have a euphoric object that belongs to the past, then anxiety represents a pathemic state which is caused by the lost of this euphoric object (this state can be a source of a certain kind of pleasure; cf. Paul Claudel's interpretation of Wagnerian aesthetics, *l'homme à l'écoute du paradis perdu*). The disjunction, or getting rid of a dysphoric object, does not bring about an anxiety, except when the dysphoria of the past has left a "trace" in the consciousness of a subject, a trace which it cannot liberate itself from, like anguishing memories.

Instead, anxiety emerges in its future-oriented form precisely from the fact that a subject has been conjuncted, or is rather going to be conjuncted, to a dysphoric object—such as death. Does the core of the whole Heideggerian philosophy lie here, in that this unavoidable conjunction to a dysphoric object becomes euphoric or is made euphoric, and is seen in general as the most appropriate possibility of man?

But how can something which is necessary be seen as possible? The possible presupposes an alternative, optionality.

The pathemic state of anxiety is therefore articulated according to the following asymmetric figure:

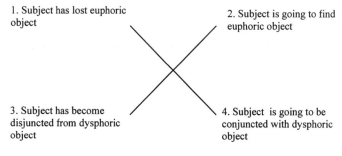

1. Subject has lost euphoric object

2. Subject is going to find euphoric object

3. Subject has become disjuncted from dysphoric object

4. Subject is going to be conjuncted with dysphoric object

FIGURE 1

Of these four possibilities, one can immediately see that only cases 1 and 4 belong to the figure of anxiety in the proper sense, and, in fact, cause it.

Furthermore, one notices that the schema includes a certain temporal structure: Case 1 represents "terminativity"—something has happened in the past and has been definitely finished, lost; whereas in case 4, something is just beginning or displays inchoativity. Cases 1 and 3 are therefore terminative, whereas cases 2 and 4 are inchoative. There also exists a "durable" anxiety, which is like a continuous state—like the aesthetic attitude of Kierkegaard.

Let us now look at the modal contents of these situations.

In anxiety directed toward the future, the case is most often one in which the subject *knows* that something is necessary, that he has to do something, but he is not able to do it. In other words, the modal articulation is: 'to know to be obliged to be not able to do something' (*savoir devoir ne pas pouvoir faire quelquechose*).

However, there is also an anxiety of ignorance, inability, lack of belief or 'will', i.e., anxiety caused by the negation of different modalities. In Richard Wagner's opera *Parsifal*, we find all these varieties crystallized into the modal competence of its various "actors."

For example, the anxiety of Amfortas is anguish of powerlessness and inability, although he knows what he should do: His *das Man sein* would require that he should share the Holy Grail with the knights; but this is what he cannot do, what he is unable to pursue. A psychosomatic sign of this anxiety of powerlessness is the wound that is never healed.

The anxiety of Parsifal himself is due to ignorance, "stupidity"; or rather it is first "unanxiety," since as long as he does not know that he has committed any crime, he does not feel anxiety. He does not feel he has done anything criminal after committing the ecological offense of shooting a swan in the Grail area, in which animals are protected. It is only through the experience of anxiety that Parsifal becomes able to free Amfortas from his anxiety. The idea of a "holy fool" (*der reine Tor*) means precisely that the hero does not carry out his task of reconciliation and mediation through his own will, but as determined by others, through others' will. Instead, Amfortas is a hero who has lost his sender Titurel in the third act, whereas Parsifal receives Gurnemanz as his sender in the Good Friday scene.

Kundry's anxiety is due to evil will, 'not-willing'. As she says herself, she never wants to do anything good to anyone. She exploits Parsifal's ignorance in the seduction scene, although without success. Her anxiety ultimately leads to complete speechlessness in the third act. The only articulated words she says are *Dienen, dienen* (To serve, to serve); she wants to reconcile her evil acts in the past by serving, like in the first act when she brings Amfortas balsam from Arabia. Not even in the baptism scene of the third act, in the Good Friday miracle, does Kundry get rid of her guilt, since at the end she sinks down lifeless when a white dove settles upon Parsifal's shoulder. This scene has often been forgotten in the staging, although it is marked in the score.

Anxiety can also be characteristic of a collective actor—the knights are freed from their anguish by enjoying the Communion from the Grail, and this is depicted in the first act.

Parsifal is therefore an opera of anxiety and its reconciliation, or of a mythical mediation which liberates man from anguish. The most impressive transformations, where the music depicts such purely inner movements of the mind, are the Communion scene in the first act and the Good Friday miracle in the third act.

Of all arts, music is one of the most effective means to express anxiety. Peter Maxwell Davies's monologue opera about a mad king portrays a kind of durable anxiety, as does Schoenberg's *Erwartung*. However, one has to distinguish between two types of musical "anxiety," depending on whether the figure of anxiety appears through musical enunciate or enunciation.

In other words, is anxiety something that the music, composition, "text" tries to describe, or is it a pathemic state that the music seeks to create, to transfer to the listener? In an opera, such as the one by Peter Maxwell Davies, the music may well describe an extremely anguished actor on stage, but its impact upon the listener/spectator may be something quite different—grotesque, cathartic, pitiful, comical—but not anguishing. Correspondingly, in the music there may not always be any "topos" or explicit factors referring to anxiety, but it may still bring the listener into a state of anxiety.

In contemporary music, the *absence* of one essential semiotic parameter, actoriality, signs alluding to the presence of a subject, can be precisely one such device causing anxiety. For example, the static music by Ligeti in his *Apparitions* and *Atmosphères* can bring about the impression of an empty space, in which the lack of counterparts of actors, musical themes, human subjects, may cause the pathemic experience of anxiety in a listener.

In the early music by Magnus Lindberg, in works like " . . . *de Tartuffe je crois*" and *Kraft*, there occurs a real Faustian anguished subject as the primus motor of the action, whereas in Lindberg's piano concerto, which does not operate so much with dramatic juxtapositions of various materials, there are no longer any traces or signs of the presence of a subject. Nor do we find them in Kaija Saariaho's recent works (this is not to be understood as a criticism but as something that forces our attention in another direction, namely toward units smaller than a modality, i.e., to kinds of "submodalities," just as there can also be proto- or subsemantic units in a musical discourse). In their musical world view, these works represent the same view of a "subject" as that found in modern artificial intelligence studies and cognitive research, a subject which has been dismantled into its fractal pieces and which has ceased to exist as a modal subject.

However, we do not need to go so deep into contemporary music, since even the classics know how to express anguish. Kierkegaard spoke of two species of anxiety: a sympathetic antipathy and an antipathetic sympathy.

In turn, Heidegger distinguished *Angst* from mere "expectation," which was a positive, euphoric transformation of *Angst*. (In his dialogue *Gelassenheit,* the teacher says: "To expect, well! But not to hope since hope is already in the sphere of representation and the represented." The learned man replies: "The expectation, however, gives it up, or rather: the expectation does not allow representation to enter. Expectation does not have any object." When the teacher comes back with, "But when we expect, we expect something," the learned man responds, "Yes, but as soon as we represent what we expect and make it manifest, we do not expect it any longer." etc.)

Think now of the slow middle movements of Beethoven's *Waldstein* and *Les adieux* piano sonatas. In both pieces, a kind of transition occurs between two "action" movements, a transformation from state *a* to state *b*. These intermediate sections do not have any independent character but just this function of transition, expectation of the future, preparation. Therefore, they are "actorially," i.e., thematically, less pregnant than the first and last parts of the sonatas.

The subject in these slow movements is not in any active function, but in a kind of latent state of virtuality, in an epistemic uncertainty, in which something is expected. However, this something is not, as Heidegger puts it, "represented," made concrete on the level of signs. Nevertheless, these intermediate movements are modalized in such a way that the middle part of *Waldstein* depicts a pure, euphoric, sympathetic expectation, whereas the transition in *Les adieux* portrays a dysphoric, anguished expectation, according to the subtitle "Absence." In both cases, we have music which has stagnated to a single point but which is still going on toward something unknown. Yet the way the "inner narrator" of the music, its subject, reacts to this existential situation is quite different. The first one represents the "sweet anxiety" described by Kierkegaard, and the latter, the "gloomy anxiety."

In the above, we considered anxiety a typically German concept pertaining to the culture of *Innigkeit,* intimacy. But in Mussorgsky's opera does not Boris Godunov also represent an anguished czar who finally dies of anguish? In his case, what is involved is an anxiety of powerlessness, which is due to the placement of a dysphoric object in the past—not so much in the future. The anguish of a *Traviata* or *La Bohème* is related to a dysphoric object (disease), which threatens in the future.

Anxiety thus also has its own temporal structure. There are even operas whose theme is the rejection of anxiety and the punishment following it: Don Giovanni, for example.

In fact, anxiety as expressed through musical tones is already public anxiety. The paradox of art lies in the fact that its deepest reality is inner, but this reality has to become external. In other words, in a psychological sense, first there is *parole* then *langue*—accordingly quite contrary to what the generativists, grammarians, and cognitivists teach.

Anxiety can also be interpreted as an incongruence between the signifier and the signified, as an imbalance between expression and content (this is a narrative figure often met in Mishima's novels: The hero cannot find a proper expression for what he has in his mind; therefore, he becomes neurotic and even criminal). In this sense, it is a genuinely "romantic" passion—which can, of course, occur during any style period whatsoever.

The issue could be formulated in still another way: We have here a conflict between two semiotic systems: the inner semiotic structure of the 'I and the outer world or "the encountered." One way of solving this is a complete adaptation to the system represented by the Other—as in the Heideggerian *das Man sein*. But in his aforementioned essay, Heidegger also introduced another model of solution, the negation of *Angst* through its positive side. There he is actually close not only to zen but to all such thinking known as quietist.

Anxiety is an essential part of the life of every scientist or artist, of a "creative" person in general. Everyone will have experienced that typical emotion of anxiety which precedes the beginning of a "creative" work, that fear which comes from the fact that one knows that soon one has to take a leap into the unknown. We do not know what will happen as the result of the action. Everyone will also be familiar with a neurotic reaction in this situation: an effort to start to do anything at all, but not just what one *should* do. This is the same psychological phenomenon as when one is looking for a certain thing: One finds in the library all other possible papers, documents, letters, things which one was searching for yesterday or earlier but not that particular thing which one is looking for right now.

In fact, to be able to do creative work requires an ability to stand this elementary obligatory anxiety, even masochistically to seek this anxiety, since without it there can be no great innovation or work of art. Of course, it may be that this is an extremely romantic view of creativity—some people work with clockwork precision during certain hours and are immediately ready for a creative process without any anguish or neurosis.

On the other hand, if anxiety is related to the psychological state preceding an act of creation, in the action itself one does not generally feel it, with the possible exception of performing artists. In performing artists, anxiety is a feature linked to the temporal process of performing. For example, a player knows that in the piece he/she is to perform, there is a technically very demanding passage. For an orchestral musician, it is sufficient to know that in a piece lasting one hour there is only one such solo that must succeed at its proper moment. This is enough to cause an anxiety that has strong psychosomatic symptoms.

Often it can be a part of a continuous performance in which the modality of 'can' is suddenly emphasized at the cost of other musical modalities, 'knowing' (i.e., information value) and 'willing' (kinetic energy). The reaction of a musician in such a situation is often to hurry, which naturally makes the passage and its performance even more difficult, thus increasing the probability of a failure. On the contrary, the right solution would be to slow down the temporal process, whereby the difficulties are lightened. Even famous musicians have this kind of nervous inclination. For example, Arthur Schnabel had the habit of accelerating at the end of scale passages and often "swallowing" the last notes unheard. A listener once came after the recital to the artist's room and asked for his money back since the pianist had not played all the notes. "I cannot guarantee anything of the kind," answered Schnabel.

All of these cases represent an attempt to get rid of anxiety by accelerating it, which in reality only causes the perceptible "sign," a disturbance in the communication.

After the action, the ready product, the object, is detached from its author and steps into publicity on its own terms. Then the author has to face the anxiety, which now of its nature recalls the anguish of *das Man sein:* Everything that is public is susceptible to criticism—to all the negative aspects which Heidegger depicts as gossiping, equivocation, etc. In science, inner intuition naturally has an important role. But science differs from private thinking in that inner intuition has to be rendered to a model to be communicated to other people. The same holds true for art, although the conditions of "communicating" are quite different.

REFERENCES

Brémond, Claude. 1973. *Logique du récit.* Paris: Seuil.
Heidegger, Martin. 1959. *Gelassenheit.* Pfullingen: Neske.
———. 1967. *Sein und Zeit.* Tübingen: Max Niemeyer Verlag.

PART TWO

In the Forest of Symbols

6

From Aesthetics to Ethics

SEMIOTIC OBSERVATIONS ON THE MORAL ASPECTS OF ARTS,
ESPECIALLY MUSIC

In the 1990s, semiotic research has come to a kind of parting of the ways. After having refound "subject," which was banished in the phase of structuralism as an object of inquiry, semiotic research can now choose the way cognition science studies the subject. There the striving for formalization that has always been inherent in semiotics bursts into flower. The human mind is seen as a huge network of nerves, as a field of their combinations. Such a model is said to "simulate" the human psyche and its functions quite truthfully. A mental phenomenon can be reduced to a certain series of numbers, which depicts its position and occurrence in the brain coordinates.

At the same time, this path paradoxically leads to the disappearance of subject and to a positivism somewhat similar to cybernetics at its time.

The other way even seems to lead outside of semiotics in a sense: It instigates one to examine the subject who makes choices. In Greimas's school, the semiotic construction of such a subject has already been clarified in detail (see, for example, Greimas and Fontanille 1991). However, one may next ask: How does a subject have to act in a given situation; which choices does he have to make?

What use can semiotics be to a given individual or a group in a certain situation? Greimas stated that the concept of sign itself is ultimately an axiological entity, and he did not avoid taking into consideration even such a "value" concept as death (an essay which remained unfinished). What do we have to do as semioticians and human beings? "What Do We Have to Do" was the title of a pamphlet published by Leo Tolstoy as early as a hundred years ago.

At the same time, we cannot exclude from the present investigation the vast domain of ethical problems. One cannot be satisfied, in general, with a study in which a phenomenon is reduced to some of its aspects, but even in a most abstract art work we have to account for the whole weight of the reality that has yielded it and which speaks therein through its own sign systems. The intentions of an author cannot be eliminated as a kind of intentional fallacy. The social context and the "ecoform" of an art work cannot be left without attention as "extrasemiotic conditions." The research paradigm is thus expanding to a remarkable extent. The change in sociosemiotics toward a direction which considers ethics and morality is a most obvious one if one juxtaposes, say, Umberto Eco's and Jean Baudrillard's analyses of American reality.

For Eco, America represents an "exotic Otherness" whose semiotic laws of functioning he makes explicit. Jean Baudrillard's reflections convey an overtly ethical tone: He talks about how Americanized information society is characterized by a shift from public to impudent and indecent, by an unrestrained, cancerous growth of the amount of communication and a falling into "ecstasy" of communication, a change of subject into a fractal field consisting of thousands of similar minimal units (the new coming of Leibnizian monadology), uncontrolled simulation, etc. Where Eco only writes a guide book to a semiological guerrilla warfare, Baudrillard is already waging it. Nevertheless, even Baudrillard's theory and vision could not exist without the cool theoretical discourse of semiotics. He only brings its tools amidst man's present situation and real action. He tries to employ semiotics in an ethical way.

The discovery of ethics seems to be related first to the problem of the subject—and, paradoxically, simultaneously to both the foregrounding of the subject and its disappearance. Without the concept of subject there is no ethical choice. Norms, external *devoirs* can be programmed into a computer or robot, whereas inner ethical 'will', i.e., deliberate choice with complicated factors and criteria with their hierarchies, cannot be inserted. On the other hand, the concept of subject must be postulated because of the notion of intention. Namely, the essential point in an act, a semiotic move, is not at all its result, but in which sense it has been done. When an art critic writes an apparently neutral text, he can leave something out, add something, or emphasize something, perhaps with bad intentions, when he wants to violate or to benefit his object for his own interests.

For instance, we are interested in knowing whether Boris Asafiev himself wanted his intonation theory to be used against Shostakovich and Prokofiev or whether this was done without him knowing or willing it. This is an essential moral question. How do the sympathies for national socialism of Paul de Man and Heidegger influence the evaluation of their doctrine? Do an artist's opinions exercise any impact on the value of his art? Do we have to condemn Wagner's music because of his obvious anti-Semitism? How do we have to relate to the interpretations of Emil Gilels when we know that he was a member of the Communist party and proud of it?

When scrutinizing these cases, it is not sufficient to deal with a subject and choice separately, apart from their context (*ça parle,* a system speaks in a man and guides his choices). It is crucial to know, for example, what was Boris Asafiev's relationship to Shostakovich and to Prokofiev, to the people in power; what were his aims, his goals—to become a great composer or what? We know, for example, how Theodor Adorno always forced all his pupils to criticize Sibelius's music—in order to raise Gustav Mahler to world fame as the only great symphonist of the century. In order to understand him, one must know that Adorno was a close friend of Alma Mahler. On the other hand, an ethical interpretation also presupposes the disappearance, "negation" of a subject. One might quote Herman Hesse's novel *The Narcissos and the Goldmouth,* in which the ideal of an "ethical," unselfish scholar is determined:

> This man . . . could have as well been a scholar, silent and rigorous researcher, who has abandoned himself to a work started by several others a long time before him, which work he would transmit further to others, a demanding and sustained work without ending and for which entire generations have devoted all their strivings and efforts. At least these aspects could an external observer notice in the face of the master: much patience, art and reflection, much self-command and understanding of what is always questionable in a human work, but on the other hand also much belief in one's vocation. (Narcissus and Rosamund)

Isn't this fragment from Hesse just a portrayal of an ethical ideal of a scholar? We have here a subject who moves the fulfillment of his own immediate pleasure to the background in order to function in his/her mythical role in the "actantial model" (Greimas's term; see Greimas 1979: 3–4; 1991: 64–66). His senders are the anonymous scholars of past generations, his helper his goodwill, and his object his knowledge.

However, the disappearance or fusion of a subject must take place in favor of some higher goals in order to say that what is involved is an ethical choice, "negation" of the self. Thus, one may ask whether the absence of a subject (actor) in avant-garde music—like in serial or field technic music—is such an ethical or unethical event?

Through all semiotics and structuralist research there passes a kind of emancipatory bass tone, *cantus firmus,* or horizon of knowledge. Yet, it is not seen immediately as actions but as a more "objective" analysis from which one can draw conclusions. Even apparently fully neutral scientific activity can contain ethical consequences—as, for example, when one gathers folklore art and mythology in the archives in the sense that people of disappearing cultures might themselves come there later to study their own lost traditions in order to rebuild their national identities. This is the moral task of museums and archives. Their task is to move the "memory" of a disappeared culture elsewhere, outside it. According to Yuri Lotman, every culture decides which texts it forgets and which it preserves, "remembers." But who decides this ultimately, whose choice is it?

Behind folk art one has often imagined a kind of nameless subject, *Volksgeist,* whose manifestation it is. Identification with this national subject also makes us consider anthropological fieldwork ethically valuable (particularly in the "peripheric," "ethnosemiotic" countries of Europe as the Nordic and East European countries). This invisible *Volksgeist* undeniably directs our interest, since such art, mythical stories, pictures, and music touches us. Even when an avant-garde painter or composer, like François-Bernard Mâche, uses a Cheremissian chant recited by an aboriginal female voice as the starting point for his synthesized music, it has its particular expressivity for all contemporary Finno-Ugric people. On the other hand, this is our own folklore, since in the end, everything is borrowing from other peoples.

In any case, the subject of an ethical interpretation is above all, in the semiotic sense, a subject provided with full *modal* competence, a subject who 'will', 'can', 'knows', 'must', and 'believes'.

What this means is revealed if we negate the thing and ask: When does a musical subject function unethically? In order to accuse someone of an unethical attitude, we should suppose that this subject has wanted to act in this way, i.e., he has had a bad intention, he must have known how to act in such a way. If he has done something without knowing it is wrong, he may be freed from criticism (at least partly). He must have been "able" to do so, i.e., he must have had the means to do so. Instead, he may have believed he was acting correctly in spite of all. Particularly, he must have acted without external forcing, without 'must'. He must have displayed an attitude of 'not-must', *non-devoir.*

One of the most obvious instances of this kind of attitude in art history and artistic life is the so-called plagiarism or fake. The semiotics of counterfeits and falsifications was studied by Umberto Eco in his essay "Fakes and Forgeries" (Eco 1987). However, the field of fakes is—at least in music—still greater, namely that of authenticity in general. What is authentic/inauthentic style is a question which I have myself examined (Tarasti 1991).

Instead, these problems have not been pondered from the viewpoint of an acting subject, i.e., one committing plagiarism or who falsifies something or argues something authentic. The essential is again, in which sense, with which intention this happens.

I shall take a concrete example: The sad and romantic composer in Latvian musical history, Emil Darzins, is connected to the Finnish composer Jean Sibelius in an astonishing way. He was accused twice of having plagiarized Sibelius. First, his list of compositions include a piano piece titled *Die einsame Fichte,* which was at the time accused of being a copy of Sibelius's similarly titled piece *Den ensamma furan.* In order to study the case, a committee was founded that was chaired by the Russian composer Alexander Glazunov. The matter was even put to Sibelius himself, but he did not give a direct answer.

From Darzins, we also know of another piece (an orchestral work, very popular in Latvia, with a subtly refined atmosphere, *Valse melancholique*), which

Darzins's competing musical critic and colleague claimed was a plagiarism of Sibelius's *Valse triste*. (I have heard this charming piece and must state that it does not remind me of Sibelius except very vaguely in its general tone.)

In any case, some years after these events, Darzins destroyed a part of his compositions, i.e., a recently written opera, and died tragically. His death was partially attributed to the accusation of plagiarism.

Nevertheless, the essential question in this composer's case was whether he willingly wrote a Sibelius fake, for which he could reasonably be accused of unethical conduct, or whether it was the case that in various artists' minds similar ideas emerge simultaneously without them knowing each other.

The Latvian musicologist Arnold Klotins has studied the case of Darzins and has been able to clarify that he started his career under signs of idealism. However, upon his return from Petersburg, Darzins encountered the general indifference of academic musical life. Thus, at closer sight, the whole myth of plagiarism is revealed not as an "unethical" attitude of the musical subject, the actor at all, but of the actors surrounding him. In the last instance, what was involved was perhaps rather an effort to falsify music history in a journalistic desire to dramatize real events. Therefore, the question about ethical/unethical behavior and intention blends into the problem of the truth value of *discourse* about music. I shall return to this problem later.

Nevertheless, let us briefly scrutinize the intentions and modalities of an author.

According to the ethics of Immanuel Kant "there is nowhere in the world, neither outside it anything which would be considered unlimitedly good, except a good will" (*Grundlegung zur Methaphysik der Sitten*).

Is the modality of 'will' the kernel of all ethics? At least in Western culture 'will' has been a problematic modality.

Whole doctrines have expressly taught the negation of 'will'. Modern novelistic art owes much to Marcel Proust's "involuntary memory" (*mémoire involontaire*). The negation of 'will' is an almost archetypical plot of theater pieces, operas, and movies. The problem of Wagner's Wotan and his gods is in fact "the will of 'will'." Wotan's "good will" strives to find some Other, an outsider, who by his own will wants the same as he, i.e., to rescue the gods from the disaster prophesized by Erda. However, it is precisely wanting what another wants, or subordination of the 'will', which leads to catastrophe. Precisely the same theme was the subject of the television film by Ingmar Bergman *Den goda viljan* [The Good Will]: Its main protagonist, the priest, wanted only good and wanted to make all other people want the same, which was the origin of all the unhappiness. It would thus seem that the Kantian ethical principle would not function in practice. The aesthetics of contemporary avant-garde art is also mostly the aesthetics of 'non-will'—one may think of John Cage, who, on the other hand, inherited his attitude partly from American transcendentalists.

The opposite ethical theory, utilitarianism, which derives the ethically correct from pleasure, will also lead one to a dead end. In Greimasian semiotic terms, it would mean that one makes a choice between euphoric and dysphoric objects, when naturally it is always correct to choose the object which is more euphoric (although Leo Tolstoy recommended the contrary in his late philosophy). This may hold true within the basic value model of an individual life, which is articulated with life/death categories (mostly life euphoric and death dysphoric). In any case, in art, say in music, in which everything depends on musical taste, the essential is precisely the question of which musical object is euphoric and which is not. Consider a common musical situation: a conflict between two actors, one of whom regards music as euphoric, and the other of whom regards it as the most dysphoric cacophony. According to deontic logic, one of the definitions of "good" is that "*p* is good, if and only if *p* is better than not-*p*." However, this seems to be senseless regarding musical objects. It is just the same if one said "Bruckner is good if and only if he is better than Brahms." Often aesthetic taste judgment is fused with an ethical choice between good and bad. György Ligeti once stated that he liked neither Sibelius nor Bruckner, since what is typical of them is their gesture (he raised his hand in a way portraying a kind of official authority or a subordinating power).

After all, the whole field of ethical values is very complex. One might quote Georg Henrik von Wright and his classification in his work *The Varieties of Goodness:*

Ethical concepts:

1. value concepts or axiological notions (related to interjections): good, evil, bad, valuable, better, best, many comparatives and superlatives;

2. norm concepts or deontological notions (related to imperatives): good, wrong, 'must', duty, obligation, justification, denial, permission;

3. anthropological concepts (related to psychological terms): act, action, behavior, character, motif, 'will', consideration, choice, intention, meaning, mood, decision, ability;

4. mixed concepts: pleasure, unpleasure, joy, sorrow, desire, virtue, vice, responsibility, etc.

One immediately notices in this taxonomy the ethics on which our "own" semiotic discourse closely focuses—in the third category or on the level of the so-called anthropological concepts. Our modality of 'will', but also 'know' and 'can' belong to it, whereas the modality of 'must' belongs to category number two.

What was tentatively understood above as "ethical" has mostly been experienced as if it were a fulfillment of the first category *through* the third one. The value concepts have somehow been reduced into more "common" anthropological notions—quite like emotions or passions.

If from the aesthetical point of view we are not interested in anything other than the art work, like the composition itself and its qualities, then from the ethical approach, we are concerned only with what was in the mind of a composer or performer when he wrote or played a work, in which sense, with which *inten-*

tion he did it. Or then we are interested in the *influence* of art or music upon the human mind and conduct.

The last-mentioned aspect has often been identified with musical ethics ever since Plato's doctrine of ethos. The aesthetic and the ethical are thus intermingled, and have taken along a third principle, that of religiosity, at least in the existential philosophy of Søren Kierkegaard.

According to Kierkegaard, the aesthetic, ethical, and religious were three consecutive world views and phases, of which the last mentioned was the highest. In fact in his "generative course," various phases could be fused with each other. He considered Mozart's *Cherubino, Papageno*, and *Don Giovanni* as concretizations of the same "actor" in its different developments.

Ethicality may appear as a particular semantic gesture, an aesthetic category—just like religiosity in music. If one says about an artist that his interpretations are characterized by an ethically uncompromising attitude, this would mean a kind of inner discipline, insisting on certain principles. *Perfer et obdura* . . . (then ethicality comes in fact rather close to the modality of "power" in John Ruskin's sense).

On the other hand, we know the case of Leo Tolstoy in which the man, having reached his "ethical" phase, completely denied his "aesthetic" achievements. If utilitarian ethics teaches (G. E. Moore) that of two acts one has to choose the one which produces more pleasure, then the Tolstoyan principle was quite opposed to it.

Moreover, it seems to be characteristic of musical discourse which lives its own life outside all ethics and ideology. When it is subordinated to the ethical, it often becomes bad music. When one reads Cosima Wagner's diaries, one feels it incomprehensible that Richard Wagner's congenial music could be created amidst this German bourgeois, chauvinist, and anti-Semite ideology.

In any case, just as the ethical can appear as a certain musical quality, as a "seme," the same holds true for religiosity.

Religiosity has often meant a kind of isolation, denial of the world. Marginality has been raised into a method. Setting oneself outside has become a new ideal in the present "ecstasy" of communication. Concerts are arranged in difficult, remote places. Sviatoslav Richter plays recitals by candlelight in monasteries, otherwise closed from the outer world. The new ideal of an artist, composer or performer is a person who avoids publicity and negates it (Arvo Pärt, Glenn Gould).

However, to what extent are these phenomena only the negative minus side of the culture of communication swollen into huge dimensions, in which it is precisely the negation of publicity which has become the source of a new kind of still greater publicity? We cannot escape from semiosis to any place after it has conquered every corner in the world.

Nevertheless, now it is time to develop these reflections further in the direction of artistic and musical practice itself and to look for the kind of model which can be derived from them.

One may take as the starting point of any artistic or musical activity that it takes place in a certain society—even when we encounter an apparently completely isolated artist, a composer writing only for himself, or a musical amateur. If one thinks of the entire field of artistic activities, in what is usually called "artistic life," one may distinguish three kinds of entities:

a) artistic actors, i.e., painters, writers, composers, performers, teachers, critics, interpreters, technicians, officials, managers, producers, etc.—each in their more or less peripheral or central role on the stage of artistic activity;

b) events, which can be either *acts* of artistic actors—for example, paintings, drama pieces, novels, poems, compositions or their performances, rehearsals, criticisms, rituals, spectacles, didactic teaching situations, etc.—or the results of *processes* maintained by artistic actors, often by multi-actorial interactions;

c) evaluations or "modalizations"—the situation can be illustrated by the following "chart" of artistic life and its ways of functioning:

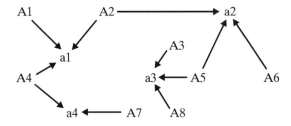

FIGURE 2. A = actor, a = act; arrows depict intentions, evaluations, and modalizations

First, one has to account in the model for the fact that both actors and acts have their own inner hierarchy, depending on the society to which we are referring. If what is involved is the magic and mythical life of an aboriginal tribe, the musical performance may be identified with a ritual, whose roles create the hierarchy among actors. If we have as our example a European town of the nineteenth century, its artistic actors may occupy various places in it according to their functional and aesthetic roles (writer, composer, conductor, actor, rector of a dance institute, listener, spectator, etc.). In such a context, "acts" are also placed in their own hierarchy: The art work itself can doubtless be considered a primary act, its performance or reception a secondary event, and a text written about a product of a "third" degree.

However, what is essential are the modal relationships among the actors and acts, i.e., the evaluations. When every "actor" in artistic life is a person provided with a modal competence, their intentions are often confronted. Conflicts in artistic life do not come from acts so much as they come from the conflicting modalizations related to them. Thus, one act may exclude another one. Some actor *A1* may argue that his "act" *a1*, a composition or sculpture, is "euphoric," whereas according to an actor *A2* it is "dysphoric." Above all, using the model one may articulate artistic life as a whole without reducing it to mere cases of individual art works (art, music, literature, "histories"), performances ("theater life," "musical life") or biographies of artists. When one reads a typical chronicle of the artistic activities of a bigger or smaller town, such as *Music and Musicians of Chicago,* one provides the reader with a whole store of separate, disconnected life stories of artists and musicians. How these people have acted in the context of Chicago's musical life remains open for a reader. On the other hand, the histories of certain artistic institutions, operas, theaters, dance companies, and publishers forget the role of individual "actors" therein.

As was said above, the artistic life often appears as a *text* (expressly as a verbal one), when such a text constitutes a *narrativization* of the aforementioned elements or their linearization as a story, a discourse. Then one does not only provide the text with a certain "logical" order, but also the "world," "the life" itself it represents. Therefore, the semiotics of texts about art is also a semiotics of artistic culture.

Texts dealing with art can be of very different kinds. They can be speeches, criticisms in newspapers, memories, evaluations of students in the matriculations of institutions, letters, histories or aesthetics, local histories, reviews, radio programs, film documentaries, etc.

The essential point is recognizing for whom the text has been written. Even if the text does not have any proper receiver, the producer of the text had in his mind a kind of hypothetical, perhaps unintentional, reader group to whom the text is addressed. Moreover, the discourse which has been chosen for the text may determine to a large extent the choices of textual strategies and isotopies. About what is the text speaking? A text can deal with the art work itself, a composition, but also with its style, the context of its creation, interpretations, etc. How does a text speak about art? It can speak about it objectively, depicting some "act" in the field of artistic life—or at least pretend to do so. Nevertheless, finally most texts about art, say music, paradoxically do not have a concrete, primary object at all. For instance the art criticisms of the nineteenth century are often such that they move only on the level of "modalizations," without giving us any information about the performance in a more precise sense. Then the text, as it were, addresses or closes to itself.

The ultimate goal of any art history is, of course, to get behind the documents to grasp the reality behind them, for which they serve as signs. What we have at our disposal are signs whose signifier, physical trace we have in front of us, whereas their signified is missing. Our task is to reconstruct that absent content, the lost meaning.

Texts dealing with arts can be situated on an axis according to the *degree of deixis:* The impression of being *hic, nunc, et ego* is naturally at its greatest in criticism of certain performances and occasions, speeches, lectures, and views, and at its smallest in theoretical, "scientific" treatises. The more deictic the text, the more "iconic" it is in relation to the artistic reality about which we are talking.

Furthermore, the actorial deixis, 'I' or 'we' is not an unambiguous category. Who is the 'I' who is speaking, or who is the subject ultimately? For example, a speaker in a festivity can use the 'I'-form not so much as a reference him/herself as an indication of belonging to a certain group: 'I' is the same a member of a group.

Again, in some texts, the receiver greatly determines the articulation of text. What is foregrounded is the Jakobsonian conative function. This is the case of letters, whose intention is not only to transmit information but to strengthen the value model common to the sender and receiver, or to persuade the receiver to adopt the intentions of the sender, or to tempt him to a more permanent communication. The emotive function can also be emphasized, i.e., the idea is to transmit emotions. (Such a function often prevails in memories written by famous artists; these texts are a kind of auto-communicative means by which they articulate their own world views and legitimize their ethical and aesthetic choices. Sometimes they narrativize "events" whose glorified hero-actor is none other than the narrator himself—say, in autobiographies from Benvenuto Cellini to Artur Rubinstein.) The essential point here is how the subjects of art history have themselves conceived their own reality and what kind of concept they have used in its portrayal.

Therefore, texts dealing with art can well occupy an important role guiding the acts of a subject. Their possible ethical content cannot be estimated or understood without texts referring to them.

In any case, one may ask whether our "semiotic" model of artistic life helps some artistic actor, painter, composer, or performer to act better. At least it can lead to a hermeneutic self-comprehension, to the conception of another type of Otherness when one realizes that no artistic actor can function outside such a field, and that his choices always involve an axiological moment.

REFERENCES

Baudrillard, J. 1986. *Amerique.* Paris: Editions Grasset.
Eco, Umberto. 1984. *Semiologin quotidiana.* Milan: Gruppo Editoriale Fabbri-Bompiani.
———. 1987. "Fakes and Forgeries." *Versus 46* (gennaio–aprile): 3–29.
Greimas, A. J., and J. Courtes. 1979. *Semiotique. Dictionnaire raisonnée de la thérie du langage.* Paris: Hachette.
Greimas, A. J., and I. Fontanille. 1991. *Sémiotique des passions. Des états de choses aux états d'âme.* Paris: Editions du Seuil.
Hesse, Herman. 1931. *The Narcissos and the Goldmouth* [Narziss und Goldmund]. Berlin: S. Fischer.
Kant, Immanuel. [1785] 1959. *Crundlegung zur Metaphysik der Sitten.* Stuttgart: Reclam Verlag.
Tarasti, Eero. 1991. "Sur l'authenticité et l'inauthenticité des arts." *Degre's 68:* a1–a26.

———. 1994. *A Theory of Musical Semiotics.* Bloomington: Indiana University Press. (In French: *Sémiotique musicale,* trans. Bernard Dublanche. Collection Nouveaux Actes Sémiotiques. Limoges: Presses Universitaires de Limoges, 1996.)

Tolstoy, Leo. 1904–12. "What Do We Have to Do." In Lev N. Tolstoy, *Works,* trans. and ed. Leo Wiener. Boston: Colonial Press.

von Wright, Georg Henrik. 1963. *The Varieties of Goodness.* London: Routledge & Kegan Paul.

7

The "Structural" and "Existential" Styles in Twentieth-Century Arts

One of the most fascinating intellectual upheavals of our century—an epistemic crisis, as Foucault would say—took place with the shift from existentialism to structuralism. In order to understand this rupture fully, one must look at the arts and related background phenomena of the time. My thesis is that the concepts of the "existential" and the "structural" are *general aesthetic categories,* which do not merely characterize the historical movements specifically called existentialism and structuralism. Rather, these categories constitute central strata in the arts of our century in general, and in all of European civilization in a broader sense.

Admittedly, I am moving in an unexplored area. For glancing at the art history of our century, one seldom, if ever, encounters styles or trends called existential or structural. Instead, one finds such commonly accepted stylistic designations as impressionism, futurism, Dadaism, cubism, surrealism, expressionism, serialism, neoclassicism, folklorism, and many more. Should my new style categories of existential and structural be subsumed into these categories? Or do they instead represent universal distinctions of any art?

While it is certainly rare to hear anyone speak of existential music, there has been much debate about structural music. Carl Dahlhaus, among others, thought it to be the most important aesthetic "school" of the music of our century. In such an aesthetic, the musical work itself—its technical aspects and form—was the focus of study. Did the fact that the existential style paralleled the development of structural analysis escape Dahlhaus's notice? Although the popular cultural critic José Ortega y Gasset spoke about the "detachment of art from the human," did art not retain some back gates through which subjectivity and actoriality slipped into the garden of art history? Emphasis on structure has, of course, been the obvious, explicit, and official canon of modernism up to our days. Yet there is also music, literature, and other art in which existential concepts such as subjectivity, limit situation, transcendence, *l'être pour soi,* thrownness, and others have found expression.

Who were the existential artists? Are they the same as the expressionists? In his *Die Musik in der Kulturgeschichte des 19. und 20. Jahrhunderts*, Hans Hollander (1967) construes the birth of expressionism as both a reaction to cubism and as a continuation of—amazingly enough—impressionism. For Hollander, both impressionism and expressionism started from experience. Yet if impressionism was receptive, sensual, and lyrical, expressionism was formative, penetrating, and intellectual. Impressionism strove for the evanescent, momentaneous state of the object. Expressionism aimed for the innermost core and permanent essence of the thing perceived. The former was typically picturesque, colorful, and sonorous; the latter plastic, form-conscious, and structural.

What are the distinctive features of expressionist art? According to Hollander, it strives for the cerebral, the abstract, and the non-sensuous. The psychoanalytic dimension is important, particularly the darker aspects of the human soul, such as fear, suffering, absence of moral freedom, social alienation, and sadomasochism. These qualities transformed the impulses of freedom and death into an "un-desire," changing them into something religious and esoteric (Hollander uses the term *Unlust,* where a French scholar would speak of a negation of *désir, khora, pulsion*). Therefore, the outer manifestations of expressionism are often irrational and unpleasant; they are irruptive, destructive, and stem from unbearable inner tensions. Precursors of the expressionist style in literature were Dostoievsky, Strindberg, Georg Büchner, and E. T. A. Hoffmann; among its subsequent representatives were Ernst Toller, Karl Kraus, Bertolt Brecht, Karel Čapek, Mayakovsky, James Joyce, and Franz Kafka. Joyce's *Ulysses* is an effort to portray the entire consciousness of a thinking and feeling soul as one huge outbreak of despair. Accordingly, expressionism is in effect a critique of the human condition in this century. In music, Janaček, Bartók, and Stravinsky were expressionists. In Schoenberg, expressionism appeared as a rejection of melody: The atonal system played as large a role in the new melodic thought as it did in the dissolution of traditional harmony. Stravinsky displayed the same will to freedom with regard to rhythm. Whereas Adorno viewed Schoenberg and Stravinsky as irreconcilable counterpoles, in Hollander's mind, both *Pierrot lunaire* and *Le sacre du printemps* conveyed expressionist ideas, inasmuch as they reflected the crisis of European man on the eve of World War I.

The Belgian musicologist André Souris also dealt with these questions in his "Existe-t-il une musique expressionniste?" (in *Conditions de la musique*). His view differs sharply from that of Hollander. To Souris, the expressionist artist does not ponder technical aspects at all, but concentrates on himself. Souris falls into even worse dilettantism when he considers "sincerity" and "human emotion" the most important content of art. He quotes from Arnold Rüdlinger's history of modern art: "Expressionist artists are less interested in art and art work than in themselves and people like them. . . . A painting, whether it describes a landscape, *Stilleben* or a person, becomes a mirror, in which the artist's feelings and psychic participation are reflected. . . . Only the expression means something." If we accept this statement, it would be easy to equate the categories of "structural" and "existential" with aesthetics that emphasize, respectively, form and content, technique and expression. However, Souris's examples of musical expressionism are so disparate that they include composers as different as Hindemith and Milhaud, as well as Charles Ives and Alexandre Scriabin.

Even on the basis of these brief descriptions, it is clear that we cannot straightforwardly differentiate between expressionist and existential styles, given the variety of views on the subject among the writers just cited. Let us instead make our own path through the various "-isms" that contributed to existentialism and structuralism.

FROM FUTURISM VIA DADA TO SURREALISM

We start with the birth of modernism itself. How did the structural/existential appear in the futurism, Dadaism, cubism, and surrealism of the beginning of the century? Or did the structural and the existential play any part at all in those movements?

The term *surréel* was first used by Guillaume Apollinaire. It meant "something which comes from elsewhere," in regards to which we have no questions, because we do not expect it at all. Apollinaire introduced this term in his play *Les mamelles de Tiresias*; he also used it to characterize the ballet *Parade* by Satie-Cocteau-Picasso. Heretofore, Apollinaire had been the theoretician and propagator of cubism, the aim of which was to create art that could be enjoyed without the perceiver grasping its meaning. The representational nature of art was deliberately blurred by geometrical forms, thereby making the level of first articulation of (visual) language disappear. In the collages of Cézanne and Braque, the main emphasis went to the play or *ars combinatoria* of objectal forms. The cubists' primary goal was to create *asemantic* art that had no immediately recognizable signification. Rather, the receiver was to appreciate the play of structures on the level of signifiers. In music, a typical cubist work was *Oedipe-Roi* by Stravinsky-Cocteau. Likewise, the music of Satie represented cubism, in its foregrounding of the geometric-plastic melodic line.

A natural continuation of cubism was Dadaism. This movement proved to be more influential in painting than in literature, particularly in the art of Picasso and Gerico. Of decisive impact, however, were works by the poet Tristan Zara—among them his collection *25 and 1 Poems*. For Zara, the basic unit of poetry was the word: "There are only words one after the other." Zara believed that a poem could be made up of words written on small pieces of paper that were then mixed in a hat. In this way, he created a kind of collage, just as in painting one could build up works from detached elements that had no obvious connection with each other. Likewise, the music of Poulenc consists of "pieces" comprised of a few measures, which are abstracted from various textures and combined so that the "edges" are quite obvious (as in his *Concerto for Two Pianos*); and in Dadaist verse one finds short poems with jazz-like rhythms. For Dada, only the material of words, colors, and tones existed. Yet Dadaism also had its own aesthetics and ideology, which partly blended with most of the modernist movements of our century. Dada declared that, for art, one had no need of any material other than that which was readily at hand. This view produced things, banal and vulgar objects—such as the utopian and unreal machines by Marcel Duchamp—which consisted of collages and functioned at the same time as purely aesthetic games. According to Dada, an art object was not to be sacralized, and anything whatsoever could serve as its building material. Dada represented the concepts of *non-sens*, whereas the surrealists preferred to speak about *sur-sens*. Nevertheless, the theoreticians searched for some signification for the concepts of Dada, which was described as "bacteriological" in nature. To its practitioners, Dada was synonymous with the expression "Qu'est-ce-que le beau? Ne connais pas, ne connais pas, ne connais pas. . . . " Dadaists felt compelled to repeat things: words, colors, and motifs. A typical Dadaist answer to a question was to avoid it by a non-answer. The real Dada was counter-Dada.

It was not far from Dadaism to—surrealism. At the same time, there occurred an essential shift from the surface and manifest level of art to the immanent and inner one. Apollinaire started to speak about the "sur-natural," by which he meant that art dealt with inner reality, and thus constituted a kind of X-ray of ordinary experience. To him the *esprit nouveau* (new spirit) was above all surprise. The poet was a discoverer of myth, even though he started from such everyday subjects as a dropped handkerchief.

Apollinaire also saw a connection between science and poetry: Poetry was to be a revelatory science, and not a cache of dated rhetorical devices. Thus, Apollinaire aimed at two kinds of poetry. One type was poetry as notation, called "automatic writing," that revealed "truth." Among his poems is one entitled *Il y a* ("There Is"). It begins with the words "There is," followed by a list of all that there is. The second species of surrealist poetry was based on the search for a mythic unity behind the poet and his adventures. The surrealists believed in myths of the modern world. For instance, the poem *Les collines* portrays a battle between two airplanes. Arthur Honegger composed *Pacific 231* to depict the sounds of a railroad locomotive, and Heitor Villa-Lobos wrote a Brazilian variant entitled *O tremzinho de caipira*. For André Breton (*Manifestes du surrealisme*), the mythical foundation of poetry included passionate love and communication, and the myths of the city, the street, and the modern world. In philosophy, Karl Jaspers wrote *Selbst die Machinen gewinnen ein mythisches Leben* [Even Machines Achieve a Mythical Life] (Jaspers 1919).

Surrealism as a movement differed radically from other modernisms. Its five sources were literature, Dada, problems of poetic language, new knowledge of man gleaned by psychoanalysis and ethnology, and the Marxist poetics and social program. The surrealists tried to replace profane significations of words with a new "authentic" and "magical" content. Yet surrealism was no mere collection of artistic techniques. It had a broad social-philosophical program that made it more of a religion than an art. The surrealist manifesto was "evangelical"—to be listened to as a gospel. (It even bears asking whether one can truly speak of surrealism without being a surrealist.) Breton pondered a surrealist truth, for which language was a mere tool. Crucial to Breton's ideas was that such a truth was not found on the surface of reality—as the Dadaists believed—but elsewhere, in dreams and in the unconscious. In this sense, surrealism anticipated structuralism, which likewise confirmed the existence of a "deep level," hiding beyond the surface and determining it in every respect.

Finally, one must note that none of these movements would have emerged without futurism, whose manifesto appeared as early as 1910. Cubism and futurism were parallel movements that never intersected. The cubist painter did not start from a topic in reality. Rather, the topic was only a pretext for painting, whose essential thrust went elsewhere—to painting as such. In contrast, the futurist painter superimposed pictures, situations, and events. If the cubist destroyed and lost reality in transforming it, the futurist praised reality and punctuated it with exclamation marks.

In Search of a Structural Style

In our paradigm of modernism, the categories of structural/existential appear in many variants and combinations. The structural view was influenced as much by cubism, surrealism, and even Dada as it was by scientific discourse on the arts. In any case, the impulse of modernism came from a general reaction against the romantic movement. To borrow Roman Jakobson's terms, this reaction replaced the *emotive* function of communication in the arts with the *poetic* function; this last denoted a concentration on the *form* of a message instead of its content. Art was technique, whose rules were to be revealed and expressed in axiomatic form, as a grammar of artistic production.

This view represented an ultra-rationalist belief that reality consistently followed the rules of a grammar. The structural view further embraced a concept of reification, inasmuch as everything pertinent was located in the object itself and its structures. One finds this attitude throughout the arts of our century. In Kandinsky's view, the elements basic to all arts were the point, the line, and the plane, from whose combinations could be inferred a grammar of the arts. Jumping ahead to Boulez's writings in the 1960s, one encounters amazingly similar reasoning. The starting points are now vertical and horizontal elements, which can be divided into three types of movement: from point to point, from one group of points to another, and finally to relationships among groups of groups. Classic polyphony and the ancient laws of counterpoint can no longer encompass these interrelationships. In Boulez's view, even temporal structures are controlled by three principles that have nothing to do with traditional conceptions of rhythm and meter; namely, the horizontal, the vertical, and the diagonal.

The keyword—structure—brings us to a conclusion voiced by the mathematician Rougier: "What we can know about the world is its structure and not its essence. We think of the world as relations and functions and not as substances and events" (quoted in Boulez). This, of course, sounds rather formal, which Boulez instinctively notices. He defends his own position by appealing to the "father" of structuralism, Lévi-Strauss, who argues that in both language and music, there is no opposition between form and content, abstract and concrete. The content obtains its reality from its structure. For Lévi-Strauss, structure is not detached from content, but is rather the content arranged in a *certain way*. With this statement we have come to the core of the "structural style" as well.

One must ask, What kind of art does such a program or aesthetics produce? Although the structuralists detested "aesthetics"—even Schoenberg had said it should be replaced by the mathematically measurable entity of *Wahrhaftigkeit*— structuralism had its own aesthetics. Roland Barthes spoke of a particular structural activity, which appeared as two phases: de-struction of an object and its re-struction. A re-structured object revealed at the same time its inner way of functioning.

I once published an essay on the films *Oedipus* and *Theoreme* by Pier Paolo Pasolini, in which I applied Barthes's notion of a "structural man" and showed how Pasolini's structuralism was reflected in the cinematographic language of these movies. Now Marxism was, of course, looming somewhere in the background, and it is true that structuralism was connected to surrealism by a similar social program. However, many a structuralist art work in the 1960s remained on Barthes's first level, that of the de-struction of signs. The films by Pasolini, as well as those by Antonioni, could be taken as structuralist experiments. For in cinema and theater direction (as well as in dance), it is none other than a structuralist idea that an actor's expression consists of "amounts" of expressiveness, and that the combinations of those amounts can be determined by a director. Renoir would first demand from his actors a completely expressionless recitation of the text, to which he would then add his "interpretation." The carefully planned composition of image and sound by Eisenstein and Prokofiev in the film *Alexander Nevsky* represented a structuralism *avant la lettre*.

Nevertheless, if structuralism in music is above all typified by Boulez's *Structures* for piano, then structuralism in music is equivalent to serial techniques. In those pieces, Boulez serialized both pitches and durations as well as "secondary" parameters, such as dynamics and timbre. Although in doing so he was able to make all musical dimensions completely predictable, the unraveling of the aural form remained the task of the listener (*énonciataire*) and not the enunciator (*énonciateur*). The fact is that such music sounds cubist. It is asemantic art, which we are supposed to enjoy although we might not know its codes and grammars. Even if at the one end of musical communication there works a structuralist, guided by a superintelligence, his messages are nevertheless coded at the other end as a surrealist, Dadaist, cubist experience. Thus, the final message is something irrational. The understanding of this message presupposes that the listener will throw himself at its mercy, and trust in the significance of a hidden, esoteric meaning—a considerable paradox! But in the interpretation of art, one can never resort to only one aspect of communication. One must account for the whole, the particular *situation* in which everything takes place.

In the 1960s, the serial and the structural were almost the same. In Umberto Eco's *La struttura assente* (1968), the differences and similarities of these two are well defined. Eco's thesis is that structuralism is an avant-garde method by which one produces so-called *open* art works in painting, poetry, and music. At that time, structuralism appeared as serial thought that tried to create polyvalent structures. In this connection, Eco refers to Boulez, who said that classical tonal thinking reflected a universe ruled by principles of gravitation, whereas serial thought was based on a universe under continuous expansion. (I shall come back to this idea when dealing with existential style, since even there one is detached from the objects of *Dasein* and shifted to the world of Nothingness and its unbearable lightness.)

Eco's analysis also helps us to understand Lévi-Strauss's ideas on the essence of non-representational and atonal music. He felt a clear repugnance toward such music, because for him it was not a language. From our contemporary perspective, Lévi-Strauss's criticism seems to be misplaced: What does it matter whether the products of modern art are "language," that is, comparable to verbal activity? In the 1960s, however, whether or not an art was a language was a crucial question. The justification and value of any phenomenon was based on its language-likeness. The condition of language for Lévi-Strauss was its functioning on at least two levels of articulation. Yet serial music as well as non-representational painting tried to function on only one. Even *musique concrète,* which attempted to make musical narration from assemblages of recorded "natural" noises, mainly wanted to render those sounds unrecognizable in order to create a system of purely acoustic differences: The listener should not be able to identify the murmur of the wind, the breaking of tree limbs, and so on, according to the concrete source, but only as part of a system of noises determined by the rules of the composition. Here one strives to detach objects from the world of *Dasein,* yet without success; for it is hard to signify anything with such music.

Thus, Lévi-Strauss's structuralism cannot be taken as a methodology of the avant-garde, since he sees this art as deprived of its most essential value. However, his structuralism has other aspects which are relevant to the discussion of the modernism of our century. Hardly anyone would consider him part of the antimodernist movements which Hugues Dufourt considers so dangerous—an almost proto-fascist phenomenon in the spiritual heritage of our century.

Let us take another example. In its display of collage techniques, Luciano Berio's *Sinfonia* (1968) clearly evokes the *bricolage* described in Lévi-Strauss's *La pensée sauvage*, a treatise which appeared a year before Berio's work. Bricolage, a sort of gathering and assembling of objects, is enacted by the so-called *bricoleur*, who operates with certain sensible qualities. When Berio mingles musical quotations from various style periods with texts by Lévi-Strauss and Martin

Luther King, he is doing precisely a kind of bricolage, inasmuch as he improvises a new kind of "language." All the aforementioned elements of musical style and words possess familiar significations, while at the same time distancing themselves from those familiar meanings. One could paraphrase Roland Barthes and say that the *Sinfonia* represents a myth of the modern world. The original signified of the quoted music—by Mahler, Beethoven, Debussy, and others—is pushed aside and replaced by a new meaning. The distanciating and estranging sign complexes in this collage create, in the first place, a surrealistic impact. Second, a Dadaist effect is involved: It is very disquieting to hear Mahler's symphonic scherzo recorded over the singing and recitations of the Swingle Singers. Here one has clearly left the conventions of the world of *Dasein.* The signs of a musical style have been shifted to another type of space, where they no longer possess the weight and dignity they had earlier. This is futurist music, since the elements of collage interpenetrate and are juxtaposed to each other; it is music provided with exclamation marks and simultaneity, on the order of Charles Ives's *Three Places in New England.* Finally, the *Sinfonia* is also cubist, in the same sense as compositions by Picasso and Braque: The pieces of the collage have lost half their previous identifications. Though quotes from Lévi-Strauss abound in the *Sinfonia,* these are not cited with a view to the primary meaning of his words, but with a conception of his text as a literary creation.

Existentialism Disrupted

Another, typically structuralist aspect of Berio's *Sinfonia,* is its subjectlessness. It would be impossible to mistake this work as existential or expressionist art. The distinction between the structural and the existential was revealed at the moment when the epistemic shift between them started. Leonard B. Meyer claims that philosophers live with their noble thoughts in a kind of "upstairs" of the history of ideas. Only some ideas escape from on high, often in popularized and distorted form, and make their way into that "downstairs" or cellar in which the artists work. In spite of this dichotomous situation, we must give some attention to the crisis that emerged in philosophy when existentialism gave way to structuralism.

Structuralism was in many ways the antithesis of existentialism. Even Sartre had argued that existentialism was a kind of humanism, but the same could not be said of structuralism. Of course, becoming acquainted with distant cultures teaches us to appreciate differences and to direct a critical eye on our own civilization. Yet in principle, structuralism was anti-humanistic, since it aimed at reducing the individual to part of an impersonal collective, the *parole* into a moment of *langue,* conscious choice to the mastery of the unconscious, and individual creativity—what Charles Taylor would later call the "ethics of authenticity"—to a mere wave in the sea of history. All could be reduced to a kind of combinatory principle, and the individual was seen as only one transformation of a system. The freedom and responsibility of the individual disappeared when man became an intersection of systems rather than an individual subject. He no longer spoke in discourse—not in his own life, in the arts, or in politics. Rather, *ça parle*—the system spoke in him, forced him to say things according to the mechanisms of codes. On the other hand, some structuralists saw in the combinatory of values the possibility for a kind of social therapy. In this therapy, one was to shed dominant, stagnated practices, and become conscious of other alternatives of the paradigm (as Greimas optimistically supposed).

In any case, the change in spiritual climate was obvious in the rupture that took place in the 1950s and 1960s. In April of 1966, *La Quinzaine littéraire* published a series of questions concerning topics of death. These questions were addressed to Foucault, following the publication of what might be seen as his most structuralist work, *Les mots et les choses.* According to Foucault, Sartre had said that sense was omnipresent. Upon being asked when he had stopped believing in "sense," Foucault answered: "The detachment took place on the very day when Lévi-Strauss, for societies, and Lacan, for the unconscious, showed us that 'sense' was probably nothing but a kind of glittering reflection of the surface. And what passed through us, what was before us, what carried us in time and space was the system." Sartre soon responded by saying that the attack of the new generation on existentialism manifested a rejection of history: "It is most important to know how people shift from one way of thinking to another. In order to do this he [Foucault] should take into account the practice of history, which he expressly repudiates . . . he replaces the movies with a magic lantern, movement with a series of motionless points."

As interesting as the advent of structuralism, was the emergence of existentialism amidst the devastating events of World War II. It engaged a human situation in which all previous supporting structures seemed to have disappeared, and where man appeared to have fallen into a kind of emptiness. When Sartre spoke of emptiness and Nothingness, his tone was quite different from Hegel's, despite Sartre's indebtedness to German speculative philosophy. At first, existentialism provoked opposition, but soon it became a fashion. As Simone de Beauvoir said in her chronicle of post-war events: "Under the title [of existentialism] were gathered all the books—written even before the war—and also by our friends . . . and moreover [existentialism] was joined to a kind of movement in painting, and to a certain kind of music." Nevertheless, her memoirs make scant reference to existentialist music, either by Sartre or by Beauvoir herself. She wrote: "Existentialism had set Ansermet and Leibowitz to quarreling; the former said that existentialism offered an explanation of all music; the latter stated that that explanation fit only dodecaphonic music. They had strongly criticised each other in *Labyrinthe.*"

Almost the only musicologist to write about the matter was André Souris, in his *Sartre chez les musiciens.* Of course, in Sartre's output, music has a certain role. The philosopher was indeed very musical, knew how to play piano, and belonged to the famous musical family, the Schweitzers. Moreover, in his *L'imagi-*

naire, Sartre had pondered Beethoven's Seventh Symphony and its existence in time (the work's possibility was in the non-reality created by the imagining consciousness). And perhaps few know that the protagonists of Sartre's first novel were Cosima and Richard Wagner and Friedrich Nietzsche.

Inquiring further into "existential" music, I wrote to my friend Daniel Charles, a leading specialist of French music philosophy. Asked whether he knew the *Labyrinthe* mentioned by Beauvoir, Charles answered (January 22, 1994): "You ask whether I know *Labyrinthe*. Unfortunately not. But after having reread the Swiss Ansermet and the Polish Leibowitz, I can say that their way of understanding phenomenology is very suspect. Gisèle Brelet, with whom I often talked about these erroneous phenomenologies, was very severe, and with reason, about them. The terrible article by Michel Filippot about Ansermet's book *Les fondements de la musique* appeared in *Critiques*. As to the relationship music/existentialism, I know only one important francophone writer, the Belgian André Souris, whose posthumous *Ecrits* puts together the essentials . . . You certainly also know Barthes's texts on Schumann. They are super-existential! About Sartre and Hegel's logic Jean Wahl wrote very clearly in his article which appeared in the magazine *Eucalion*."

Sartre's fundamental idea was the same as that of other existentialist thinkers, such as Kierkegaard, Heidegger, and Jaspers. Human existence precedes one's essence. One has been thrown into the world, into emptiness, amidst Nothingness. Elsewhere in this anthology I have pointed out the possibility of interpreting the signs of this condition (especially with regard to Walt Disney's American-ness). There I suggest that one can delineate a completely new theory that I call "existential semiotics." Subsequent to that essay, my theory has ripened into a tentative model, by which I sketch the change of the semiotic subject into an existing subject. The essential aspect of existentialism is that of "becoming": One can never definitely determine oneself as long as one is under the temporal process of one's existence. A contradiction prevails between *l'être en soi*—fixed, clear-cut, determined objects—and *l'être pour soi*—continuously developing and changing entities.

Along with my theoretical reflections, I have pondered what would be the existential style in various arts. Perhaps it might be based upon the idea that art does not exist as such, but that it is only incessantly sought after. The existential style would be a property similar to that of femininity in the arts: It would be almost impossible to define as an objective quality of a musical, literary, or visual artistic text or utterance. Such a property would exist only as a particular communicative situation, as a relationship between sender and receiver, in the act of enunciation and being enunciated, in the interaction of coding and decoding. For instance, one might not conceive of a musical work such as Ravel's *Concerto for the Left Hand* as evoking something existential. But our attitude changes when we learn about the work's historical background. Ravel dedicated the piece to Paul Wittgenstein, a pianist who lost his right hand in World War I. In addition,

Paul happened to be the brother of the philosopher Ludwig. Thus, the work is related to a family in which a particularly strong sense of existentiality and extreme situations were felt.

I assert even more: There exists art which reflects a typical existential experience, and from which the existential style stems. It is always opposed to the structural style as defined above, in that the latter is primarily interested in a world of objects without subjects. The structural style, as its title declares, operates with subject-less structures, whereas the existential style represents subjects without structures. A precise portrayal of the colorful impressions of the world of objects could hardly be taken as particularly existential.

In literature, the existential modus is *je,* 'I'. A book like Bernanos's *Le journal d'un curé à la campagne* might well be considered to exemplify the existential style, as do Camus's *La chute* and Sartre's *Nausée.* Bernanos's novel appeared in 1936, before the books just mentioned were published and before the breakthrough of French existentialism in the proper sense. Still, its themes of human loneliness, social indifference, and the quest for authentic existence are all purely existential. The young priest arrives at his first parish with a sincere determination to perform his tasks to the utmost of his ability. Soon he faces the austerity and hostility of his environment, and all his good intentions produce grotesque antitheses of the results he had hoped for: The young girls tease him; the lady of a noble family breaks down and dies after their conversation; and so on. The contrary figure, that of the older priest of Thory, is taciturn and well-to-do. The stomach pains that afflict the young man force the older priest to nourish him with only wine and bread, which leads the villagers to regard the younger man as a drunk. Finally, the young priest leaves for town, where he is diagnosed as having a cancer from which he later dies. The impressive narrative mode of this novel is its usage of 'I'. In this story, everything is seen through the eyes of an anguished Kierkegaardian subject.

Thirty years later, in his *La sémantique structurale,* A. J. Greimas produced an analysis of Bernanos's book; this analysis is a paradigmatic example of the structuralist approach. The protagonists, or actants, of the novel are not the young priest, the priest of Thory, the countess, and so on; rather, they are the lexemes of life/death, lie/truth, and the like. After classifying the most essential lexemes and semes of the Bernanosian universe, Greimas puts them into a transformational model that reveals the basic values of the author. His study clearly anticipates the content analyses later realized by computers, in which key terms are put into the machine's memory and then reordered according to a specified program. Greimas's method is too reductive and objectifying. It does not take into account the fact that the semes and lexemes of the novel are ultimately the fantasy of the protagonist. The subject is surrounded by other actants, such as opponents and helpers. The priest suffers from a kind of semiotic inability to interpret the messages sent to him by reality. He takes them to be essentially hostile expressions, as signs from a dysphoric reality. Those signs depress him— perhaps he even wants to be depressed, since he is seeking hedonistic pleasure as a release from his sufferings. At the same time, the young priest is unable to see what kind of sign he himself presents to others. For instance, the girl communicant says that she learned her homework only because the priest had such beautiful eyes. He believes himself to be authentic when he insists on fulfilling his duties to Christ, which, however, have catastrophic consequences for the world around him. The young priest would have done well to heed the warning issued by the American philosopher Charles S. Peirce, in his essay "How to Make Our Ideas Clear":

> Many a man has cherished for years as his hobby some vague shadow of an idea, too meaningless to be positively false; he has, nevertheless, passionately loved it, has made it his companion by day and by night, and has given to it his strength and his life, leaving all other occupations for its sake, and in short lived with it and for it, until it has become, as it were, flesh of his flesh and bone of his bone; and then he has waked up some bright morning to find it gone, clean vanished away like the beautiful Melusina of the fable, and the essence of his life gone with it. (Peirce 1992: 127)

Bernanos's priest, who in Greimas's structural analysis seems to live in the world of an "objective lie," has, from an existential point of view, created that lie himself. He lives in a world of illusions, whereas the actants surrounding him immerse themselves in real life. Above all, Greimas's structural analysis takes into consideration neither the particular nature of the story—its touching portrayal of human fate—nor the temporal-processual character of the narration. Greimas's interpretation is an effort to reduce the existential to the structural.

Is Bresson's film rendition of Bernanos's novel in an "existential" style? In the film, the 'I'-centered narration becomes more objective than in the book; even the use of music to evoke a certain atmosphere is not enough to render the screen version as subjective-existential as the original. There are, of course, films made as if they were from the point of view of a narrator-listener-ego. In one effort of this type, only the narrator's hands are seen on screen. In a musical work, one would certainly expect to encounter traces of an existential subject, accordingly, a kind of actoriality.

However, the relationship of the existential style to the structures of *Dasein* is problematic, because "existing" involves an act of "transcending." Sartre speaks of only one kind of transcendence: a step into Nothingness. However, the movement of a subject probably does not stop there, but continues as the realization of Nothingness's counterpole, which is plenitude. I have sketched my model of this process in another essay in this collection (see "On the Paths of Existential Semiotics"). The journey of our subject continues beyond his having located the *Ground*. This *Ground* is not the same as the isotopy of signs nor their semiosphere, that is, something similar to objective signs in the innocence of their worldliness (*Weltlichkeit*). From the *Ground*, a more fundamental significance radiates outward to all signs. When the subject thereafter returns to his *Dasein*, he creates new signs, which are purely existential. Their meaning is understood only by a subject who has himself passed the same way. Accordingly, I have come to a theory of existential signs. What kind of signs are they? They are signs unbound by gravity, floating upward from the world of *Dasein* to the state of Nothingness. This kind of sign "levitation" is seen in Chagall's paintings, in which things hover freely in the air. These signs then move into the universe of "plethora" or "world soul," where they become laden or heavy, as it were, with the meanings of that place.

The existential style in the arts reflects these two transcendental acts. Serial music imitates the transcendence of negation: Its signs are sounds which have lost their signifieds. But there is also music that reflects affirmative transcendence. There, in contrast, the old content may be provided with a new signifier, a new tonal figure, by abandoning itself to deeper laws of music. We should thus speak of two kinds of existential style: The one—negation—is anguished and rebellious; the other—affirmation—is transfigured, blending together with the harmony of the spheres. It is clear that this style category is not bound to any particular period or time, but can appear anywhere at anytime. The existential— as little as the structural—is not just the invention of twentieth-century modernism. Nevertheless, without the avant-garde of our century, both in the arts and in the sciences, we would perhaps not have become aware of the existence of those two aesthetic phenomena.

REFERENCES

Apollinaire, Guillaume. 1965. *Les Mamelles de Tiresias.* Paris: Lettres Modernes.
Beauvoir, Simone de. 1990. *Ajan haasteet.* Helsinki: Kirjayhtymä. Published originally as *La force des choses* I, 1963.
Bernanos, Georges. 1936. *Journal d'un curé de campagne.* Paris: Librairie Plon.
Boulez, Pierre. 1971. *On Music Today.* Cambridge, Mass.: Harvard University Press.
Breton, André. 1924, 1930. *Manifestes du surrealisme. Idées.* Paris: Gallimard.
Dahlhaus, Carl. 1980. *Musiikin estetiikka.* Helsinki: Suomen Musiikkitieteellinen Seura. Published originally as *Musikästhetik,* 1976.
Eco, Umberto. 1971. *Den frånvarande strukturen. Introduktion til den semiotiska forskningen.* Lund: Bo Cavefors Bokförlag. Published originally as *La struttura assente.* Milano: Bompiani, 1968.
Eribon, Didier. 1993. *Michel Foucault.* Tampere: Vastapaino.
Foucault, Michel. 1970. *The Order of Things. An Archaeology of Human Sciences.* London: Tavistock Publications. Published originally as *Let mots et les choses,* 1967.
Greimas, A. J. 1980. *Strukturaalista semantiikkaa.* Helsinki: Gaudeamus. Published originally as *Sémantique structurale.* Paris: Larousse, 1967.
Hollander, Hans. 1967. *Die Musik in der Kulturgescichte des 19. Und 20. Jahrhunderts.* Köln: Arno Verlag.
Jaspers, Karl. 1919. *Die Psychologie der Weltanschauungen.* Berlin: J. Springer.
———. 1948. *Philosophie.* Berlin, Göttingen, Heidelberg: Springer Verlag.

Kierkegaard, Søren. 1993. *Päättävä epätieteellinen jälkikirjoitus.* Porvoo, Helsinki, Juva: WSOY. Published originally as *Afsluttende uvidenskabelig Efterskrift yil de philosophiske smules,* 1846.

Meyer, Leonard B. 1989. *Style and Music. Theory, History and Ideology.* Philadelphia: University of Pennsylvania Press.

Peirce, Charles S. 1992. *The Essential Peirce: Selected Philosophical Writings.* Vol. 1 (1867–1893), ed. Nathan Houser and Christian Kloesel. Bloomington: Indiana University Press.

Picon, Gaetan. 1973. Lectures on surrealism at the Ecoles des Hautes Etudes en Sciences Sociales, Paris.

Solowjew, Vladimir. 1965. *Philosophie, Theologie, Mystik.* Deutsche Gesamtausgabe VI. Freiburg: Erich Wewel Verlag.

Souris, André. 1976. *Conditions de la musique.* Bruxelles: Editions de l'Université de Bruxelles.

Tarasti, Eero. 1972. Article in *Ylioppilaslehti* [Student Weekly Magazine] (Fall). University of Helsinki.

8

On the Authenticity and Inauthenticity of Art

The problem of authenticity came to the fore in semiotics some years ago, when Umberto Eco published an article on "Fakes and Forgeries" in the Italian journal *Versus*. Although in this article Eco presents a consistent theory of *in*-authenticity (that is, of fakes in various fields), no one has yet seriously pondered the entire problem, which includes the positive aspect—that of originality, genuineness, and authenticity.

Nearly all of Eco's examples came from the visual area, despite the fact that authenticity in music has been under scrutiny for a good while. Therefore, as a musicologist, I thought it tempting to try to formulate a semiotic theory of at least musical authenticity. I noticed rather soon, however, that the problem cannot be solved by resorting to musical sources alone. This is because a kind of "infiltration" takes place in music, as it does in the other arts. That is to say, authentic musical interpretation takes place in an intertextual field; thus, the performer of music should also become acquainted with the philosophy, painting, literature, and other arts of the time. It is claimed that interartistic competence increases the authenticity of interpretation. Yet exactly how such competence does so remains a mystery.

Authenticity is found almost everywhere one looks. Thus, one can with good reason speak of authenticity as an *anthropological* phenomenon. In his conversations with Georges Charbonnières, Claude Lévi Strauss dealt with levels of authenticity in society. In that context, communication is at its most authentic in small communities where everyone knows each other. In so-called primitive societies this is the only kind of communication; such societies provide a global view of all human behaviors, as performed daily by almost every member of the society.

Yet life is not so simple for most of us. Levels of inauthenticity are on the increase, according to Lévi-Strauss: People are interconnected and disconnected via various mediating agents and systems, by various means of administrative power, by different ideologies, and so on. For Lévi-Strauss, an effective anthropological argument for social planning would be to decentralize activities on all levels, so that as much social activity as possible takes place at that level of authenticity on which the members of a given group have concrete knowledge of each other.

If such a view of authenticity were applied to the arts, it would realize the position that Aboriginals take toward artistic life, a position which considers every member of the tribe as an artist. In the history of Western art, such authenticity emerges now and then, as in small societies such as the seventeenth-century literary salons of Paris, and the Viennese "Schubertiads" of the Biedermeyer period. In both cases, artists created for a small, responsive public, which also consisted of the artists themselves. However, the main trend, both in the arts and elsewhere in society, has been toward inauthentic communication, a situation in which the sender and receiver do not know each other. The more that art is produced by machines, the more it has something "unhuman" or inactorial (as Greimas would say) about it.

If this last statement is true—which is strongly denied by defenders of the avant-garde—then how can the arts return from the present state of inauthenticity to one of authenticity? Would this mean a return to artistic styles of earlier ages? Or is there in every man a kind of universal source of authenticity, which only waits to be revived? Doubtless there are and have been efforts to return to authenticity in both the objective—in time and space—and subjective senses. My question is simply, Can semiotics help analyze this situation?

THE TOOLS

One might begin by juxtaposing the opposition authentic/inauthentic with the semiotic concepts of signifier/signified or manifest/immanent. In that case, "authentic" indicates something that has a meaning, a content, a signified; whereas "inauthentic" designates something without content, and which moves "merely" on the surface of reality. In addition, the term "authentic" contains a temporal shifter, inasmuch as one considers authentic to be something pre-existent or prior, as if it were more original. Usually the authenticity of a "later" object (token) or phenomenon is tested by comparing it with the supposedly "original" model (type) or occurrence. Eco proceeds in precisely that manner:

> Thus the *necessary* conditions for a forgery are that, given the actual or supposed existence of an object Oa, made by A (be it a human author or whatever) under specific historical circumstances t1, there is a different object Ob, made by B (be it human author or whatever) under circumstances t2, which under a certain description displays strong similarities with Oa (or with a traditional

image of Oa). The *sufficient* condition for a forgery is that it be claimed by some Claimant that Ob is indiscernibly identical with Oa. (Eco 1987: 9)

Therefore, Eco's theory of forgeries and his conception of inauthenticity are based upon comparison between *two* objects which are claimed to be similar, but which have a certain difference between them. On the basis of this difference, it can be proved that one is "authentic" or "original," and the other is a copy or a fake.

These two objects are often situated on two completely different levels: In most cases we are only faced with the latter object *Ob*, a copy, which is thus something manifest, something which 'appears' or 'seems', while the first mentioned object *Oa* only 'is' or rather 'has been', as is the case when we try to reconstruct a "lost" style or art form. Accordingly, A. J. Greimas's categories of *to appear/to be* might be useful for classifying and describing problems of authenticity. These concepts can in turn be placed in the so-called semiotic square, in its "veridictory" articulation: truth to appear to be lie; secret not to be, not to appear Here "truth" is something which both appears and actually is. That which only appears or seems, but is in fact not what it appears, is a "forgery" or a "lie." If an object or phenomenon is known to exist, but does not appear in any way, then it remains hidden or a "secret." Something which neither is nor appears to be, is something "untrue." In what follows, I shall use these categories when analyzing various cases of authenticity/inauthenticity.

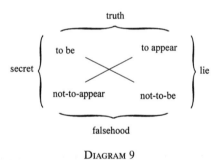

DIAGRAM 9

Let us begin with a case taken from the cultural history of Finland and Germany. In 1840, the great Finnish statesman of the nineteenth century, Hegelian philosopher Johann Wilhelm Snellman, published a book entitled *Tyskland, skildringar och omdömen från en resa 1840–1841* [Germany: Descriptions and Judgements from a Journey, 1840–1841]. The book described his travels in Germany during the years he had pursued his philosophical studies. The following year saw the publication of Snellman's most important philosophical work, a dissertation defended in Tübingen and entitled *Versuch einer Spekulativen Entwicklung der Idee der Persönlichkeit.* This strongly Hegelian treatise had a decisive impact on the development of the awakening national culture in Finland. In his travelogue, Snellman is united with the Romantic "episteme" of authenticity, as his description of the cathedral of Cologne shows:

> The state in which a spectator now sees this wonderful building perhaps increases that feeling of unsatisfied expectation and melancholy; [that feeling] always distresses one who has returned from observing the cathedral. It is not merely a wonderful ruin that bears witness to times past; in it one can see an incomplete effort, a started work which to him [the builder] was overwhelming, since it was effected at the same time as that spirit was defeated which had laid its foundation; it was a work whose fulfillment would have signified the abandoning of the spirit of the time during which it had occurred.

Let us first analyze the narrative and modal processes of this text. Two subjects can be distinguished therein: Subject 1, the "enunciator," or constructor, of the ruins; and Subject 2, the "enunciate," or observer, of the ruins. The building itself constitutes an object in which we can distinguish two layers: (1) a signifier, which in the description is evaluated in principle as euphoric, as suggested by the adjective "wonderful"; (2) and a signified, which for the spectator is dysphoric, since it evokes the feeling of "unsatisfied expectation and melancholy." In the text, one can clearly distinguish two phases: The first is a static state of being, a state in "which a spectator now sees this wonderful building." The second is a state of dynamic doing and action, which is portrayed by the words "work" and "effort." Thus, in the narrative sense, there is a phase that conveys a state of being (*énoncé d'état*), within which there is an embedded phase that projects a state of doing (*énoncé de faire*).

Each of these phases is modalized differently. The state of being is depicted by "unsatisfied expectation and melancholy"—a 'want to not-be' and its overmodalization by the modality of 'know'. A spectator knows when he looks at the ruins that even though they are felt on the level of signifiers as "wonderful" or euphoric, on the level of signified the ruins represent a wanting or longing for something that does not exist—hence, a kind of dissatisfaction. The state of dissatisfaction, as such, could be interpreted as an articulation of the aspectual seme of "perfectivity," here in its negative manifestation of "unachieved," "incomplete," "unfinished," "imperfective." More essential to notice, however, is that the spectator is led to deeper semiotic speculation about *why* this is so.

The modal state of dissatisfaction and melancholy that comes upon the spectator is explained by a historical reference or temporal shifter to the category of "before." The ruins are simultaneously a euphoric and dysphoric object, but at the same time, they communicate about something else. In order to explain this "else," a phase depicting the state of *doing* is embedded in the phase depicting *being*. The former state belongs to the "before." Another subject, the once-upon-a-time constructor of the building, serves as Subject 2. The efforts (doing) of this subject have been negated, in the sense that they have remained unfinished, as the words "incomplete" and "overwhelming" in the text indicate.

This action is depicted in the first place by the modalities of 'can' or, more precisely, 'not to be able to do'. The actor in question, who remains nameless, was unable to bring his work to fruition because "the spirit was defeated which laid its foundations." In other words, during construction of the signifier (the building), there occurred a change of spirit (the signified): The Middle Ages turned into another age, and at the same time, the semiotic reason for the existence of the building vanished. This transformation on the level of content produced an inability to continue the action. The phase can be put in the following formal scheme:

$$S1 \longrightarrow Fm \left(Ov^1 \ \frac{Sa}{Sé} \ [S2 \longrightarrow Fm \ Ov^2 \ \frac{Sa}{Sé \longrightarrow non \ Sé} \ ]\right)$$

"to observe"   "to build"

DIAGRAM 10

Snellman, however, does not believe that any activity of reconstruction can bring back what was original and *authentic*. In Eco's terms, Snellmann's view of authenticity is that no object (*Ob*) can be taken as the previously-created object (*Oa*), since what he calls the spirit of the time—in semiotic terms, the signified—never stays the same but always changes. The signifiers, or material objects, remain the same, as do the material aspects of the cathedral; but the content of the cathedral, which that material reflects and signifies, does not. Snellman is a typical romantic, insofar as he starts from the signified. Yet he is also anti-romantic, in his belief that the lost signifieds can never be revived as "authentic" cultural units. In this respect, Snellman's discourse may serve as a prelude to our explorations in the area of authenticity and inauthenticity.

A HEIDEGGERIAN EXCURSION

Although scholars who study authenticity focus mostly on the past—as do historians and archeologists—we must also remember, as Lévi-Strauss, that there is a special kind of authentic subjectivity or subjective authenticity, which can characterize one's activities at any time and in any place.

When one acts, feels, and thinks in a certain way, one's behavior is authentic; that is, it follows one's essence. Otherwise that person must be considered alienated, representing *falsches Bewusstsein*, or false consciousness. Is one way of living more authentic than another? This was the question asked by Leo Tolstoy, Henry Thoreau, John Ruskin, and other thinkers, and it has maintained its currency. It still makes people search for their "roots"—in their birthplaces, in the countryside, or wherever else. As far as such a "return to authenticity" takes place via memories, diaries, or correspondence, it constitutes a discourse of its own. Such a process may be called "auto-communication." Compared with such authentic auto-communication, any external communication is something "inauthentic." Marcel Proust said that the company of even the most ingenuous and gifted people only disturbs our fundamental ego, since that company leads us outside ourselves, into "inauthentic" being, one might say.

Accordingly, there are two forms of authenticity. The first is objective, which can be easily analyzed by concepts provided by Eco, Greimas, narrative analysis, and the like. The other is subjective. This last cannot be excluded from a semiotic investigation. To begin such an investigation, it will prove useful to look first at what Heidegger says about subjectivity in his existential philosophy.

Heidegger uses the concepts of *Eigentlichkeit* and *Uneigentlichkeit*. To him, existence is not a thing-like matter, a being of something present, because such an "existence" is indifferent to its own 'being'; such an existence merely 'is'. Instead, existence can become my own 'being' only if it conceives its being as its "own possibility." Existence is always its possibility; it does not "have" or possess this possibility by virtue of some property or thing. Since existence is in essence its own possibility, this entity can, in its 'being', "choose" itself, so to speak; it can find, conquer, or even lose itself. The two modes of 'being'—*Eigentlichkeit* and *Uneigentlichkeit*—are based upon the fact that existence is most often determined by its *Gemeinigkeit*. The inauthenticity of existence does not, however, connote a lesser or lower degree of 'being'. *Uneigentlichkeit* can rather signify existence in its highest and most complete concreteness, in its full activity, energy, enjoyment and interests.

Heidegger further reasons that the basic mode of 'being' in everyday life is *Verfallen* (fallen). This term does not signify as such a negative judgement, just as the "negations" in Greimas's semiotic square, non-*s1* and non-*s2*, need not indicate any anything pejorative. Rather, *Verfallen* only denotes the existence that is nearest and mostly in the "world." By its nature, this 'being-in-something' means, in turn, a blending into the public-ness of social man (*das Man*). Existence has fallen from its essence, from its proper (authentic!) mode of 'being', and has been thrown into the world. Being fallen into the world means a sinking into 'being-with others', in the realm of chatter, curiosity, and equivocation. What was above called the "inauthenticity" of existence finds here its more precise definition. "Inauthentic" here means nothing like 'not being', in the proper sense of actuality, as if existence in this modus would lose its 'being' altogether.

Inauthenticity is in no way the same as 'not-to-be-any-longer-in-the-world', since, contrarily, it has completely abandoned itself to the world and to 'being' with others. 'Not-to-be-oneself' serves as a positive term of a being who loses itself to the world in concerning itself with the world. Hence, the fallenness of existence must not be taken as "falling" from some purer and higher "original" state of being. Existence has already, as it were, fallen out of itself in its factual 'being-in-the-world'. And it has not fallen into any other 'being', which it would only then encounter; rather, existence has fallen into a world that belongs to its own 'being'. Fallenness is thus an existential property of existence, and does not say anything about existence as 'being-there' or its relationship to the 'being' from which it has "lost its way." For Heidegger, such a 'being-in-the-world' as fallen means a perpetual striving. At the same time, this striving is so self-evident that in all its aspirations and desires such an existence is experienced as something quieting. Acquiescence to this inauthentic 'being' does not mean a state of rest or of inactivity, but an unrestrained desire and impulse.

Heidegger provides the fallen 'being-in-the-world' with a third property: alienation. Alienation does not mean that existence is torn from itself. On the contrary, such a state is characterized by self-deception. The movement among these states—striving, acquiescence, alienation, and self-deception—is called by Heidegger "being thrown" (*Sturz*). Existence is thrown from itself into the bottomless depths of inauthentic and inappropriate banality. However, such a thrownness escapes its own attention and is concealed by explanations or rationalizations that declare this phenomenon to be "progress," "advancement" (cf. Ruskin's "advancement in a career"), "elevation," and "concrete life."

One can easily see that Heideggerian analysis deals precisely with inauthenticity in the subjective sense. Here he is not far from Greimasian semiotics, insofar as inauthenticity represents the categories of 'seem'/'not-be'. The Heideggerian analysis can be well illustrated by examples from literature (for instance, the portrayal of the Guermantesian circle in Proust's *Remembrance of Things Past*). But it can be also seen as a criticism of any research that does not take into account the "fallen" nature of existence, its 'being' thrown into inauthenticity, and that only provides a taxonomy of the surface phenomena of reality. Sometimes scientific theories may function as "official explanations" of fallenness; such explanations are justified when the totality is legitimized as "concrete life."

This brief discussion of Heideggerian subjectivity leads one to ask the following questions: To what extent has the art of our time fallen or been thrown into an inauthentic 'being' which serves as its expression? Do we want the arts to serve as tools of inauthenticity? Or do we want them to guide us in our journey toward the spheres of authenticity?

HIC, NUNC, ET EGO

To help answer these questions, let us now continue our analysis of authenticity with semiotic tools. Applying Greimas again, one can speak of authenticity of time, place, and subject (or "actor"). Centrifugal and centripetal forces operate these three dimensions. Greimas calls the centrifugal force, which makes a text move in the inner or outer sense, *débrayage* (disengagement), and the centripetal force *embrayage* (engagement). Theoretically, authenticity is at its greatest when complete engagement prevails in all three dimensions: (1) the temporal—'now' (*nunc*); (2) the spatial—'here' (*hic*); (3) and the actorial—'I' (*ego*). Such a state has often been considered the ideal; it is the utopia of philosophers. Such total engagement would represent the typical quietism, which appears both in the German romantics to whom the most complete life was mere 'being' (cf. *Heinrich von Ofterdingen* by Novalis), in the American transcendentalists Emerson and Thoreau, and in the ideas of their contemporary followers, such as John

Cage. Yet such a complete engagement might not be very desirable either in daily life or in the arts. (Please note that "engagement" should be understood in a strictly semiotic sense, and having no necessary reference to, say, "political" or "moral" engagement.) If we accept the Greimasian modalities, then there are two that are basic: 'being' and 'doing'. In both life and art there must be not only a steady state of engagement, but also a kind of tension and movement; that is, there must be a disengagement—a shifting away from the temporal, spatial, and actorial centers.

Yuri Lotman argues that culture is always oriented beyond itself, from the sphere of organization to one of disorganization. In stories, some "disengagement" always takes place, motion from a 'now' moment to a 'then' moment, from 'here' to 'elsewhere', from 'I' to other actors. Even in arts that one would not take as narrative in the proper sense, such as music, disengagement plays an important role. For instance, minimalist music, which contains very little "disengagement" may sound extremely "authentic" (i.e., static), but this hardly satisfies aestheticians who value dynamic form, motion, and the regulation of tensions. How indispensable to any narrative is the breaking of such a completely "authentic," almost autistic, state is illustrated by the film *Padre padroni* by the brothers Taviani. In this film, music serves as a tool of *débrayage,* as a message from the other world; this world awaits the subject of the film's narration, a shepherd who leads an extremely monotonous life in Sardinia. He hears a waltz from Strauss's *Fledermaus,* played by the accordion of a strolling musician. Hearing this music triggers a process in the shepherd, a process which no one can stop—not even the father who functions actorially as the mythical sender and receiver in the story; this process is none other than the disengagement of all three dimensions of narration.

In fact, the whole breakthrough of modern arts at the beginning of the century can be seen as a process of disengagement from the stagnated state of *la belle époque.* The ideal of avant-garde texts, until the postmodern time, has been maximum disengagement, or inauthenticity. The principle of repetition—which always characterized authenticity—presented the worst obstacle to the creation of a completely disengaged, subjectless, placeless, and timeless art work. Therefore, repetition was the most taboo artistic device. It was even attacked using psychoanalytic criteria, with Adorno calling it a form of regression and infantilism. Yet one consequence of complete disengagement could be seen in the isolation of art from the public, in a form of elitism. As Jacques Attali says in his *Les bruits:*

> This impersonalisation of static scientism leads to the elimination of a style, even to the demand of its complete disorientation . . . one has to write music in deculturalised forms that threaten to disappear into general statistical abstraction. . . . A modern musician does not say anything, does not signify anything other than the meaninglessness of his time. . . . Freed from the constraints of ancient codes, [the musician's] discourse is therefore unlocalizable. (227)

One need not take as pessimistic an attitude as Attali does toward "modern" music. One would rather adopt the Ruskinian view that just because the great majority of people do not understand and appreciate something, it does not follow that it is without value or merit. Ruskin also said that opinions that are wrong individually cannot become right when taken altogether (Attali's main argument against modern music was that it has no mass market). Yet we must admit that total disengagement—chaos—cannot remain the permanent state of the arts. In other words, disengagement must be followed by engagement, a return back to the center of narration, at least in one dimension, in order for one to experience an art work as being constructed in an aesthetically satisfying way. Engagement need not be total, however, as in the reprise of sonata form or the refrain of a rondo; it may be only partial.

In fact, Hegelian dialectical aesthetics presupposes that upon returning we may encounter the same time, place, and subject as at the beginning; yet these are somehow qualitatively transformed so as no longer to be the same, but reflecting a certain degree of *différance,* as Derrida would say. Accordingly, to return to our example from the Taviani movie, at the end the protagonist returns home to Sardinia, but now as an educated linguist; he is no longer the same subject, but a subject whose modal competence has changed. Therefore, engagement can occur even in "modern" texts, but it can prove to be only apparent, as in Proust's *A la recherche du temps perdu.* With the passing of time, there occurs a slow actorial disengagement, since the whole novel depicts precisely the transformations of the protagonists' sense of time, although one always returns to the level of the narrator-subject. The narrative plot has been dilated so vastly, into several volumes, that no one can read the novel as a "normal" story. At the same time, the whole novel expressly portrays various degrees of authentic and inauthentic existence. Indeed, the Proustian narrator-subject is still the internal and soulful romantic subject, who represents the nineteenth-century "culture of the inner" (*Kultur der Innigkeit*). What is involved is the modus fulfilling the aforementioned subjective authenticity; although on the surface level of his narration, Proust still searches for the greatest possible objective authenticity. Even from his sickbed, Proust sent his secretaries to various galas to inquire what kind of evening dress this or that countess had worn, or what decoration this or that ambassador had displayed. In this way, Proust succeeded in uniting subjective and objective authenticities in a congenial manner.

One can of course ask whether inner subjective authenticity (in semiotic terms, actorial authenticity) is in the end nothing but a "meaning effect" (*effet de sens*), which in turn is produced by a certain sociosemiotic situation (for Proust, that of bourgeois nineteenth-century culture). Still, certain kinds of discourse in modern media society also maintain this kind of subjective authenticity, which aims at actorial engagement: American television's Sunday ceremonies in churches, or programs like *Mr. Rogers' Neighborhood.* In this last, every segment of the series starts with the same music, and shows Mr. Rogers saying to his audience, "There is nobody like you," "You are a very special person," and the like, in an effort to make them believe just that. These examples display a striving for authenticity, and they use the techniques of discourses created particularly for this purpose.

ONCE AGAIN, RUSKIN

From the great British art historian John Ruskin (1819–1900) we have inherited a very consistent theory of authenticity and inauthenticity in painting—and in arts in general—although as far as I know Ruskin did not use these terms, at least not in his main theoretical work, *Modern Painters.* If we accept the Greimasian definition for the concepts of authenticity—by using the categories of 'seeming' and 'being' and supposing some relationship between them—then they can be used to interpret Ruskin's various definitions for different "ideas" that art can convey and to which its language is bound. For Ruskin, there is no doubt that art is a kind of language: His view represents a hidden semiotics, like that of many another semiotician *malgré lui.* Says Ruskin, "Painting or art generally, as such, with all its technicalities, difficulties, and particular ends, is nothing but a noble and expressive language, invaluable as the vehicle of thought, but by itself nothing." Yet soon after this general "semiotic" statement, which launches the entire series of *Modern Painters,* he also says, as a genuine romantic, that "It is not by the mode of representing and saying, but by what is represented and said, that the respective greatness either of the painter or the writer is to be finally determined."

In other words, in art there is always a "signifier" and "signified," of which the signifier is the visible "language" and the signified the invisible, belonging thus to the category of 'being' (on the other hand, it is peculiar that for Ruskin the language-likeness of art does not imply its capacity to transmit content). In Ruskin's view, art conveys the following "ideas": power, imitation, truth, beauty, and relation. These categories are basically semiotical and can be interpreted in the light of Peirce's sign categories.

Ideas of power concern the production of signs such as art works (legisign, sinsign, qualisign), and expressly so, in the sense that in the final product one distinguishes a trace of how it was made. One could also argue that they constitute indexical signs, which are still "in touch," in a contiguity relationship, with the process of their making; such signs have not yet been completely detached from their producer, or from the energy and means of elaboration that he has used. Clearly, here the notion of authenticity applies only in the sense that some techniques can be more authentic than others. For instance, take Ruskin's example of a hand-carved Indian canoe whose artisanship we admire. It is doubtless more authentic than, say, a motorboat produced on an industrial assembly line. Live concert performances on stage are somehow more authentic than the finest digital recordings. The passion for facsimile editions can be understood in this sense, for they can be taken as authentic inasmuch as they are viewed as transmitting original techniques or "ideas of power."

Ideas of imitation come closer to the semiotic definition of authenticity offered above. As Ruskin says: "Whenever anything looks like what it is not, the resemblance being so great as nearly to deceive, we feel a kind of pleasurable surprise, an agreeable excitement of mind . . . [W]henever the work is seen to resemble something which we know it is not, we receive what I call an idea of imitation." In fact, here we encounter the opposite pole of authenticity: something which seems what it is *not*. Ruskin admits that ideas of imitation are the most inferior that art can produce—semiotically they represent a kind of transformed iconicity. They are "contemptible," first of all, because in them the mind gives up the impression it has received and concentrates on the presented matter. Thus, it is impossible to represent higher or more noble emotions, since the attention is caught by sensual pleasure. Second, they prevent the observer from noticing the inner beauty of things and lead the attention only to subjects of less value, because it is impossible to imitate anything really great. We can paint a cat or a violin so that we would almost like to touch it, but we cannot imitate a sea or the Alps.

Instead, the concept of authenticity in Ruskin's theory can be connected with the next species of ideas, namely, those of truth. Ideas of truth differ from imitation in the sense that the latter can only concern something material (therefore, what is seen and thus belongs to the category of 'seeming'), whereas, ideas of truth are connected not only to material qualities but also to feelings, impressions, and thoughts. There is both moral and material truth, which is why truth is a concept that has a universal field of pertinence. Therefore, one can say that art is authentic when it conveys Ruskin's ideas of truth. It also realizes the semiotic nature of every art work in an ideal way. Here Ruskin's sign theory becomes axiology: "Truth may be stated by any signs or symbols which have a definite signification in the minds of those to whom they are addressed, although such signs be themselves no image nor likeness of anything. Whatever can excite in the mind the conception of certain facts, can give ideas of truth, though it be in no degree the imitation or resemblance of those facts. But ideas of imitation, of course, require the likeness of the object. They speak to the perceptive faculties only: truth to the conceptive." Ideas of truth refer to symbols, in Peirce's sense, in which signifier and signified are separate, yet are united in their task to transmit a "truth." When signs are transmitting ideas of truth, Ruskin believes, they carry their message simply and clearly; and it is just this message the mind grasps, regardless of the language in which the truths are conveyed. Therefore, Ruskin identifies "language" with the mere signifier aspect of signs.

Ruskin's definition of ideas of beauty is as follows: "Any material object which can give us pleasure in the simple contemplation of its outward qualities without any direct or definite exertion of intellect, I call in some way, or in some degree, beautiful." Nevertheless, Ruskin argues, in reality even these ideas greatly depend on the intellect. The highest among ideas of beauty are those which transmit intellectual beauty—which is in fact already the same as his last category of ideas (those of relation). From a semiotic point of view, however, ideas of beauty are in Ruskin's theory conditioned by culture, albeit implicitly. There is no reason to ask why we like sugar and not worms. Hence, the idea of beauty proves to be a rather unsemiotical category. It becomes semiotical only when we attain the ideas of relation, which start with the sign operations of inner iconicity and indexicality. This involves "everything relating to the conception of the subject and to the congruity and relation of its parts." Consequently the concept of authenticity—as far as it is sought in Ruskin's theory—is included in the ideas of truth, since in them the immediate sense impression is transcended and 'seeming' is juxtaposed with the unsensual, spiritual category of 'being'.

SCHOLARLY DISCOURSE

In no other area do the categories of 'seeming'/'being' create the aura of authenticity or inauthenticity so much as in scientific discourse. Semioticians—particularly in the Paris School—have taken great pains to show that even the so-called objective discourse of empirical sciences, which aim for a direct description of reality, is in fact only a "language" in which the effect of realism and the "true" is created by certain discursive mechanisms. Even the natural sciences are to some extent at the mercy of the linguistic-semiotic conditions of the authenticity of their discourse. Of course, there "authenticity" emerges quite concretely from the correspondence of "words" and "things": If the test results are erroneous or non-existent, but the scholar's text leads one to understand otherwise, then his discourse is "inauthentic."

One can attempt to increase the authenticity of scientific discourse by embedding in it iconic, indexical, and symbolic sign relationships. Iconicity in science appears above all as citations, which may even come from outside of the scientific discourse itself. For instance, in anthropological studies, the speech of an informant is transliterated and annotated as such, since the way in which the information is given may be even more important than the message itself. This occurs in broadcast interviews of speakers of a dialect, in which the interviewee is asked to tell a story, although the main attention of the listener is not on the narrative but on the intonation, rhythm, and other paralinguistic aspects of the speech itself.

Citations may also be inside the discourse; in this case, the discourse "proves" its authenticity with correct citations, demonstrating not only the scholarship of the author but also the intertextual connections within the *langue* of the discipline. To quote another's text without mention of the source is the height of inauthenticity, a forgery in Eco's sense, since in that case, one causes the text to "*seem* to be written" by something other than its own "*is.*" However, as late as the seventeenth and eighteenth centuries, a scholarly text was not supposed to be authentic in the sense that it was to be the writer's "own" discourse, but it had to be based upon the quotation of accepted sources. This standard is illustrated by the dissertations of the time—but this type of "iconicity" is just as rife in texts produced under totalitarian regimes in the Europe of our century. Inner iconicity naturally increases the redundancy of a text and thus serves the autocommunicative function. To a lesser extent, inner iconicity can be encountered in scientific schools that require certain quotations in order to prove that the discourse belongs to a certain community.

Indexicality is realized in the outer sense by the fact that behind a scientific text there looms some authority, to which that text is directly connected. Moreover, a scholarly discourse that emerges as an immediate response to a given situation can contain indexes. Indexicality is thus related to the "motivation" (in the Saussurean sense) of the scientific study, which means that certain external interests are guiding a discourse. Most often, the value of a scientific discourse is considered to be diminished if that discourse has a strong indexical connection to some "command," whether it comes from the business world or some other social group. Many a scientific discourse—not the least semiotics or aesthetics— needs indexical connections in a given socio-semiotical situation in order to justify itself. Medical semiotics and environmental aesthetics respond to the question of the utility of semiotics or aesthetics. And indexicality is also related to the use of power, since most often the index is established by the influence of the group that has it.

In the inner sense, indexicality can also cause the growth of authenticity by intensifying the internal coherence of a text. This coherence simply refers to how well a scholar can narrativize his study. Everyone knows that even a scientific text has its various types of "plot." The structural norm of a dissertation dictates that it must begin with a Proppian "introductory" function, which reports on what all others have said about the matter. Then follows the functions of "Problem" and "Method." The whole should end with the function of "Conclusion." In some cases, it is expressly the inner indexicality of the text which becomes the central factor in making it authentic. For instance: A scientific biography is written in the form of a novel, a semiotic treatise in the form of a detective story, and so on.

In the symbolic sense, scholarly discourse becomes completely independent and follows its own autonomous laws. In the outer respect, the choice of topic is "arbitrary," in the sense that a scholar adopts it by purely scientific criteria; that is, the topic is interesting exclusively in the scientific sense. No connection to outer reality (indexical and iconic requirements) should be present to diminish the discourse's "authenticity." In the inner regard, all the concepts used in the discourse must be based upon their own definitions within the "system" ("I use the term x in the sense y"). What these definitions are does not matter—you only have to keep to them. One might imagine that abstract mathematical or logical discourse would fulfill this symbolic inner demand most efficiently. Yet the Roumanian mathematician and semiotician Solomon Marcus has shown that emotion, and thus indexicality, exists even in mathematics. Mathematicians even speak of how some algebraic solutions are more "elegant" than others, which would more properly concern inner iconicity and indexicality than it would symbols.

Nevertheless, the categories 'seeming'/'being' are the ultimate criteria in judging the authenticity of science. Some writing handbooks suggest that to make a text seem scientific, one should not use such expressions as "never," "always," and "absolutely" but favor terms like "perhaps," "maybe," "to some extent," and "possibly"; do not say "I" or "we," but use the neutral "one"; use the passive voice; and so on. Among scientific institutions, inauthentic 'seeming' has its own agents, which market titles and degrees. One English institute sends circular letters saying that the recipient has been chosen from among those very few who deserve the degree of "Ambassador of Achievement" or "International Order of Merit," including an "Illuminated testimonial, a hand-calligraphy of the member's name, and a personal and exclusive citation on parchment," with "a photograph ready for framing and hanging on the wall." All this on the condition that a certain number of dollars are invested in the account of the institute.

STYLE AND TASTE IN THE
INTERPRETATION OF MUSIC

Authenticity in music may be divided into the following cases: the inner properties of a musical work, and the qualities of its interpretation or performance. In this area, we again meet the symbiosis of 'seeming' (performance) and 'being' (score). Yet even these categories are not quite obvious. First, we may ponder the problem as Eco does in "Fakes and Forgeries." Can we tell that the end of Mozart's *Requiem* is not written by himself but by his pupil? Do we hear in his C minor *Fantasy* that its middle section is not authentic Mozart, but written by someone else? Is the finale written by Philipp Jahrnach to Busoni's *Doktor Faust* more authentic than that written by Anthony Beaumont? How can we decide which one of the thousands of compositions bearing the signature of Pergolesi really came from his pen? In the latter case, something may be said by comparing the handwriting, but other cases must be inferred by means of structural analysis.

Here one encounters the problem of determining to what extent the score authentically represents the original composition. The farther back we go in music history, the less reliable are notations, since behind them loom as their 'being', unseen or unheard by us, an enormous amount of tradition, mostly oral, which in a certain age was taken for granted. Tradition is something whose existence—when at the height of its power—is so invisible that no one notices it. When tradition is disturbed, there emerges the semiotic problem in the proper sense, namely, the issue of interpreting signs and symbols. At the same moment, the question of authenticity/inauthenticity arises.

Tradition only "is"—and typical only of our time is the fact that nothing any longer "is" unless there exists a verbal or other kind of *trace* of its occurrence. In the theoretical sense, it must 'seem' or 'appear' also on the level of a scientific discourse. For anyone still living in the original tradition, semiotic commutation tests are of course senseless. One thinks of the video in which the ethnomusicologist Simha Arom tests melodic structures of the pygmies by asking them to say which intervals are the same and which not. That is a very inauthentic situation, indeed. A similar case is found in Bruce Chatwin's novel *Songlines,* in which an Aborigine is able to paint dreams of his forefathers. An art dealer then sells these paintings, at great profit, to American art galleries. In this case, authentic subjectivity is exploited by means of inauthentic consciousness. Tradition seems to lack the ability to divide its discourse into an object language and metalanguage, and further into a meta-metalinguistic view of itself—unless one considers myth as such the particular "metalanguage" of a primitive authentic consciousness reacting to originary experiences.

Musical authenticity is also related to performance. Certain schools of interpretation owe their existence to the transmission of certain "authentic" oral traditions from artist to pupil, to the pupil's pupil, and so on. This is one of the last cases of oral tradition in modern music culture, which is otherwise completely dominated by electronic communication. Since the teaching of music is still a tactile activity that takes place in direct contact between teacher and pupil, a certain feeling of "authenticity" has survived there. At the École Normale de Musique in Paris, Professor Jules Gentil claimed that his method of piano teaching was directly inherited from Madame Boissier, who took notes at piano lessons with Franz Liszt as to the position of hands; the principle of *la main morte* (relaxed hand) was one example found in her notes. The Pole Jan Hoffman could add to the authenticity of Paderewski editions of Chopin's works certain fingerings used by Chopin himself (such as the gliding of the little finger from one key to the next, against conventional rules, in order to produce a particular sonority). It is thus understandable why musicians and other artists think it important to situate themselves in a certain professional genealogy: Appeals to their artistic inheritance guarantee performers the "authenticity" of their interpretations.

It is easiest to deal with the authenticity of artistic texts which have as their background a clearly defined *style.* Style can be conceived as a set of rules that function as a mechanism for producing new texts, in the same way as a grammar generates language. Semiotics has enjoyed its greatest triumphs in producing such grammars, whose validity, however, has been limited by the fact that they have been constructed only for relatively simple styles, especially in the folk and popular fields. There the quest for individuality has not gone so far as in Western arts of the last few centuries. Such generative grammars have produced quite authentic-sounding Eskimo tunes, Argentinian tangos, Swedish children's songs, Finnish fiddle music, and Bach chorales. Nevertheless, in semiotics a distinction must be made between structures of communication and those of signification for any text or discourse. One can say that such grammars as described above only reveal the communication structures of the texts they "generate," leaving out entirely what these texts signify and what kind of meanings are experienced when one deciphers them. Beneath the "shell" (signifier) of every such sign or text remains the inner "core" (signified).

The signified is crucial to any sign process. Sociological analyses of art, like the taxonomies by Pierre Bourdieu in his famous work *Distinction,* grasp only statistical facts; for instance, the fact that Bach's *Well-Tempered Clavier* and

Ravel's *Concerto for the Left Hand* are primarily enjoyed by highly educated people and not by lower class workers. Such an approach says nothing about the kinds of meanings that take shape in the cognition of these pieces. Even for artistically low-level products, we can never know what kind of aesthetic processes they catalyze in the minds of their receivers: In a skewed communication situation, Bach's music might cause the most trivial of significations; whereas in a certain context, a popular tune can precipitate a very sophisticated aesthetic experience. Therefore, the signification of a work can easily escape the authenticity discussion.

Even Bourdieu would hardly claim that the various social classes—manual workers, domestic servants, craftsmen, shopkeepers, clerical and commercial employers, teachers, and art producers—possess their own authentic artistic style and taste. The reduction of art to its communication structures—whether it takes place in the sociological or linguistic sense—represents the imperialism of One Great Discourse, which for the most part has been abandoned in our postmodern time (though the information society, in turn, still actualizes such a hegemony). Some sociologists, linguists, and psychoanalysts still believe in the positivist reduction theme, in the sense that they try to reduce everything to σ (sociological), λ (linguistic), ψ (psychological), and ι (information) phenomena and systems.

Hence, the authenticity problem cannot be limited only to communication structures. However, authenticity and style are connected insofar as one asks what we gain by reconstructing a style so accurately that we can determine what is authentic/inauthentic within it. Some specialists of early music argue that most important to its interpretation is not scientific authenticity but deep musical experience. Nicolas Harnoncourt states that a lively musical performance is always preferable over a scientific, faultless, yet lifeless one. Before him, Wanda Landowska was saying the same thing. According to her, until the first half of the twentieth century, early music had been interpreted in two ways: either from the standpoint of one's own time, where the changing of tempos and dynamics and exaggeration of expression were condoned, or in the so-called traditional way—heavily and monotonously. Faced with these two alternatives, Landowska would prefer the first, since it is less boring. Traditionalists or protectors of "authentic" style forget that, although they want to follow strictly the signs given by composers of the past, the meanings of these signs change through the years. Even though Landowska seems to reject "semiology" in the following quote, she is basically a semiotician stressing the importance not only of the signifier but also of the signified: "It is true that the spirit of a performance depends more on taste than on signs, but before saying anything, an artist must be aware of what he has to say in order to subordinate the expression of the sounds to that of the thought. An interpreter must penetrate all the composer's ideas in order to feel and be able to convey the fire of expression and all the refinements of detail. There are a thousand different ways of interpreting a piece without getting away from its character."

Landowska's words encourage us to consider in our semiotics such matters as "taste" and "fire of expression." Furthermore, authenticity does not mean that one should strive for only one correct interpretation. Although we might have determined a generative grammar for a style, say that of Bach, there remains much to be done in the field of significations that are enacted in live performance via various modalizations of a musical piece. (For instance, take the C-sharp minor Fugue from Book I of the *Well-Tempered Clavier*: Sviatoslav Richter played it extremely slowly and meditatively, which shocked the Vienna Conservatory professors. One of them, Bruno Seidlhofer, reacted by saying that when Bach wrote something for five parts, he certainly did not intend it to be "silent" music.)

Authenticity is often erroneously associated with a kind of abstinence and asceticism in interpretation. In his book *Du Chant,* Reynaldo Hahn, music adviser to Marcel Proust, analyzed what it meant for one to have a "style." We might imagine that to have style means to have simplicity, accuracy, and modesty. We often reason that the more simple and modest the singing is, the more "stylish" it is. The more reserved the expression (though the lyrics may be most passionate), the more uniform the articulation. In a word, the dryer and cooler the performance, the more "style"—in our sense, the more "authenticity"—a singer is said to have. Now the style may be dry and passionless if that is what the composer intended, but it may also be flamboyant and exercised should the text demand it.

CULINARY CODES

Even in cooking an essential dichotomy is formed by the categories of 'being' and 'seeming': Food is often made to look more like "food," more delicious and tempting, than it really is. Sometimes such a 'seeming' even conceals 'non-being'. But what, then, is the 'being' of a food? It can mean various things, depending on who is the sender and who the receiver of the food. For a health-food enthusiast, such 'being' is equivalent to health value, low-calorie, low-fat content, and the like. In contrast, for restaurant operators of large institutions, such 'being' is the minimal value of nourishment which the food must contain. (So if a client complains about the food, the restaurateur can say, "But it meets all the requirements!") If not prepared according to the traditions of the region, something may even be classified as non-food. Food can also make its recipient move in narrative space, from a heterotopical to a topical area. For instance, food brought from home and eaten abroad can give one the feeling of being "engaged" to home, which is the topical or originary place.

Iconicity in cooking means that one tries to keep the food material in its unelaborated, original state. For instance, the case of a pig's head served on a platter demonstrates how live-looking food aims for authenticity. *Indexicality* appears when food is intended to produce a certain kind of behavior, as occurs for foods used to improve athletic endurance. In the film *Rocky,* Sylvester Stallone slurps raw-egg cocktails in order to improve his fitness for a boxing match: The task of the food is clearly indexical, in the same manner as the magic potion enjoyed by Siegfried in the court of the Gibichung, which causes him to lose his memory and forget Brünnhilde.

Symbolicity in food means that food signifies something completely different from what it is iconically or how it is indexically connected. Examples include dining on turkey in the United States on Thanksgiving Day, on Madeleine pastry in Proust, eating pea soup on Thursdays in Finland (because that is the day on which it is served in the army), consuming Russian pashas and blintzes at Eastertime, and the like. It is most often precisely the symbolicity of a food that spurs the most debate about it. One thinks of the famous law case in Vienna, prompted by a debate as to whether in the Sacher Torte the apricot jelly should be immediately under the chocolate cover or in between the two halves of the cake. When the famous cook Julia Child prepares "French" food, like Croque monsieur, on American television, the audience partakes of the illusion that they are participating in some way with the French spirit—an illusion that is emphasized by Child's signature closing remark, "Bon appétit," spoken in a thick accent. In the same way, a visitor to Brazil feels he has absorbed the spirit of that country when he has tasted the *feijoada* black pea sauce.

It is also possible to use in the semiotics of cooking the Peircean concepts of legisign/sinsign/qualisign. The legisign is ultimately a model for preparing food: It can be verbal advice, which serves as the norm of cooking; but it can also be a model plate kept visible in a restaurant (the meal one is going to eat should look like it). In some restaurants, pictures of such portions serve as iconic legisigns. In the same way, cooking demonstrations on television programs serve as iconic models; primarily, however, they function as indexical legisigns: Do as the cook does and you will get the same result. Cooking can also be an autocommunicative process, when the cook combines available elements and creates a meal from them. This is the activity of the *bricoleur*—the creation of a structure from ready elements. This *bricolage* is opposed to behavior that follows a certain symbolic/iconic/indexical legisign, in which the agent provides certain ingredients in order to create a pre-established structure. The result is guaranteed but lacking in surprise, and it involves less creativity than in the improvisation of a bricoleur.

There are two actors in cooking: agent, the one who "acts" by preparing the food; and patient, the one who enjoys it. Naturally these actors can be united and syncretized in one person, when the cook is also the consumer. As a situation of communication, however, it is of poorer nature than the case in which the cook assumes the "sender" role, such as that of a mythical actant: The value object he prepares is important not only with respect to the concrete qualisigns it contains, but by being a sender, he opens the channel for conveying other significations as well. Giving a dinner party in someone's honor is also a glorification of the hero subject. It is a kind of narrative situation, such that the sender is the cook; the subject is the person who is the object of celebration; the object is the meal itself; the receiver the invited guests; the helpers perhaps the waiters—all of whom may also be syncretized into the same person. For instance, the sender is equivalent to the helper when the meal is offered at home, where the host also acts as waiter. Correspondingly, the opponent can be manifold as well. For instance, the object of celebration can be difficult to please (many stories in Finland attest to this about Marechal Mannerheim); the guests might be dissatisfied or lack the competence to receive the "message" (for instance, in a movie based on Karen Blixen's short story, the provincials cannot admit that the food tastes heavenly, but instead convey their euphoric state after the meal in non-verbal behavior culminating in a moon-lit circle dance around a well).

Food is indeed a complicated semiosis, but what aspects of it are actualized with regard to authenticity/inauthenticity? As in music, literature, and dance, the authenticity in popular forms of cooking can be most easily stated in cases having generative rules that produce the correct, authentic result. Just as by merely judging the signifier we cannot distinguish original tunes from those artificially produced; food can be "generated" by such rules. But just as a synthetic Bach chorale lacks several essential subtleties, industrially produced traditional food likewise misses the mark in crucial aspects. Even in cooking, authenticity can be made only partially explicit by means of rule systems. There are unwritten rules and techniques in any musical performance, and the same holds true for cooking, whether we follow the directions in a cookbook by Julia Child, by Paul Bocuse, or by the Mennonites in Pennsylvania.

Gastronomic aesthetes try to devalue authentic folk food by claiming that only the genius of great cooks has created significant dishes (similar to the view that great music does not come from a people's soul but from the pen of a great composer). Many dishes now recognized as national were the invention of one person, Chateaubriand—the steak of Dumas, the Mazarins, and others. This theory rejects the idea of a *langue* of cooking and believes that *parole* is everything. In fact, food has its *langue,* since one can easily show how food is based upon a social order upon which agent, patient, and other actors must agree in order to communicate with each other.

But how can we reveal the authenticity or inauthenticity of a food? If we adopt Eco's theory of forgeries, we should be able to compare the object *Ob*, which we have in front of us, with some earlier object *Oa* (a dish or meal), in order to say that *Ob* is authentically the same as *Oa*. Sometimes this can happen within the same community. But how to handle those cases, common but undeniably fascinating, in which a disengagement takes place in all three dimensions? Exotic restaurants tempt people to take "food trips" to distant countries (via a spatial disengagement). How to test the authenticity of such a food if one has never visited those lands? Some places advertise historic meals, as in the Marseilles restaurant whose menu consists of forty dishes made exactly according to the recipes inherited from the Middle Ages. In such cases of temporal disengagement, we can make even fewer comparisons and tests. The least possibility we have of uncovering forgeries is by making comparisons in the actorial regard; it is extremely difficult to decide whether a particular meal has been prepared by a famous chef.

With food, though, we can aptly illustrate the functioning of engagement/ disengagement, which in some cases may also serve as the key to elucidating the food's authenticity. In many countries where the shift from an ethno-semiotic to a socio-semiotic state has not yet become obvious on all levels and in every social class, as is the case in Finland, life is still structured cyclically, that is, according to certain seasons and festivities. Such cyclicity is also manifested in foods prepared at given times, which already serve as signs of temporal disengagement. It is argued in favor of large metropolitan areas that in those places, one can eat anytime and almost anything, but from the standpoint of semiotic authenticity, such areas are uninteresting phenomena of decline. The same holds true for countries without cyclicity created by holidays.

In Finland, the memory of our national poet, Johan Ludvig Runeberg, is celebrated on his birthday (February 5). One semiotic sign of this day can be seen in the display windows of bakeries all over the country, which are full of one and same kind of pastry—the Runeberg torte. Yet if one visits a shop, buys one of those tortes, and prepares oneself to experience associations similar to those imagined by Proust with his Madeleine cookies, one usually meets with disappointment. On the level of the signifier (that is, of taste) there is almost nothing in the torte that might transport one to the Finland of the early nineteenth century, to that atmosphere of scantiness, where only such poems as "Saarijärven Paavo" could emerge and the life of a poet beyond a university profession was still quite unsure. How could Mrs. Fredrika Runeberg then have had at hand all those ingredients, produced by today's hyper-industrialized society, which the present so-called Runeberg tortes contain?

The semiotician's judgment is quite clear: Such tortes must be forgeries. But where is the authentic recipe? In this case, it was still possible to make inquiries "on the actorial level," from an informant carrying traditional knowledge. This actor was Mrs. Heidi Parland, by her maiden name Runeberg, the poet's great-granddaughter, who, to our surprise, told us that the authentic torte was not sweet at all but salty and taken with vodka snaps. Whether that is true or not, one semio-gastronaut found in his archives a recipe, following which the meaning-effect of the "texts" (the pastries) was much closer to that which could be taken as authentic: 200 gr butter; 200 gr sugar; butter and half of the sugar are whipped together; 2 eggs and the other half of the sugar are whipped. Butter-sugar mixture and egg mixture are joined plus the following ingredients added:

2.5 dl wheat flour
1 teaspoon baking powder or soda
6 dl grinded dry breads, of which 1 dl sour rye bread, about 2 dl so-called "pepparkakor" (special biscuits prepared for Christmas) and the rest ground dry wheatbreads.

The dough is portioned into small baking pans and grilled in an oven of 150–175 degrees. They rise rather quickly. When cool they are decorated with powdered sugar-water mixture and raspberry jam.

Nevertheless, because of the lack of the authentic object Ob, we can ask on what basis this recipe can be claimed more authentic than several other compet-ing recipes. Our answer is: The most important factor here is the temporal en-gagement. If Runeberg tortes are prepared only once a year, in early February, then they must be logically connected, or "engaged," with this time of year.

Let us imagine ourselves in the home of the Runeberg family at the begin-ning of the nineteenth century, and in any Finnish home at the end of the twen-tieth century. What are the differences and similarities between these two situa-tions? The common point is that at the beginning of February, almost every household has leftovers from the bakings of the Christmas season. Such rem-nants include, for instance, pepparkakor, a special kind of biscuit. Pieces of these biscuits constitute an essential ingredient in this "authentic" recipe. Their usage limits the production of this pastry in the spatial sense to Finland or at least to Nordic countries, and temporally to the beginning of winter. Another distinctive feature is that the recipe uses ground breads, especially rye. The latter is also necessarily connected with the North, Russia included. On the other hand, the use of ground bread is a reference to the poverty of the early nineteenth century, to the poor Finland, which can be felt also in other texts of the period, such as the austere paintings by Hjalmar Munsterhjelm.

As was said at the beginning of this paper, often involved in the authenticity phenomenon is a kind of infiltration, in which aspects and traits either support-ing or diminishing the authenticity of the text in question are filtered or blended. In the cooking example above, everything that can be joined to the seme of "poverty" or "scantiness" supports the identity between *Ob* (a torte prepared according to the recipe above) and *Oa* (authentic pastry at the home of the Runebergs): The ground rye bread serves as the signifier of the same signified in the Finland of both the nineteenth and the twentieth centuries.

REFERENCES

Arom, Simha. *Polyphonies et polyrythmies instrumentales d'Afrique centrale,* vols. 1–2, *Structure et méthodologie.* Paris: Selaf 1985.
Attali, Jacques. 1977. *Les bruits.* Paris: Presses Universitaires de France.
Boulez, Pierre. 1985. *Orientations: Collected Writings.* Cambridge, Mass.: Harvard Univer-sity Press.
Bourdieu, Pierre. 1986. *Distinction: A Social Critique of the Judgement of Taste.* London and New York: Routledge & Kegan Paul.
Charbonnières, Georges. 1969. *Conversations with Claude Lévi-Strauss.* London: Jonathan Cape.
Chatwin, Bruce. 1988. *Songlines.* New York: Pan.
Eco, Umberto. 1987. "Fakes and Forgeries." *Versus* 46 (January–April): 3–29.
Greimas, A. J., and J. Courtés. 1979. "Véridictoires (modalités)." In *Sémiotique. Diction-naire raisonné de la théorie du langage.* Paris: Hachette.

Hahn, Reynaldo. 1990. *On Singers and Singing: Lectures and an Essay.* London: Christopher Helm.

Harnoncourt, Nikolaus. 1985. *Musik als Klangrede.* Salzburg und Wien: Reisdenz Verlag.

Heidegger, Martin. 1967. *Sein und Zeit.* Tübingen: Max Niemeyer Verlag.

Novalis. 1958. *Heinrich von Ofterdingen.* Goldmanns Gelbe Taschenbücher. München: Wilhelm Goldmann Verlag.

Restout, Denise, ed. 1973. *Landowska on Music.* New York: Stein and Day.

Proust, Marcel. 1934. *Remembrance of Things Past.* 2 vols. Trans. C. K. Scott Moncreiff. New York: Random House.

———. 1954. *A la recherche du temps perdu.* Paris: Gallimard.

Ruskin, John. [1905?] *Sesam and Lilies.* In *The Complete Works of John Ruskin.* New York: T. Y. Crowell and Co.

———. 1987. *Modern Painters.* Edited and abridged by David Barrie. London: Andre Deutsch.

Showalter, Mary Emma. 1986. *The Mennonite Community Cookbook: Favorite Family Recipes.* Scottsdale, Penn.: Herald Press.

Snellman, Johan Wilhelm. 1841–42. *Versuch einer spekulativen Entwicklung der Idee der Persönlichkeit.* Samlade arbeten vols. 1-2.

———. 1842. *Tyskland, skildringar och omdömen från en resa 1840–1841.* Stockholm.

PART THREE

The Social and Cultural Field of Signs

9

On Post-colonial Semiosis

Post-colonial analysis covers an amazingly broad field of phenomena, ranging from imperialistic to other ideologically subordinating discourses.[1] Even Europe itself is internally divided into colonizers and colonized. Semiotically, Saussure's signifier/signified relationship must be broadened to include the one which—or who—signifies or makes something signify (*signum facere*), that is to say, the one who has the modal competence to provide something with a meaning. The signified, in turn, is that which *has been* provided (notice the tense!): that which has *de facto* become the signified or object of a particular exercise of semiotic power. He, she, or it has had no control over what significations have been joined to it. Therefore, post-colonial sign analysis is always the rebellion of the signified, or *colonialisé*, against the signifier, the *colonialisant*. For the Modernist project, it was typical of signifiers—things or thing-like signs—to revolt against the signifieds that had been forced upon them. The Russian Formalists discovered that art was the sum of artistic devices; and Raymond Queneau, with his *Exercises stylistiques,* in turn showed how the message (the narrated) depended completely on the narrating elements or signifiers.

Colonializing discourse is omnipresent throughout the collective memory of history. Any message can become part of the colonializing act of signification, and it often proves futile to try to change this situation by emphasizing the inherent value of the colonized. The fault does not lie in the content of the sign, but in the ways in which another sign system grasps, frames, defines, and finally deprives it of use by the larger "Great Society" (this term comes from Josiah Royce, American philosopher and a contemporary of Peirce). To be colonized, however, does not mean that one would have no access to the *langue* of the Great Society. Without a *langue*, one cannot communicate at all. Rather, the colonizing language, while accessible to all, at the same time abducts the *langue* into its own possession and denies others any right to it.

As it has taken shape in the last several years as part of post-structuralist thought, post-colonial theory contains discussions about experiences of various kinds: migration, suppression, resistance, representation, difference, race, gender, place. The theory also discusses responses to the influential master discourses of imperialistic Europe, such as history, philosophy, and linguistics, and the fundamental experiences of speaking and writing by which all these come into being (These are discussed in detail in the *Post-colonial Studies Reader*; Ashcroft et al. 1995; for the above list, see p. xx). None of these characteristics is "essentially" post-colonial, but together they form the complex fabric of the field. Stephen Slemon, in his contribution to the *Post-colonial Studies Reader*, "The Scramble for Post-colonialism," defines the concept as follows:

> Post-colonialism, as it is now used in its various fields, describes a remarkably heterogeneous set of subject positions, professional fields, and critical enterprises. It has been used as a way of ordering a critique of totalising forms of Western historicism; as a portmanteau term for a retooled notion of "class," as a subset of both postmodernism and post-structuralism (and conversely, as the condition from which those two structures of cultural logic and cultural critique themselves are seen to emerge); as the name for a condition of nativist longing in post-independence national groupings; as a cultural marker of non-residency for a third-world intellectual cadre; as the inevitable underside of a fractured and ambivalent discourse of colonialist power; as an oppositional form of "reading practice," and—and this was my first encounter with the term—as the name for a category of "literary" activity which sprang from a new and welcome political energy going on within what used to be called "Commonwealth literary studies." (Ashcroft et al. 1995: 45)

Post-colonial theory has emerged in societies under the sway of European imperial power, although it has not always appeared in the form of theoretical texts. As a rule, the term has been used to indicate the process of imperialist suppression in the institutions and discursive practices of all the relevant societies. Moreover, no community is so small and subordinated that it would not, in its turn, become the colonizer (for examples, consider the Finnish in the Baltic countries and Carelia, and the Estonians toward the *inkeriläiset* and *setukaiset*).

One colonizing technique is that of silencing. Pre-colonial practices are suppressed simply by the fact that one no longer talks about them. The colonized subject keeps silent, since that is his only possibility for transcendence: The colonizing discursive practice has taken the voice into its possession. The "natives" either fall silent and talk about "tacit knowledge," or they attempt to turn weakness into a virtue.[2] The truth of the matter is that a discursive space has to be taken in the same way as physical space (Le Corbusier once said that the first cultural act of man is to take space into his possession). One result of discursive practices which have a silencing or muting effect can be seen in international public discussions. There, the representative of a peripheral, colonized country is not supposed to take strongly held, principled positions; the voice of such a representative must not speak too loudly. Instead, such voices are occasionally permitted to speak on a symbolic level, as representatives of the domain of "art," where their exotic qualities can be admired (many years ago Lévi-Strauss spoke about this role of "art" as the "savage mind" of our time).

The position of a colonialized object cannot be improved by its being shifted to the status of a colonializing object, that is to say, by subordinating others to it or by trying to emphasize the excellence of its inner qualities. The only real solution would be the dissolution of the relationship of signifying—that of subordinating/subordinated, or dominant/dominated—which in most cases is an impossible venture. In fact, every semiotic act—at the same moment one identifies, delimits, and fixes the relationship of signifier/signified—includes within itself the relationship of dominant/dominated. Knowing this helps us to peer into the hidden power mechanisms of those non-verbal discourses that represent so-called "tacit" knowledge. (A cautionary word: The dominant/dominated distinction should not be identified with gender dichotomies, although in certain phases of Western history it does coincide with them, such that masculine = dominant, and feminine = dominated).

Here is the essential problem in the post-colonial situation of the "colonized" nations of Europe—and this concerns all peripheries, i.e., the so-called "nationalistic" cultures, since the dominant cultures usually do not represent themselves in the colonizing discourse as national but as universal types. Sometimes the problem is pushed into the background by the use of other dichotomies such as German/Latin (as Adolphe Appia has done): How can we distinguish, within the European cultural heritage, its colonizing elements from its real *langue,* which even the "natives," we as Europeans, have the right to speak? For we naturally do not want to adopt the values of colonizing discourse when expressing our innermost experiences. The answer is this: One has to leave space around every subject and society, a space which transcends words, gestures, signs, and objects. That space must be, first of all, empty; it is not the same as the semiosphere, which is already filled with signs and signifying units. Therefore, liberation from the sign relations of dominant/dominated starts as early as with the creation of an empty space, in which signs can be detached from their earlier, fixed signifying relations. Consequently, the first semiotic act is not that of signifying. Rather, it is an event that has already taken place before the subject grasps the sign. A semiotic act is the negation of the signified, an abandonment of the ready-made meaning. Thus, it is also an existential moment, it is choice, it is a breaking free from the power of the signified and the creation of a new (transcendental) space. Post-colonial theory is therefore intimately related to existential semiotics, which always emphasizes the situation of an individual and his abilities to influence the signifying process. A subject can change his or her own position as a subject, define him-/herself, and so escape the power of dominant signs.

In this connection, it is worth noticing the hidden anti-existential nature of many postmodern theories, a kind of pessimism, which could be called our *mal de siècle,* a sense of hopelessness. Georg Henrik von Wright once described this situation as the "dictatorship of conditions." Moreover, postmodern society is qualified by too much everything: a surfeit of communication, knowledge, words, or in the words of Baudrillard, an "ecstasy of communication." Vattimo, in turn, argues that we can no longer speak about reality and truth, but only of their imitations, their *simulacra.* It has been further said that semiotics cannot represent a so-called "first philosophy," because of its inability to deal with ontological and metaphysical questions. Yet existential semiotics is precisely first philosophy. The real problem is that the world of *communication* has attained such an exaggerated position that one has forgotten the other side of the semiotic project, that of *signification,* from which entirely new theoretical avenues are opened. The world of communication can be colonized, but there are always ruptures, from which the voice of the subordinated subaltern breaks through. This voice must be encouraged to speak. For only in such a way can it understand how its *Dasein* opens into transcendence and how it is capable of comprehending transcendent ideas, the categories that throw light on communication in such a way that the semiosis appears in a completely new critical aspect. In this way, postcolonial theory is also existential semiotics.

It is also argued that we live in a world of interpretations and interpreting. We do not speak about matters of truth directly, but dwell upon what has been said about them. (Greimas said this decades ago, when he stated that there is no *vérité* but only *véridiction.*) Thus, the present media world is a kind of reified nominalism. It runs contrary to the ideas of existential semiotics, which go deeper into the moment before the formation and fixation of discourse, before the act of signifying—which always includes a certain exertion of power.

Always when we signify or provide something with significance, we create a sign which serves as a tool of power. This is particularly the case if this signification becomes a type or legisign to some token sign occurrence. The Venezuelan writer José Manuel Briceño Guerrero, in his essay *L'enfance d'un magicien,* depicts how one goes beyond words and dissolves the act of signifying.[3] In the same way, the creation of the social sphere (semiosphere) is portrayed in the novel *Friday*: When it does not exist, it must be invented by a solitary man on a deserted island. Yet the lack which Robinson soon notices is that the signs he creates do not have any Other; they do not have the subordinated or dominated content before the man Friday appears. The author, Tournier, shows how Western society is quintessentially based upon a colonial experience. At the end of the story, there remains a kind of Other: The Estonian boy who stays on the island after Friday has left, and becomes emancipated.[4]

The post-modern situation may be put into the following dichotomies, which indicate the shifts from one category to another:

• We have moved from representation to production (this means almost the same as the above comment on the difference between the semiotics of signification and that of communication);

- from realism to a reified nominalism (we cannot reach the truth but only *simulacra*, not Plato's ideas, just shadows in a cave);
- from an authentic message to a media message;
- from the optimism of a unique experience to the pessimism of repeated mechanical experiences;
- from one whole subject to many fragmentary subjects, which appear without any unifying factor;
- from explicit colonialism, in which the dominant/dominated aspect is determined conspicuously and unequivocally, to implicit colonialism (often called post-colonialism)—a state in which the relationship dominant/dominated still prevails, but masked as the less noticeable power of the media.

In the emancipation of a subject, it is essential which of the following alternatives he/she chooses: (1) hybrid communication, whereby he tries to change the colonial signifying process from within: The subject assumes the dominant *langue* by which to express his/her own Otherness; (2) or going outside the whole relationship of dominant/dominated by establishing one's own *langue* and producing one's own *parole* within it. The latter case brings with it the danger that the subject will exaggerate his/her own *langue,* i.e., will elevate it, in turn, to a colonializing status (for instance, a text created on the "periphery" is raised to the level of having a national-patriotic originality).

How do nationalism and patriotism relate to this situation? In the first phase, the colonial state, they are positive forces. But in the second phase, or post-colonial state, aggressive and marked nationalism becomes negative, since by defining itself as national, a state, at the same moment, establishes itself as the external "Third World" and not the authentic "First World." The whole process can be taken as the background for the formation of icons and idols.[5]

According to Abdul R. JanMohamed, colonial literature scrutinizes and represents the world at the borderlines of civilization, the world which European signification has not yet tamed or encoded in a detailed way with its own ideology. This world is conceived as uncontrolled, chaotic, unreachable, and basically evil. In his will to occupy and rule, the imperialist conceives the colonial reality as an opposition, which is based upon differences among race, language, social habits, cultural values, and ways of production.

> Faced with an incomprehensible and multifaceted alterity, the European theoretically has the option of responding to the Other in terms of identity or difference. If he assumes that he and the Other are essentially identical, then he would tend to ignore the significant divergences and to judge the Other according to his own cultural values. If, on the other hand, he assumes that the Other is irremediably different, then he would have little incentive to adopt the viewpoint of that alterity: he would again tend to turn to the security of his own cultural perspective. Genuine and thorough comprehension of Otherness is possible only if the self can somehow negate or at least severely bracket the values, assumptions, and ideology of his culture. (JanMohamed, in Ashcroft et al. 1995: 18)

JanMohamed further argues that "if every desire is at base a desire to impose oneself on another and to be recognized by the Other, then the colonial situation provides an ideal context for the fulfillment of that fundamental drive" (ibid.: 20). On this view, we could say that post-colonial theory is connected to many other post-structuralist doctrines of psychoanalysis, gender theory, the Kristevan definition of the subject, and the like.

According to another writer in the anthology, Homi K. Bhabha, colonialism does not simply refer to a "person," to a power struggle between self and the Other, or to a distinction between a mother culture and alien cultures. The trace of a disapproved culture is not repressed but repeated as something different, as a mutation, a hybrid (the Derridean *différance,* which indicates both "differing" and "deferring," applies to this situation). This view parallels those of the cultural semiotic school around Yuri Lotman, whose scholars speak about the integration of such completely "different" elements (representing the non-culture) into the culture in the proper sense: Those elements must remain "exotic" in order to fulfill the function of non-cultural counterforce, by which the culture, properly speaking, can measure or be seen to constitute its own sameness.

Colonial praxis is therefore not only an unambiguous repression, but a subtle, mixed, and ambivalent discursive practice. What is involved in colonialism—and its flip side, nationalism—is often precisely the subjectivity, suppression of an individual, and his/her emancipation. Among other questions, one might ask, What is that suppressive element in the colonized cultures that quite often makes the careers of their artists, politicians, and intellectuals finish prematurely? It is the colonializing, subordinating discursive practice, the invisibly masked Power as the Other, which exhausts the resources of those whose energy is consumed in their endless fight against it.

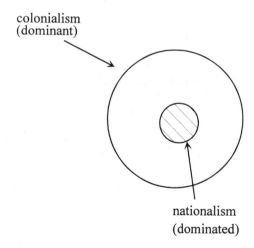

FIGURE 3

Nationalism can be seen as the flip side of colonialism. To the latter it is a counteraction, a resistance phenomenon to the dominant, colonializing culture according to the following scheme, which puts nationalism in the place of the dominated phenomenon:

One must further ask, What kinds of signs, in this broader dichotomy, occupy the place of dominated? That is to say, What kind of sign practices can this relationship absorb into its usage? The case is somewhat analogous to Roland Barthes's model of the mythical sign system, in which the signified of the original sign is pushed aside, and is replaced by the new signified of bourgeois ideology. In this case, the relation dominant/dominated does not influence the contents of the relation signifier/signified: The sign remains as sign, but instead has an impact on the relation indicated by the slash (/) between signifier and signified. Those signs in which this relationship has solidified into something more stable are susceptible to getting into this subordinate position, the more fixed the relationship is. In the extreme case, this appears as marked stereotype signs, which have been elevated to the position of an icon or even an idol. They do not permit any kind of space to move to the signified. If this relationship is already sedimented in the sign, the subordination is easily realized. In those signs in which it has not yet been crystallized, the falling to the right-most position in the scheme dominant/dominated puts the signs in their subordinate position.

The dominant/dominated relation also concerns the relationship of *langue/parole*. Very often the subordinated voices can speak—have their voices heard—only after they have adopted the *langue* of the dominant culture. *Langue* is, however, always a collective contract, which the dominant society has signed for the dominated before it can even think about it. In Heideggerian terms, the dominated is always "thrown" into its lower position. The revolt of the dominated signs takes place as the detachment of the signified from its signifier, as its opening to redefinitions. Yet it can also occur as a rebellion of the signifier, as a new physical quality, appearing as subversive to the dominant, who forces itself into a reevaluation. Therefore, we face a chain of three sign relations:

FIGURE 4

In the first instance, a dominated voice can make itself heard by dissolving the signifier/signified relation within the conveyed *parole*. For example, in the music of Jean Sibelius, there appears a new aesthetic quality that is distinct from "European rationality," a quality one could only call the voice of Nature. Even a quite newly published Sibelius study, by Englishman Guy Rickards, launches with this statement: "More than any other single factor, the music of Jean Sibelius is quintessentially the product of the natural landscapes (physical, ethnic, historical and political) of his native country" (p. 9). A more typically colonializing statement one could hardly find. In it, Sibelius is articulated strictly as a peculiarity to be found in a certain place. Thus, one cannot apply to him those normal categories of the rationality of Western art music, by which we evaluate the so-called universal composers such as Beethoven, Brahms, Mahler, and the like. The phrase is also racist—with its reference to physical ethnicity—and chauvinist, by stating that Sibelius manifests the history and politics of a certain, particularly peripheral nation: In a word, the composer is situated as part of the colonial discourse. The only thing missing here is the gender definition. But even this is found, among other places, in Charles Ives's statement about the effeminate quality of Sibelius's music.

One must remember that categories of dominant/dominated are not only an umbrella concept for subordinated sign processes, but they represent the positions of two different subjects. The dominant one is the colonizing subject, who sees all sign processes from its own point of view. The dominated position, in turn, is occupied by the subordinated subject, who either accepts the situation without question, or who itself wants to occupy the dominant position. It may strive to gain this status by fulfilling all the requirements of the colonizing discourse as "by the book" or as thoroughly as possible, or by transgressing them— in which case it wants to revolt. This rebellion or resistance is possible on levels mentioned earlier. For one, the signifiers can refuse to carry the signifieds thrust upon them from above. This is a kind of subversion of *Firstness*, an outbreak of qualities and phenomena by their own weight, their detachment from the heaviness of the signifieds forced upon them, and riddance of the *langue* guiding them. For instance, certain gestures may no longer sublimate into a "spiritualized expression" within the limits of the prevailing aesthetics, such that sound colors do not find enough place within conventional musical frameworks, or rhythms and melodies may abandon traditionally accepted codes (for instance, those of periodicity and quadratic phrasing). Also, in the background an entirely new signified may arise. If emancipation from the gendering sign relationships occurs, then the whole unlimited field of *khora*, body, desire and inclination rises up in the foreground.

Resistance can also appear if the *parole* as a whole is so penetrated by new signifiers and signifieds that it becomes an idiolect, a new species of speech, which cannot be decoded with the rules of the dominant *langue*. This shuts the dominated into a tragic and devastating loneliness, unless he or she can find for this new speech a community, even the smallest, in which it would be accepted and understood. Thus, the rebellion of the *parole* and its success depends on the social semiotic conditions, in the form of the response which the dominated, rebellious subject can receive from other individuals in the same position.

Yet another possibility for revolt would be to grasp directly the *langue* that is determined by the dominant and thus properly sanctioned. This—to become oneself a reformer of language—is the most difficult task. It is much easier to adopt the *langue* of a new content or *parole,* with its own fresh signifiers and signifieds. This is the only way an artist born in the periphery can become accepted by the dominant colonializing society. The fact of being approved also implicitly justifies the dominant *langue,* its extraordinariness and exquisiteness and stability: "Look, he came from such a remote country, with no civilized traditions or institutions. But in spite of this, he rose to the top of our art." So long as he keeps within the boundaries of the *langue,* such an artist is willingly permitted to convey his "picturesque" ethnic and racial features. For the dominant culture, this only shows forth its tolerance and all-encompassing nature—its ability to accommodate the most varied cultures within itself.

From the dominated subject's point of view, this often manifests the attitude of "he showed the world, he ran, played, painted, drew us a map." But then one does not ask what or who that world is, to whom something is shown. One does not realize that it is the colonializing, dominant world in which the signs are stationed at those places where the dominant had once put them. Therefore, our scheme should be corrected to the following form:

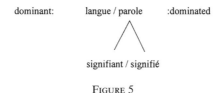

dominant: langue / parole   :dominated

signifiant / signifié

FIGURE 5

Stephen Slemon equates post-colonial discourse and postmodernism, and quite rightly, since the postmodern thesis that "everything has been said" is only a variant of colonialism's view that nothing new can exist outside of the dominant culture, beyond the prevailing systems of communication. No new meaning can emerge from the process of signification. There is no freshness of *Firstness* for postmodern man.

In the postmodern era everyone is (or experiences themselves as being) dominated, but the dominant is nameless. Sign relations have been established by some agent prior to the dominated subjects. This agent is not a precise media figure or spokesperson, nor all of them together; it is not one of the pundits or opinion builders, from Bernard Pivot to Larry King, but rather their "ideal type" (in Max Weber's sense). The meanings of media and communication are already fixed and ready; the much touted freedom of choice in programming is a ridiculous fiction. Modern media technology has colonized the entire globe. All are dominated and forced to look at the stream of communication from this position. Therefore, post-colonial theory extends to the whole sociosemiotic situation of contemporary man. The only exit is the semiotics of the resistance and de-subordination, as discussed above. Clearly, one can see how the various aforementioned solutions are already being used by different groups: (1) those who wish to reform the *langue* of communication (are semioticians among them?); (2) those who want to provide communication with either a new content or new *parole* ("dissidents," "village idiots," and other "oddballs," whose thoughts are met with amusement, since by allowing their speech, the dominant power justifies the functioning of the system and its "democracy"); (3) those who want to explode the relationship of signifier/signified, either by believing in the power of new "qualities"—certain kinds of avant-garde art, displaying "roadkill" (the carcasses of animals that have been struck by cars) as art, shock effects in the movies, experiments with new musical timbres, new culinary signs, and so on—or by putting faith in the force of new signifieds; for example, in new ethical and religious movements.

Moreover, the absolute majority is formed by the dominated, who want to distinguish themselves at meeting the conditions of the dominants and by doing so attain the latter's status. One sees this in the case of the news photographer who went to Sarajevo and Tshetshenia with the sole intent of obtaining a Pulitzer prize. He did not stop to question the dominant media ploy, in post-colonial countries, of producing a certain amount of catastrophes in order to titillate the dominated receivers (television watchers, readers, listeners, etc.) so that they do not become bored (this is the interpretation of Jean Baudrillard). Sports and musical competitions also exemplify ways in which dominant cultures try to legitimize themselves.

If one thinks of the dominant and dominated as juxtaposed subject positions, they could be easily identified with sender and receiver. For a seed of subordination is latent in any communication, nurtured by the fact that the sender forces the receiver to "read" his/her message. And yet the situation is not so one-sided. That is to say, the dominant could be the receiver and the dominated the sender. If I say, "Your Excellency is so kind; do allow me to add cream to your coffee," then I am a sender who, by the content of the message, tries to show that he considers the receiver to be of a higher status than himself. A semiotic act as such does not contain the articulation of power into signifier and signified, but can also include it. As a semiotic act one may take that activity whereby something immanent is made manifest. I have an idea in my mind, and I realize it through my act. Is, then, any act whatsoever a semiotic act? No, since according to the term itself, an act has to be significant—it has to create, destroy, promote, prohibit, preserve, frame, elevate, reward, punish, or glorify something meaningful. In other words, it has to be related with a meaning. (On the other hand, signification can be also of a completely inner nature. But rather than engage that issue now, I shall consider it below, with a theory of the semiotic act.)

The idea of the dominant and dominated can be generalized to cover one basic situation in existential semiotics, in which a subject treats another subject as an object. This always involves the reification of the Other in the terms of the dominant. Thus, we have here an essential application of existential semiotics to the social field. By contrast, the Bakhtinian concept is that in a dialogue the sender is not necessarily the dominant and the receiver the dominated, but both subjects construct themselves freely during the communication process. The meaning effects (Greimas's *effets de sens*) which emerge during this process result from the transcendental values of both subjects. Someone might argue that no transcendental values are needed for the creation of significations. The social significations are those which simply are yielded in this process and nothing else; they only have validity in this dialogue, not outside of it. One might even take this as a particularly existential semiotic standpoint, viewing the resultant significations as completely immanent and unattached to any preexisting categories. Yet this is not true, since the criteria for social significations are not their functionality, efficiency, and fruitfulness in social communication, but that the partners of the dialogue both compare them to their own transcendental categories and their own positions between the two transcendences of Nothingness and fullness or plenitude (both as a distance and proximity, as well as the inevitable changes of the corporeal life between life and death in the bio- and psychosemiotic process; on the axis of inchoativity, durativity, and terminativity, to use Greimasian terms). In a certain sense, such a comparison is also a semiotic act which establishes a relationship to the encyclopedic store, as Umberto Eco puts it.

What is essential in the emancipation of the subject is naturally which alternative he or she chooses: (1) hybrid communication—the attempt to change the colonial signification process from within by adopting the subordinating *langue* in order to express his/her own Otherness in its context; or (2) communication which transgresses the whole relationship of dominant/dominated by creating its own *langue* and by producing its own *parole* in this framework. In the latter case, there is the danger that the subject exaggerates his own *langue,* i.e., elevates it to the colonizing position.

We can try to define nationalism and patriotism from this viewpoint. They are positive forces in the colonial state (phase 1), but in the post-colonial state (phase 2), the aggressive, marked nationalism is transmuted into the negative, since by defining itself as national it also consigns itself to an external "Third World" and not an authentic "First World." This whole process can also be seen as the background process of building so-called national "icons" and idols.

How then should the dominant and the dominated encounter each other, such that communication and signification would fulfill the emancipatory function which is immanent in existential semiotics? Must the dominant continually make the dominated aware of the hierarchical difference between them (as in some universities where the professor prohibits the students to address him in familiar terms in order to make plain their subordinate status)? Or should the dominant conceal or mask the difference as carefully as possible, although both parties remain aware that it still exists? How should the dominated behave; in what manner should he/she approach the dominant?

He may try to identify with it, despite the fact that *Quod licet Iovi, non licet bovi* [What is appropriate for Jupiter is not appropriate for an ox]. Or he may try to position himself in clear rejection and resistance, perhaps by foregrounding those signifiers which he/she knows will irritate the dominant as something alien to its sameness (*épater le bourgeouis*). Or one can absolutely refuse to communicate and withdraw into one's own world—which does not, of course, abolish the colonialist relationship as such.

The communication between the dominant and the dominated is also influenced by their position in the *Dasein*. If they inhabit the same *Dasein*, in the society or community, they cannot avoid interaction, and encounters are unavoidable. If they live in different *Daseins*, as in different "worlds," they may encounter each other only on the discursive level. This may be illustrated by the following diagrams:

1. dominant and dominated occupy the same *Dasein:*

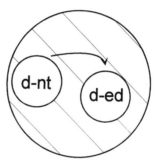

FIGURE 6

2. the dominant is outside of the *Dasein* of the dominated (where the emphasis lies on the *Dasein* of the dominated):

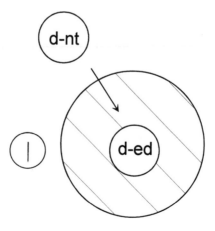

FIGURE 7

3. the dominated is outside of the *Dasein* of the dominant (where the main stress lies upon the *Dasein* of the dominant):

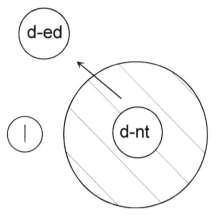

FIGURE 8

Construed as a theoretical problem, the semiotic act, as such, consists of two aspects: rendering something manifest and making a decision immanently, within one's mind, such that this solution is the origin of a change. These differences could also be connected to other categories, namely to the distinction between communication and signification. An act can be a communicative act; it can be addressed to another subject or to the destinator of the communication; it can be an act solely creating significations, and not directed toward communication, i.e., the world of various subjects acting in the *Dasein*. A semiotic act thus takes shape differently in various discursive practices and semiospheres. In aesthetic discourse, when a semiotic act is addressed to another subject, a message is produced which is an artwork addressed to a certain community as partners in a dialogue. But when merely experiencing the aesthetic meaning is involved, then we limit ourselves to the area of aesthetics, such that the parallels are as follows: aesthetics = signification; art = communication.

As to ethics, when we do something moral to another subject, for instance an act of goodness, we are dwelling in the world of ethical communication. But when we only get a moral idea, conceive the moral content of some event or phenomenon, then we are trying to grasp its moral and ethical meaning or signification; as seen, for instance, in notions such as solidarity, compassion, reverence, and so on.[6] The objective of an ethical act of communication can naturally be some reward allotted to the community of communication, some benefit or pleasure, but in the last instance, the only content of such an act lies in itself, i.e., in the transcendental category which opens via one's grasping the signification of the moral act. Moral acts are thus realized in the world threatened by Nothingness. Their background of resonance is emptiness, which recognizes neither good nor evil. Still, one can perform a moral act as its own reward (in fact, in the world of *Dasein* a moral act just as often brings disadvantage to the actor and thus does not lead to any conspicuous glorification).

In the religious dimension, the semiotic act can be realized in communication as a cult or prayer. But in signification it appears as the "illumination" of the world in relationship to what is called *"pleroma."* In that case, the objective of such an act is the experience of a particular grace attained by realizing the plenitude of 'being'; i.e., experiencing that one has not been thrown into the emptiness of 'being', but that 'being' is carried on by a plenitude greater than oneself.

In the economic realm, the semiotic act can be realized in communication as an exchange of things; and in the sense of signification, it is the experience of its value, the compensation for work performed. In the linguistic area, the act of communication is naturally the production of discourse via *langue*. Signification here means that the intention of the speaker is enacted in the form of its particular meaning effect.

In all these cases, the issue is to what extent the world of communication or *Dasein* penetrates to the world of signification, and to what extent the act of signification can again change the world of communication. The concept of act always carries the idea of a certain energy invested in the act by the actor. Two questions to be addressed come to mind immediately: How is this determined in the various cases above, and how does it influence the situation? (It is likely that the theories of Italian semioticians Ferruccio Rossi-Landi and Augusto Ponzio can offer us help in this field.)

In any case, according to Aijaz Ahmad (see Ashcroft et al.), such a theoretician of the postmodern as Fredric Jameson divides the world into those who make history and those who are its objects. Ahmad argues that anyone who believes in the theory of three worlds (not in the Popperian sense)—where the Third World has been defined purely with the terms of colonialism and imperialism—has to admit that one of the strongest counterforces to it is nationalism. With only a slight exaggeration, one could claim that every text of the Third World is inevitably a national allegory.

Yet even more interesting is the contrary thesis: Are all the manifest national texts logically "Third World" texts? For instance, nationalism in Finland necessarily relates it to colonialism and determines the position of Finland as one of being colonialized, dominated, subaltern, and then leads to a result completely different from what was desired. The more national celebrations, the more patriotism is underlined; such (auto-)communication purports to strengthen the inner feeling of coherence of the dominated society. Seen from outside, from the position of the dominant, it is a clear-cut sign that the dominated nation is in its proper place in the colonial hierarchy of nations—as an inferior, subordinated people, which is not capable of a really "universal" act of communication in the semiotic sense. As a rule, nationalist activity and emphasis are, of course, communication that conveys to somebody outside (to the dominant or the aspiring

dominant) that what it is planning—the other's subordination—will be useless:
It is strong enough to withstand such a threat. Nationalism thus is a rejoinder to
the sense of being threatened.

To conclude we may ask, In what historical phase do the texts produced in a
colonized country become "Third World" texts? Naturally, it is only the reading of these texts which makes them such. But it is also a function of space. Are
texts that are classified according to their geographical place and origin already
"Third World" texts? Consider the texts produced in Finland, the Baltic countries, Russia, Hungary, the Czech Republic, Poland, Bulgaria, Portugal, or
Greece—are all these to be considered "Third World" texts? As having something "national" in their relation to the central axis in Europe, which represents
the universal culture and only to which the categories of European rationality
are applied? Sometimes such an argument can be masked in beneficent tones, as
may occur when one praises a country and its people, applauds how faithfully its
artists and poets reflect its nature, and the like. But it is precisely by this technique that excludes text from the "universal" community, from what Goethe
called the *edle Geisterschaft,* the noble society.

NOTES

1. This essay is part of a larger text in which I mostly focus on European nationalism
and on Finland particularly, with special emphasis on Jean Sibelius as a cult figure in the
North as well as elsewhere. The whole text stems from the idea that many phenomena of
contemporary European cultures, like Finland, are understood only if one takes into account a remarkably broader context.
    That broader aspect is simply colonialism—and post-colonialism as its continuation.
The latter typically belongs to the conceptual arsenal of the 1990s, along with deconstruction, postmodernism, gender studies, etc. Post-colonialism is a notion particularly associated with English literary studies. It has not yet often been applied to music. I had encountered similar ideas earlier, when studying Brazilian culture, and found in one treatise
dealing with Latin American literature, the term "colonialized imagination." It meant
that Third World people do not know to appreciate their own achievements, their own
leaders and "icons," but believe only in the pertinence of the values and models imported
from outside, from Europe. As early as that time, it dawned upon me that the term also
aptly portrayed certain phenomena in Finland, particularly the Finns' sense of inferiority
and their worship of everything foreign. But only now have I realized that the colonial
heritage concerns as well and expressly my own country. The theme is now more topical
than ever, since Europe can be divided into colonizers and colonized. There is no doubt
in which category a country like Finland belongs.
    Thus, post-colonialism is the right term to depict not only such cases as Finland, but
also Estonia. In Estonia, the years 1944–1990 saw not so much the sovietization of the

society as its colonialization. The Finns believe that colonialism does not concern us, at least after 1917. In fact, however, it has concerned and still concerns us. Patriotism is a reaction to colonialist ideology, which is distinctive, racist, and essentialist.

Nevertheless, when the physical threat of colonialist suppression has been removed, there remains the imagined post-colonial threat. The anti-subject is imagined since patriotism must always have it. Nationalism in all its forms is an ideology of distinction, which determines itself as a subject, i.e., the people in relation to something not-subject or anti-subject. The situation is very much similar in other European countries as well. Nothing threatens them physically, thus one has to ask, Where does this zeal of national distinction originate? From inner uncertainty. Patriotism, which serves to replace the lack of inner certainty, is as dangerous as colonialist-expansionist patriotism, i.e., the intruding of one's own culture into others. In Finnish neopatriotism, nationalism is not expanded to anywhere; it is communication which fulfills the function of pure auto-communication.

2. See the recent studies in Finland about the semiotics of silence, by Pirjo Kukkonen (1993) and Hannele Koivunen.

3. I am indebted to Drina Hocevar for bringing this interesting author to my attention.

4. For many of these ideas, I am thankful to the attendants of my seminar on semiotics at the University of Helsinki during the school term of 1997–98. Among others attending were Kristian Bankov, Drina Hocevar, Luiz Fernando de Lima, and Mikko Kuusimäki.

5. I have discussed the formation of icons and symbols elsewhere; see Tarasti, "Jean Sibelius as an Icon of the Finns and Others."

6. See the categories of Josiah Royce and Vladimir Soloviev.

REFERENCES

Ashcroft, Bill, Gareth Griffiths, and Helen Tiffin, eds. 1997. *The Post-colonial Studies Reader.* London and New York: Routledge.

Barthes, Roland. 1957. *Mythologies.* Paris: Editions Seuil.

Briceño Guerrero, José Manuel. *L'enfance d'un magicien.* La Tour d'Aigues: Edition de L'Aube.

Eco, Umberto. 1975. *A Theory of Semiotics.* Bloomington: Indiana University Press.

———. 1992. *Les limites de l'interprétation.* Paris: Bernard Grasset.

Fisch, Max H. 1986. *Peirce, Semeiotic, and Pragmatism.* Essays by Max H. Fisch, ed. Kenneth Laine Ketner and Christian J. W. Kloesel. Bloomington: Indiana University Press.

Kukkonen, Pirjo. 1993. *Kielen silkki. Hiljaisuus ja rakkaus kielen ja kirjallisuuden kuvastimessa.* Helsinki: Yliopistopaino.

Rickards, Guy. 1997. *Jean Sibelius.* London: Phaidon.

Royce, Josiah. 1951. *Royce's Logical Essays.* Iowa: Dubuque.

Solowjew, Wladimir. 1965. *Philosophie, Theologie, Mystik. Deutsche gesamtausgabe der Werk von W.S.* Vol. VI. Freiburg: Erich Wewel Verlag.

Tarasti, Eero. 1994. *A Theory of Musical Semiotics.* Bloomington: Indiana University Press. (In French: *Sémiotique musicale,* trans. Bernard Dublanche. Collection Nouveaux Actes Sémiotiques. Limoges: Presses Universitaires de Limoges, 1996.)

———. 1996. *Heitor Villa-Lobos. Life and Works.* Jefferson, N.C.: McFarland Publishers.

———. 1999. "Jean Sibelius as an Icon of the Finns and Others." In *Snow, Forest, Silence,* ed. E. Tarasti, 221–246. Acta Semiotical Fennica VII. Imatra: International Semiotics Institute.
Vattimo, Gianni. 1985. *La fine della modernità. Nichilismo ed ermeneutica nella cultura post-moderna.* Milano: Garzanti.

10

Semiotics of Landscapes

The landscape is a crucial factor in the aesthetic judgment of man's living environment. In the history of both Western and non-Western civilizations, conceptions of the landscape have varied, from a natural or mythical world view to the environmental perspectives of industrial and automated societies. The present situation of environmental aesthetics displays a great need for a general theory that takes into account with the highest accuracy the manifold historical and cultural nature of landscapes. Such a theory might form the scientific basis for a deeper examination that would not only study the beauty of the countryside and of raw nature, but would also comprehend the poetics of cities. For the landscape theory which strives for such generality, a semiotic approach offers a fruitful perspective. The science that would study the landscape as a kind of sign language should thus be called *landscape semiotics*.

First, one should determine the relationship of this new discipline to landscape aesthetics, its concepts and methods. Since landscape aesthetics can be taken as a sub-branch of environmental aesthetics, the concept of "environment" would also serve as a point of departure for landscape aesthetics. In his *Structural Semantics,* the semiotician and linguist A. J. Greimas defines the environment as follows: "The environment means at the same time the center of something and that 'something' which surrounds this center." In our conception of landscape, a "center" is constituted by the observing subject whom the landscape surrounds. The interaction between the environment and its observer can be interpreted as a communication relationship in which surrounding nature serves as the sender of a message, the landscape as an experience (the message itself), and the observer as the receiver of the message or sign language of the landscape. Thus, landscape semiotics concerns communication between nature and man: The landscape "talks" to man.

Let us first study this communication relationship from the viewpoint of the receiver of the "message." It is clear that in this case, the receiver can greatly influence the content of the message. An important factor is the concrete situation, the position from which the receiver scrutinizes the landscape. The messages of certain landscapes can be grasped only by a receiver in motion, as when one journeys by sea or wanders in the desert. On the other hand, the landscape itself may be in motion with respect to the observer. Good illustrations of constantly shifting landscapes can be found in Goethe's descriptions of his travels, as found in his *Dichtung und Wahrheit* and *Zur Farbenlehre*. In the latter, we find the following aesthetically impressive description of a landscape in the Harz Mountains:

> Once, on a winter's journey in the Harz Mountains, I made my descent from the Brocken as evening fell. The broad slope above and below me was snow-covered, the meadow lay beneath a blanket of snow, every isolated tree and jutting crag, every wooded grove and rocky prominence was rimed with frost, and the sun was just setting beyond the Oder ponds.
>
> Because of the snow's yellowish cast, pale violet shadows had accompanied us all day, but now, as an intensified yellow reflected from the areas in the light, we were obliged to describe the shadows as deep blue.
>
> At last the sun began to disappear and its rays, subdued by the strong haze, spread the most beautiful purple hue over my surroundings. At that point the color of the shadows was transformed into a green comparable in clarity to a sea green and in beauty to an emerald green. The effect grew ever more vivid; it was as if we found ourselves in a fairy world for everything had clothed itself in these two lively colors so beautifully harmonious with one another. When the sun had set, the magnificent display finally faded into gray twilight and then into a clear moonlit night filled with stars. (Goethe 1988: 181)

Likewise in paintings, one can distinguish static depictions of landscapes in which the observer views the scenery from a fixed position, or in which the movement of the observer in the landscape has been, as it were, "internalized." Movement can occur simultaneously in time and place, as Goethe's wanderings in the Harz Mountains, or non-concomitant events and landscapes can be presented in the same painting. Such non-concomitance is well-illustrated in certain paintings by Nicolas Poussin, particularly in the one that takes as its subject Orpheus and Eurydice, in which the artist blends spring and autumn in the tree leaves thereby presenting in the same work disparate temporal orders of the same landscape. Such "surreal" movement is an essential device in many paintings by Marc Chagall.

Landscape semiotics cannot be defined, however, simply as a dialogue between man and nature. Other factors intervene between these two basic elements, and the analysis of those factors is our proper task. When putting the observing subject at the center of our approach, we must consider that he or she is not an isolated, idealized individual, but a being who acts in and is conditioned by society and culture. As Rousseau said: *"Qui dit homme, dit language et qui dit langage, dit société"* [Whoever speaks of man, speaks of language; and whoever speaks of language, speaks of man].

If landscape is a kind of sign language, as proposed above, and if we replace the more restricted notion of society with a broader one of culture, then landscape can be articulated as a cultural unit: Landscape is a cultural fact. The most extensive definition of landscape might be accomplished by the anthropological categories of "nature" and "culture" if the emphasis were shifted from the receiver (observer) to the message of the landscape. Yet this message is greatly dependent upon how each culture interprets landscape, and more generally, upon what each culture generally takes to be a landscape. Furthermore, a culture's conception of landscape is connected to the borderline between the two spheres of nature and culture. The broadest definition of the whole problem might be put as follows: Landscape is that part of nature/culture, the border area, which a culture views from its own area and on which a culture projects its own structures and attitudes. The concept of landscape is thus based upon the dialectic between nature and culture: It is the humanization of nature and, above all, the transformation of nature into culture. Such humanization (or domestication) occurs frequently in the history of landscape painting. For instance, although in Poussin's paintings we encounter vast and wild nature, that nature is nevertheless anthropomorphized by a mythological topic that underlies the painting. In turn, impressionist landscapes represent nature completely tamed and possessed by man; yet these are but pieces of nature, atomistic impressions of a single moment.

Cultures not only define landscapes, they also show which kinds of landscape they consider the most appropriate, which landscapes are for them ideal, beautiful landscapes, and which ones are ugly or inappropriate. Thirdly, cultures can be characterized according to *where* they situate their own ideal landscapes—whether these last are situated within or outside a culture, in a close or distant sphere. Finnish Carelianism at the turn of the century exemplified a culture that was strongly oriented to the "extra-cultural" sphere. Corresponding to this general cultural orientation, artists sought to depict, as an "ideal landscape" from Carelia, a peripheral area of culture. In opposition to Carelianism stands a culture whose ideal landscape is neither temporally nor spatially "outside," but within itself; such is, for instance, the culture reflected by French impressionism.

A landscape can thus be situated in the outer or inner sphere of a culture. In the former case, landscape represents a culture's Otherness, and in the latter case, that which is the Same. When to these localizing criteria the principles of evaluation, either positive or negative are added, we arrive at the rudimentary frame or "elementary structure" of landscape semiotics, by which we can in principle classify and deal with the landscape concepts of any culture:

Landscape as a cultural unit

evaluation localization	positive	negative
inside, Sameness		
outside, Otherness		

It is not hard to find examples to fill the categories of the above scheme. For example, the inner, positive landscape of a culture is precisely described by French impressionists and by Dutch painters of the seventeenth century. An inner, negative landscape of a culture is seen in the satirical pictures by Hogarth or any turn-of-the-century naturalist. There are abundant examples of landscapes which are outside of culture but are nevertheless positive: the Carelian deserts in the age of Carelianism, the Tahitian landscapes of Gauguin, or the ruins so widely depicted in romanticism. Negative extra-cultural landscapes are manifest in descriptions of stormy seas or shipwrecks (see Delacroix's "Medusa," the Russian realists, some French romantics); and in literature, certain travel descriptions, such as those by the Swede Linné in Lapland or the French traveler the Marquis de Custine in his "eternal Russia."

It might prove interesting to apply the concepts just presented to the study of a single culture, in order to avoid too great a variety of illustrations. Let us take the cultural landscapes of any Nordic country in the 1990s; these may be classified as follows: (1) *Inside* (of culture) *and positive*—environmentally, aesthetically, and functionally well-planned urban landscapes, or organically developed village communities; (2) *inside and negative*—the urban industrial suburb or the arbitrarily created "modern" village; (3) *outside* (of culture) *and positive*—a desert landscape in Lapland, or a marsh landscape, which only recently has achieved a positive evaluation; (4) *outside and negative*—any polluted natural landscape.

Above I have spoken without making a clear distinction between landscape proper and its depiction in painting or literature. The semiotics of landscape itself should not be mixed with the semiotics of landscape depiction; these levels should remain separate. In the landscapes themselves, as well as in their pictorial renderings, one has to distinguish between "representational" landscapes, which are felt to convey an emotional state or other cultural unit, and landscapes which represent only themselves. In the former case, the landscape can be considered a sign with two levels: (1) the level of representation; that is, the landscape in its physical form; (2) the level of represented content, that is, of an aesthetic image or emotional state, which can be called the content of the landscape. In the latter case, in which the landscape is not interpreted as an expression of a psychological entity, there is only one level—that of the landscape itself. Yet even this last case does not escape the organizing impact of culture. Following Greimas, one can conceive of landscape as being constructed analogously to other discourses of a culture. A baroque garden is a good example of such a conception: The interrelationships of its various parts are structurally homologous with relationships within the social or theological system of that era. A baroque garden and the hierarchy of the society are arranged according to the same "syntax."

The problem of landscape semiotics is not clarified by a simple dichotomy between representational and non-representational landscapes. The question remains, What is the relation of landscape sign language to the signs that depict it, such as in painting, literature, and music? The sign language of the landscape itself could be taken as the "primary modeling system." A landscape description that mirrors this primary language would be called a "secondary modeling system." Any landscape painting consists of at least these two levels of articulation. How the object of description is chosen, in what colors it is represented, how it is evaluated—these manifest the proper language or primary level of landscape, its *semiosis*. The visual composition of a picture, which in painting is an artistic representation, can be regarded as a secondary system; this system can be delineated quite independently of the primary level. Structural analysis of any landscape depiction should distinguish between these two levels, in order to decide to what extent the depiction really represents a culture's views on landscape— that is, the semiotics of landscape proper, not of its description. This is an important methodological distinction if we want to compare various ideal landscapes of different cultures.

In order to illustrate these reflections, I take an example from early romanticism. The French writer Etienne de Sénancour published in 1804 an epistolary novel entitled *Oberman,* which consists of a kind of dialogue between the protagonist and the landscapes of the Swiss Alps. While hiking in the Alps, Obermann projects his own sentiments and musings on surrounding nature, sometimes in a tone of almost Rousseauian melancholy:

> The fantastic excites lively and animated imaginations; the romantic is only for profound souls with a true sensibility. Nature in primitive countries is filled with romantic impressions; a long culture destroys them in old countries, especially in the plateaus, which man easily subordinates to his power. The romantic impressions are like accents of a language which no one knows and which in many areas become foreign. One ceases to listen to them as soon as one does not live among them. . . . In society, man no longer recognizes any of these impressions, which are too far from his customs. . . .

And elsewhere:

> But this view—the mountain tops in front of me, this great, powerful view, which is so far from the monotonous emptiness of the landscapes of plateaus— was not yet the one I was searching for in free nature, in silent immobility, in

pure air. In flat countries it is indispensable for natural man to change inces-santly when breathing that stormy social atmosphere . . . whereas here, in these deserted mountains, where the sky is immense, where the atmosphere is more stable, time slower and life more sturdy, here all of nature eloquently expresses a higher order, a more visible harmony, an eternal unity.

The protagonist of Sénancour's novel resembles two other well-known romantic heroes, Goethe's Werther and Chateaubriand's Réné, as George Sand points out in her preface to *Oberman*. As in Goethe's *Werther,* in Sénancour's work long descriptions of nature alternate with melancholy expostulations, which make the "valleys" of Obermann genuinely romantic pictures:

> Imagine a transparent lake with light coloured water. It is broad but surrounded by mountains; longish and a little oval, it reaches toward the west. The high tops of mountains, in majestic series, enclose it on three sides. You sit on a mountain slope, above the northern beach of sand, from which the waves rebound and spool. Behind, you find abrupt rocks; they rise up to the clouds; the sad polar wind has never blown in this happy strand. On the left side the mountain opens up and a silent valley pushes into its depths, a brook descends from snowy tops, which surround the valley; and when the morning sun again appears behind the frozen points of the mountains and sounds bespeak alp cottages, up above, where there are still meadows, we see a primitive country, a monument of our unknown fortunes!

Sénancour's *Oberman* is closely connected with the *Vallée d'Obermann,* written by Franz Liszt in 1835 for his *Années de pélérinage,* that part of the collection of piano works which portrays Swiss nature. It was no wonder that Sénancour's writing inspired the composer—and not, say, a painter—to create an artistic ex-pression for Obermann's valley. Sénancour lets his protagonist declare in one place:

> It is in tones that nature has best expressed its romantic essence; it is precisely the sense of hearing which can be made sensitive to the features and strong character of peculiar places and creatures. Perfumes evoke quick and vigorous but vague impressions; observations by sight seem to interest more the spirit and heart; what is seen is admired, but what is heard is felt. . . . The tones which make places noble produce deeper and more stable impressions than do the forms of those places.

The story of Liszt's composition of the piece is as romantic as the novel that inspired it. In the year Liszt wrote the *Vallée d'Obermann,* he and Countess Marie d'Agoult left Paris for Lake Geneva. For part of their travel reading they took along Sénancour's novel, which described precisely the landscapes that sur-rounded them. Liszt depicts the Obermann valley "iconographically," with a sinking and syncopated melody that forms the main theme of the piece:

espressivo

MUSIC EXAMPLE 1

This theme serves as a kind of *idée fixe,* recurring in varied forms throughout the piece, just as in Sénancour's novel the valley of Obermann is portrayed in various ways according to the states of mind and feelings of the hero.

For the semiotics of landscapes this episode from early French romanticism is very interesting. What is involved are two aesthetic portrayals of the same painting: The one has been realized in the form of a literary narrative, the other as a musical narration. It is also noteworthy that these two descriptions can be said to represent a similar interpretation, namely, the early romantic view of the same landscape, although they were written more than thirty years apart. The novel and the musical work represent a very similar interpretation of a landscape—it is taken as a metaphor of certain emotions—and this becomes convincingly clear to a reader or listener. One should also mention that most of the Sénancour passages quoted above are likewise included in the collection of piano pieces by Liszt. Neither listener nor pianist can fail to recognize the source of inspiration. On the other hand, the juxtaposition of Sénancour and Liszt can be questioned, due to the fact that the composition was created partly under the influence of the novel and therefore does not directly convey to us the landscape itself. Thus, the composition does not form a representation of its own, but is at least partly an interpretation of the description offered by the novel.

In the case of "the valley of Obermann," we can discern four levels:

(1) the original landscape as physical nature—to be localized as a mountain landscape in the environs of Lake Geneva; (2) the early French romantics' view of Swiss Alp landscapes as romantic as sublime and sentimental; (3) the novel by Sénancour, which situates the early romantic, idealized landscape as a mountain view of Geneva; (4) the composition by Liszt, which has all the previous three levels as its components.

For landscape semiotics, the second level is of primary pertinence, since the concept of landscape can be defined by reference to the romantics' view. That is to say, the landscape, in that view, is understood as a culture's way of scrutinizing the borderline between nature and culture, the line that marks the "inner" and "outer" bounds. Perhaps just as important are levels three and four, in which the landscape is realized as a cultural unit; that is, the landscape appears as texts that interpret and comment on it.

Following from our analysis thus far, one might also argue in a more general way, that the sign language of a landscape has two forms of manifestation on the level of signifier (or more simply, two signifiers): landscape as physical nature, and the description of landscape by various sign systems. On the level of the signified, in turn, we can speak of landscape as a cultural unit, which seems to remain a rather transcendental area. However, through those signifiers, it is doubly united with external reality: with nature as a physically and geographically determined landscape, and with culture through a painting, novel, or composition that describes it. As a whole, these aspects constitute the semiosis of landscape:

Landscape as cultural unit (level of signified)	
Landscape as physical nature (level of signifier I)	Landscape description (level of signifier II) painting, novel, composition, etc.

The above model has the same status of generality as our previous elementary structure of landscape semiotics. Therefore, both schemes could be used for comparison of various cultural views on landscape, and within one culture for examining historical changes in different ages. The content of the "boxes" can thus have much variety: Idealized European landscapes vary greatly according to geographical region, and, further, are quite different from non-European landscape types. Yet even in cases of similarity, there remain basic differences. Claude Lévi-Strauss compares the landscape of the Brazilian plateau to the European landscape in his *Tristes tropiques:*

It is like entering another world. The coarse grass, milky-green in colour, barely conceals the white, pink or ochre-coloured sand produced by the surface breaking-up of the sandstone floor. The vegetation consists of only a few gnarled and scattered trees with thick bark, glossy leaves and thorns to protect them against the drought which prevails for seven months in the year. But it only has to rain for a few days and this desert-like savannah is transformed into a garden: the grass becomes green and the trees are covered with white and mauve flowers. However, the major impression is always one of vastness. The ground is so level and the incline so gradual that there is an unbroken vista to the horizon dozens of kilometres away: it takes half a day to cross a landscape that one has been looking at since morning, and which is an exact replica of the one traversed the day before, so that perception and memory are fused in a kind of obsessive immobility. However far the land may stretch, it is so uniform and so featureless that one can mistake the distant horizon for clouds in the sky.. The landscape is too weird to be monotonous. From time to time the lorry fords bankless streams which flood, rather than cross, the plateau, as if this territory—one of the oldest in the world and a still-intact fragment of the continent of Gondwana, which linked Brazil and Africa in the secondary era—were still too new for the rivers to have had time to hollow out their beds.

In a European landscape, you find clearly defined shapes bathed in diffused light. Here what we consider as the traditional roles of the sky and the earth are reversed. Above the milky expanse of the *campo*, the clouds build the most extravagant constructions. The sky is the region of shapes and volumes, while the earth retains a primeval softness.

What causes difficulties for landscape semiotics is of course the variety of its physical bases—the incredible multiplicity of nature and its structure throughout the world and hence in different cultures. One might be tempted to hypothesize that there are no constant features for a general theory of landscapes.

Next, I shall still try to elucidate the semiosis of landscape on the level of its description. Above, the expression "message of landscape" was used. But what does this mean? As we know, there is no message without a code, or the rules according to which a message can be interpreted. Roman Jakobson has shown that communication can be oriented toward the message, the code, or to other elements of communication. Correspondingly in the arts, for example in painting, one could speak of *code-oriented* pictures, in which the spectator's attention is seized by the content of the message. One might test the appropriateness of these definitions for the problems of landscape. Is the distinction only possible on the level of their description, or can the landscapes themselves be conceived in these two ways? Can we speak of landscapes as if they serve as "codes" and "messages"?

Let us take four cases: (1) The landscape and its description are oriented to codes; for instance, when a baroque garden is represented in a ghost-like texture. (2) The landscape is a code, but its description is a message, as when a modern urban landscape is represented in a surrealist painting. The two other cases I shall examine more closely. (3) The case of both landscape and its description *qua* message. And (4) landscape *qua* message, whereas its description is equivalent to code.

These last two cases can be illustrated by styles of different painters. In the Golden Age of Finnish art, at the end of the last century, we had two great painters: Albert Edelfelt, from the older generation of realism, and the late-romantic, almost symbolist, Axel Gallen-Kallela, who became a "Carelianist" and proponent of l'art nouveau. Edelfelt was well known as a great portrait painter (for instance, see his portraits of Louis Pasteur and other famous Europeans of the time); Gallen-Kallela was appreciated for his mythological, *Kalevala* paintings. In the North Carelian landscapes by Gallen-Kallela, the topography of a culture's outer sphere is depicted on the basis of its Otherness with respect to Finnish (or European) culture. He strove for representation of the *message,* in the particularity of Carelian desert vistas. Contrarily, Edelfelt's descriptions of the outer archipelago in the Bay of Finland refer to Sameness, or that which is similar to the culture: There the culture projects the rules and codes of its own discourse. In his archipelago landscapes, Edelfelt sought for and represented those features that were consonant with the ideal-positivist value system of his cultural context. Therefore, his paintings catch the spectator's attention primarily by the *code* by which the landscape and its figures are painted. Thus, Edelfelt and

Gallen-Kallela differ from each other on the level of description of the landscape. For the semiotics of landscapes, their positions are, however, similar: Both painters depict landscapes external to a culture, whose message for this culture lies precisely in their being "outside." An austere desert and an archipelago landscape were negative spheres in the value system of nineteenth-century Finnish culture.

Nevertheless, Edelfelt and Gallen-Kallela provide such landscapes with a positive judgment. Edelfelt does so by treating the landscape according to the codes of the culture's "inner" sphere, which has a positive evaluation. For instance, the archipelago's sea landscape is "modalized" by perseverance and determination, which via the foreground figures in the painting attune the entire view. In turn, Gallen-Kallela aims to draw out the peculiar beauty of the landscape, the message based on its own charm, as in his painting *Palokärki* (*The Woodpecker*). In both cases, the result for landscape semiotics is the expansion of positive cultural values to cover even the outer spheres of that culture. It thus seems that the aesthetic description of a landscape can in practice guide and greatly influence the semiosis of a landscape.

REFERENCES

Charbonnier, Georges, ed. 1969. *Conversations with Claude Lévi-Strauss.* London: Cape.
Eco, Umberto. 1968. *La struttura assente.* Milano: Bompiani.
Goethe, Johan Wolfgang von. 1963. *Zur Farbenlehre. Didaktischer Teil.* München: Deutscher Taschenbuch Verlag.
———. 1988. *Johann Wolfgang Goethe: Scientific Studies.* Trans. and ed. Douglas Miller. New York: Suhrkamp.
Greimas, A. J. 1966. *Sémantique structurale.* Paris: Seuil.
———. 1970. *Du sens: Essais sémiotiques.* Paris: Seuil.
Jakobson, Roman. 1963. *Essais de linguistique générale.* Paris: Editions de Minuit.
Lévi-Strauss, Claude. 1970. *Tristes tropiques.* New York: Atheneum.
de Sénancour, Etienne. [1804] 1892. *Oberman.* Grenoble: B. Arthaud.
Sollers, Phillipe. 1972. "La lecture de Poussin." *Cahiers théoriques* 8/9.

11

Poetics of Place (Particularly in Music)

"Place" is a more specific term than "space." It is part of space; yet it is a space with borders—in a sense, a space within space. The essence of place requires that it distinguish itself from the space surrounding it, or to put it in Greimasian concepts, it is *englobé,* surrounded by something else. Therefore, a particular relationship obtains between place and space. Place may symbolize the space surrounding it, functioning as that space's sign, and some places may transcend the space around them. Insofar as the space where the place occurs is already as such "symbolic"—somehow semiotized, as the universe of human activities of the narration always is—the place existing in space is a kind of supersign that alludes to the signs surrounding it. To use Greimas's terms again, a place is like an isotopy within an isotopy.

Is such an imaginary place, then, a kind of interpretant sign to the primary space in which it is located? Actually no, since an imaginary place is a rupture or a transcendence of a primary place. Such a space is not an interpretant that evokes the primary sign, but something else. Sometimes such a place can be completely hallucinatory. (A good illustration is the scene in Léon Minkus's ballet *Bajader,* in which the prince takes opium and imagines seeing his beloved as if through a prism, as twenty beings.)

Always crucial is the return from secondary places, back to the basic or primary state. In a story, however, just any shift from one place to another does not necessarily constitute the phenomenon of double representation. Such a poetics of double space appears when, for instance, something is presented in a performance or other kind of representation. An example of this can be found in Richard Strauss's opera *Ariadne auf Naxos*, in which a mythological play is performed, thus creating the phenomenon of a double enunciation. The spectators are the primary enunciators, whereas on stage a secondary enunciator acts. A movie or a novel that tells something by means of someone else's consciousness constitutes such a double enunciation. The Proustian narration is an ideal example. The places in Proust's novels (Balbec, etc.) acquire the status of double symbolism in the narration, since they are experienced through the consciousness of the narrator. Also poetic in this sense is the beginning of Evelyn Waugh's novel, *Brideshead Revisited,* which returns the reader to the main place of the whole story, but several years later. Common to the examples above is the fact that the poetics of place does not exist without actors feeling and functioning therein.

In music, the poetics of place can appear in the sonorous iconic portrayal of a locale. The most primitive case is the musical landscape, in which music directly refers to the spirit of a place and evokes that spirit faithfully by means of musical imitation (a process that is essentially realistic, as Michel Butor notes). One finds such instances in Albeniz's suite *Iberia,* whose various movements depict different regions of Spain, and in Milhaud's *Saudades do Brasil,* whose individual movements portray different districts of Rio de Janeiro, such as Ipanema, Copacabana, Leme, Payssandu, Sorocaba, and Tijuca. Smetana's *Moldau* attempts to paint places along a certain river; the same holds true for his symphonic poem *Ma vlast,* which "describes" the Bohemian countryside.

Music can also describe an actor without a place—such an actor is precisely the nostalgic atmosphere in Smetana's *Ma vlast*—or a place without actors, a landscape without personages—such is the association often evoked by the music of Jean Sibelius. Yet these cases differ from what I really want to ponder, which is the poetics of place in music. The development section in sonata form, a form in which one always returns to the basic isotopy, is one musical process that engages such techniques of place. In a sonata, we always feel that when the development starts, the music "moves" us into another isotopy, from which we return when the recapitulation arrives. Such a detour or deviation always constitutes a special kind of semiotic transcendence.

In Karl Jaspers's philosophy, "transcendence" receives a category of its own: "Real transcending thus means a shift from something concrete to non-concrete. . . . Transcending is not a fact, which would have been given with existence, but it is a possibility of freedom within it. . . . A transcending thought can be understood as a formula: an object without a subject" (1948: 32). Semiotic transcendence accordingly means that when we are already in a symbolic "understanding of being," the movement of thinking and being does not stop there, but continues further and transcends itself. That is why sonata design is a transcendent form and why, in a sense, music represents in itself the act of transcending, rendering transcendence concrete and perceivable by means of certain signs. Hence there exists a poetics of special transcendental places. Using particular devices, a composer can "modalize" a transcendental place as illusory—as a lie, from which one returns to the "real." For instance, in Tchaikovsky's Fifth Symphony the happy illusion of the waltz scherzo is shown to be a wish fantasy, an illusory place, by the return of the fateful leitmotif in the clarinet at the end.

It is also essential to clarify whether the musically existing subject is "present" in (whatever) place. Gabriel Marcel has poignantly described such a category of presence:

> One has to note right at the beginning that the distinction between presence and absence is not the same as the one between attention and absent-mindedness. A most attentive listener can give me an impression that he is not present; he does not give me anything, he does not give me place within himself.... The problem is perhaps elucidated by a statement that a person who is at my disposition is the one who can be with me with the whole cogency of his being when I need him; instead, the one who is not my empathizer seems to offer only a provisional loan of his resources. To the first-mentioned, I am a present being; to the latter, I am an object.... It is typical of the soul who is present and at the other's disposition, that he cannot think of this as a mere case. In his eyes there do not even exist any "cases."

The last sentence of the above quote emphasizes the particularity of an existing subject. It is also characteristic of a mythical place, according to Cassirer. Such a place is always concrete, qualitatively present. We can therefore be present in some place in a physical sense, while at the same time mentally or psychically absent. The poetics of place always emerges from an existing subject who is present.

Some historical locations, buildings, and so on are inhabited by people who are physically there but not in the proper sense. A space or place whose history is unknown to us, to which we are not bound by any memories, is an indifferent space to us. In Lévi-Strauss's view, one of the most acute problems of our time is the fiction that man can be present simultaneously in various places. Modern life strives on all sides to create the impression of an omnipresent, nomadic subject. Portable telephones make people available everywhere, and virtual reality machines try to erase totally the feeling of existential presence.

All this can also be noticed in musical "places." One problem for interpreters of modern music is that they can execute their performance perfectly without being present existentially. What, then, would be a *sign* of existential presence in a musical piece? A disturbance, or a noise, of course; in the sense that the more faultless and "correct" the interpretation is, the less lively, the more machine-like it becomes. Yet contemporary aesthetics strives for precisely this condition. Attention is paid to the "correctness" of a performance, the absence of which is immediately noticed by critics. Of course, a performance error can also be a sign of the lack of presence, but paradoxically it can be a sign of a contrary aspect as well. Therefore, even computers can supplement a "perfect" sonic combination by means of a particular "humanizing" filter, which purposely makes the overall synthesis sound less perfect.

When music reflects the poetics of place, it must carry signs of the presence of a subject. The above-mentioned works by Albeniz and Milhaud attain their value not merely as iconic illustrations of places, but because in those pieces, we feel the presence of a subject, one that mirrors an authentic experience by means of indexes and modalizations.

The role of place in music is therefore connected with the particular space to which the musical enunciator is brought. Not without pertinence is where the music is performed; and vice versa—the music performed there may identify the place. Places have "memories," as Yuri Lotman says, which means that what certain actors have done in these places has remained, in the retained consciousness of history, as a trace in the semantic field. Rooms, salons, concert halls, and theaters are isotopies in themselves; that is to say, they create meanings. When we go to such places, our feeling of presence, the qualitative degree of our existence, becomes amplified and more intense. Hence, to listen to Wagner we journey to Holy Island in Scotland, to the original *Tristan* landscape, or to Bayreuth. Puccini's *Madame Butterfly* is performed in Japan, Verdi's *Tosca* in Rome, and the Brazilian *carnaval* should be experienced only in the streets of Rio de Janeiro.

A cable television studio or stage set, as a theater hall, provides a certain urban avant-garde tone, regardless of what one may perform there. As another example, recitals and other performances are furnished with a sublime connotation in the amphitheater of the Sorbonne. Fans make the pilgrimage to Memphis on Elvis Presley's birthday in order to listen to the music of their idol in its "original" environment. In music, in theater, and in spectacles generally, the poetics of place is based upon continuous interaction among various enunciators. Such a double representation contains subjects on many levels. 'Being-in-itself' (*l'être en soi*) and 'being-for-itself' (*l'être pour soi*)—these categories in Sartre's philosophy are also central to what I call "existential semiotics."

Is semiotics a science of objects in the Kierkegaardian sense? Does it study subjects as objects among objects (Jaspers)? New paths open for semiotics, when one takes into account the 'being-in-itself' and 'for-itself' of signs. There is semiotics that only names and classifies; such is the semiotics of objects. Peirce defined his signs in relationship to objects, but at the same time he succeeded in seeing *beyond* his object-bound, triadic sign categories. In a way, Peirce "humanized" the categories of Hegel's logic by transforming them into the movement of a subject cognizing reality by means of sense data gathered from empirical objects, from the immediacy of *Firstness* to more transcendental ways of thought.

Still, the fact remains that the situations to which semiotical concepts are applied are almost never exhausted nor totally encompassed by these concepts. A tension always prevails between real, significant existence, and the fate of how this existence is crystallized into an objective sign. What is crucial is precisely the tension, the virtual space in which the signs live—the space *before*, or preceding, signs as objects (an aspect also emphasized by Floyd Merrell in his recent studies). The problem is the following: From the point of view of a subject, we can reconstruct the process that ultimately leads to the sign (e.g., icon, symbol, index, seme, isotopy, chronotopy, topos, and so on). But after this crystallization has taken place, the existence from which such a sign emerged may have changed, and the sign no longer corresponds to the reality in which the subject who created it now lives (Goethe once said to his secretary, Eckermann, that many people saw in *Faust* such things that had never occurred to him).

Even when a subject produces a sign only for himself, a sign to serve as the Archimedean point of his own existence or the key to interpreting his own inner world, that sign nonetheless exists in the world of other subjects, in the space of non-ego. How can a "foreign" subject interpret a sign presented to him? Can he understand it? Only on condition that those mechanisms which function within him at the moment of decoding are to some extent the same as those that created the sign. Of course, an alien subject may not care about the processes that brought about the sign, and may unscrupulously use the sign for building his own existence. Everyone has the right to understand and interpret artistic signs in his own manner.

Nevertheless, if we encounter a sign whose original meaning it is essential to know, then we must resort to the foregoing hypothesis. One has to presume that the way we experience signs from the inside also justifies our interpreting them from the outside. When we read a myth from antiquity, for example, we have to suppose that it refers to psychic processes similar to those that we still experience. A sign seen from the inside is like the shell of continuously swelling dough that encases baking buns.

By contrast, when we scrutinize signs from the outside, we can never be sure that we are applying the right rules in decoding them. If we name the sign phenomenon, we have experience by means of a certain concept; in that case, we confine the sign only to its 'being-in-itself'. Behind it remains the 'being-for-itself' of the sign, which always contains numerous potentials.

Let us take an apparently simple sign, such as a Coca Cola bottle. It can be easily classified as a certain product, whose legisign is seen and revealed easily. Yet, the ways different people in different cultures use this product vary immensely. We cannot know what meanings existing subjects will associate with the Coke bottle or most other cultural objects. Therefore, every semiotics must respect the realm of 'being-for-itself' which looms behind every sign. In the same way, when we treat other persons as signs, we ought not classify them as certain types, since man can always change and is free to determine himself again and again. (Gabriel Marcel has well elucidated this Sartrean distinction.)

Accordingly, in our existential semiotics we are located between objects and subjects—between fixed and delimited concepts of 'being-in-itself', and possibilities, continuous becoming, existing, indefiniteness, 'being-for-itself'. To some people, 'being' itself is synonymous with 'being-in-itself'. For instance, for a philosopher such as Quine, the real is only 'being' as such—determined, fixed, empirically observable. Also, the cognitive-science view of the human mind is that of 'being-in-itself'. This last likewise comes close to a structuralist world view: 'Being' is being as part of a system. In the same way, a Hegelian speculative philosopher considers the subject as part of dialectical movement, and Augustine would take him as a citizen of *civitas Dei*.

The antipode of all these systems is the Kierkegaardian ego, whose only worry is how to become an existing subject: "The one who exists is continuously in a state of becoming. A really existing subjective thinker always imitates in his thinking his own existence, and tunes all his ideas to the state of becoming. . . . The situation is the same as when one speaks about a style. Only the one has a style in a proper sense, who never has anything ready, but who always when he starts 'moves the waters of language', so that the most commonplace expressions in his use becomes to the world as original as a newborn. . . . Constant becoming represents the uncertainty of life on the earth, in which everything is uncertain" (1943: 98). So, we can never be sure whether the presence of a subject is realized or whether the poetics of place emerges as its consequence. Therefore, this is the phenomenon of the aesthetics of uncertainty, whose occurrence must always be understood as a kind of gift, which, in fact, the subject does not deserve.

SOME ANALYTIC SKETCHES

Following are some brief analyses of indexes of places in music, of how "place" is indicated by musical signs. The analyses take into account the presence or absence of a subject (i.e., whether there is any trace of a subject in the music), the distance of a subject from the place, the level of *deixis* of the place, whether it is any place whatsoever, whether it is distanciated, imagined, faded, nostalgic, idealized, hallucinated, here or elsewhere, surrounded, alluded to, changing, approachable, and the like.

Robert Schumann, "Eine verrufene Stelle" [A Frightening Place], from *Waldszenen,* Op. 82: The setting is a forested place, the main significance of which is that, owing to its past, the place horrifies a subject. A pastiche in the baroque style indicates temporal distance; and the strange melodic curves and un-liedlike phrasing produce a distorted, frightening atmosphere, as in a story which one dare not tell, but can only hint at.

Isaac Albeniz, *Le chant d'Espagne*: The place represents a broad area—the whole of Spain—and its contrasts of religious idealism, Iberian melancholy, and sunny nonchalance. A subject who is satisfied with his object wanders through the place and is astonished by various associations he meets, one after the other.

Modest Mussorgsky, "Il vecchio castello" (from *Pictures at an Exhibition*): Italy and antiquity are seen through the eyes of a Russian; thus, the basic mood is *modo russico.* This is a pastiche rather than the "linear" remembrances of a subject. The subject of enunciation has the object (a painting) in his possession, and he enjoys the nostalgic scene presented therein. Yet the subject is disjuncted from an object, in the sense that he is charmed by the memory of times past as a kind of secondary enjoyment. This is a place distanciated by the visual representation, a place within place, a metalevel place, a transcendent place.

Vincent d'Indy, *Symphonie montagnard*: Without the cue of a certain index—a modal melodic interval—we would never guess that we are in the mountains of France. Thus, what is involved is an indexical place, in which the subject is not present in the proper sense.

Antonin Dvořák, Adagio, from the *"New World" Symphony*: The subject of enunciation looks at his own topos through the eyes of a foreigner, or vice versa, at the foreign topos with nostalgic feelings for his "own" place. This is the New World as seen by a Czech. The object longed for by the subject can thus be either a topos or a heterotopos.

Ferruccio Busoni, *Finnische Ballade*: Finland seen in 1887 through the eyes of an Italian-German, rationalist artist. The music is a cultural semiotic description of a place in which a subject is present, having style features all its own, without being fused with the landscape itself. Among the traces of a subject are a fugue, the vague major/minor tonality of the melody, the clash of two cultures—the Italian harmonious sense of form versus the extremes of Finnish culture, which include a rough, dance-like character, extreme slowness, austerity, and an overall static quality.

Charles Ives, *Three Places in New England*: The associations evoked by the place are present simultaneously, superimposed. The plenitude of meaning is overwhelming and chaotic. The subject is in a place whose various aspects he only registers as an immediate *Firstness*, without having time to modalize them.

Darius Milhaud, *Saudades do Brasil*: a musical landscape and atmosphere as a kind of system of differences, contrasts, and similitudes. This is Rio de Janeiro as seen through European eyes. Bi-tonality acts here as an alienating index of strange atmospheres, registering types and attitudes that are foreign to Europeans. Rather than in the modalizations of a subject, the atmosphere of place here is situated in the properties of the object itself, which alludes to various districts of Rio. The music functions almost as a realistic discourse, such as a travelogue or tourist pamphlet.

Claude Debussy, *L'isle joyeuese*: a dim, faded place. According to tradition, the piece depicts Watteau's painting *The Embarking on the Isle of Cythere*. Thus, strictly speaking, this is not a description of a place but of the approach to it. The place is seen through a mythological *sfumato,* the vaguest impression of a place without any concrete indexes of it.

Maurice Ravel, *Vallée des cloches*: The feeling of place is strongly iconic and physical, like the presence of the musical narrator observing it; however, this is not a particular valley, but a generalized valley of bells.

Franz Liszt, *Vallée d'Obermann*: a wandering in a place, its contrasts, its peaks and valleys; exaltation about a place, a story that deals with movement within a place.

Léon Minkus, *Bajader*: an imaginary place, a profound shift to a heterotopos, in which the hero, intoxicated by love, sees his beloved as manifold, as if looking through a prism. This is a completely inner and imaginary place that in reality exists nowhere.

Magnus Lindberg, *Action, Situation, Signification*: Places are strongly indicated by various elements of nature, physically present, but which have been universalized as places of whomever, wherever, and whenever. It is precisely to these types of sites that one may apply Gaston Bachelard's poetics of place; they are places of a universal, psychoanalyzed subject.

REFERENCES

Butor, Michael. 1964. "Musique, l'art realiste." In *Répertoire II*. Paris: Editions de Minuit.
Hardwick, Charles S. 1977. *Semiotic and Significs: The Correspondence between Charles S. Peirce and Victoria Lady Welby*. Bloomington and London: Indiana University Press.
Jaspers, Karl. 1948. *Philosophie*. Berlin, Göttingen, Heidelberg: Springer Verlag.
Kierkegaard, Søren. 1943. *Päättävä epätieteellinen jälkikirjoitus* [Closing Unscientific Post-scriptum]. Finnish trans. of the Danish original *Afsluttende uvidenskabelig Efterskrift* (1846). Juva: Werner Söderström.
Marcel, Gabriel. 1927. *Journal métaphysique*. Paris: Editions Gallimard.
Merrell, Floyd. 1995. *Peirce's Semiotics Now: A Primer*. Toronto: Canadian Scholars' Press.
Sartre, Jean-Paul. 1943. *L'être et le néant. Essai d'ontologie phénoménologique*. Paris: Gallimard.

12

Walt Disney and Americanness

AN EXISTENTIAL-SEMIOTICAL EXERCISE

The fantasy industry created by Walt Disney, with its inherent Americanness, forms an inseparable part of the media world that emerged after World War II. The Disney phenomenon is so far-ranging that no one who studies the media or postwar events can ignore it. It is no exaggeration to say that most people in the industrial world have at some time in their lives come under the influence of Disney.

Several inferences have been drawn from this fact. Some consider Donald Duck and Mickey Mouse harmless entertainment that even an adult can permit himself to enjoy in certain situations, such as in the barber's waiting room, in the army, at the beach. Some orchestral musicians keep Donald Duck open on their music stands while awaiting their next entrance—Disney entertainment is fun that does not require too much concentration. Others are convinced that Disney represents a covert intrusion of American ideology—an intrusion that plants the laws of capitalism and colonialism in young and supple minds. In 1971, the Chileans Ariel Dorfman and Armand Mattelart published a now-classic pamphlet entitled *Para leer al Pato Donald* (*For Reading Donald Duck*). According to them, Disney colonializes reality by playing with children's fantasies. Though Dorfman and Mattelart speak about cartoons, what they say concerns in principle the whole Disney phenomenon. From a contemporary point of view, their book tends to come off as extremely moralistic finger-pointing. Naturally, behind Disney stands a huge, rationalized entertainment industry, but it is impossible to explain the success of Disney's products by mere capitalist exploitation. There must be something in the semiotic mechanism of the product, something in the message itself, that has an almost universal appeal and persuades people to believe in it. If we could explain the property that enables the functioning of a message in any society, we could reveal something essential about the success of American culture. This last has often been called a "culture of experience," but it is better described as a "culture of persuasion."

It seems to me that European explanatory methods and analyses are often helpless before the American phenomenon. We of course have the colorful portrayals of America by Umberto Eco and Jean Baudrillard. Yet I wonder if an approach that departs from European structuralism might provide us with more efficient tools for understanding Americanness and Disney. One would have to start from a deep level, from the philosophical ground of the concept of sign. We cannot begin with the concept of structure, with symbols that constitute part of a "continuum of signs," since for American culture, we cannot assume the existence of the structures and continua that are valid in the European context. We have to find the moment or level *before* the formation of structures. To engage that level, the existentialist opposition between 'being' and Nothingness might serve as our point of departure. This leads me to some reflections on a new sign theory, which I call *existential semiotics*.

The basic situation of man is that he is surrounded by 'not-being'. This might sound dangerously Hegelian, and would not rid us of the hold of structuralist binary or ternary thought, unless Nothingness were understood differently from its interpretation in German philosophy. Hegel's *das Nichts* is not a frightening or anxiety-ridden entity, since it is only one step in reality's move toward a synthesis on a higher level. It is somehow ironic that not even the American Charles Peirce was free from this three-phase dynamic of thesis-antithesis-synthesis, when he construed the gradually deepening cognition of reality as taking place via *Firstness*, *Secondness*, and *Thirdness*.

The existentialist distinction between 'being' and Nothingness, however, differs quite radically from the Hegelian model. In the existential model, a human being first "is," and then attains his being amidst Nothingness. His life is bordered by two voids—before and after. I call this initial distinction the *primary negation* of reality. Now when the 'being' becomes conscious of itself in relation to Nothingness, it realizes its fate in the arms of the void, and, enriched by this experience, it returns to itself. At this point, the 'being' already represents a viewpoint in which it has been seen, namely by itself, after having become a sign to itself. Therefore, the very concept of sign may be fundamentally irrational. The sign emerges from emptiness, from Nothingness; it is a happy fortuitousness. One might say that the sign appears in Nothingness like a torch that lights the darkness for a while. The concept of sign is an effort to erase 'not-being' for a time, an attempt to create something of permanence.

The sign always emerges when *'the being'* is temporarily detached (the Greimasian disengagement) from its *'state of being',* and becomes conscious of its place amidst emptiness, aware of the Nothingness surrounding it on every side and awaiting it at all times. In its movement toward Nothingness, the 'being' reflexively turns to itself and sees itself from the viewpoint of Nothingness. By then it has shifted to another level, to a new degree of consciousness. The 'being' has internalized the Nothingness, it has taken the void into itself; hence the 'being' becomes to itself a *sign*. Sign, therefore, always means a leap from a concrete 'being' to the unknown, abstract emptiness, and at the same time an effort to conquer this 'not-being' by the possibility of becoming *recurrent*. Recurrent signs become part of social practices; but there are also non-recurrent signs, which are signs only to the 'being' itself. It is characteristic of precisely these "non-recurrent" signs that they are unique and individual. The concept of inner meaning, of signification, is fundamentally based on this uniqueness. Uniqueness is bound with *temporality*. The Nothingness appears precisely as temporality, by virtue of the fact that every sign carrying an inner meaning is doomed to extinction at the next moment. Hence, there is nothing stable in this sense. The sign receives its meaning precisely from its relationship with the temporal process, by becoming conscious of its own disappearance, momentariness, and uniqueness. Full meaning is achieved at the moment when one realizes that one has to give it up. In the view I am forwarding here, the sign emerges only secondarily from a continuum of signs. There may well be a semiosphere, but where and how was it born? The origin of the sign is in the experience of Nothingness.

This last premise has sociosemiotic consequences. Structures, which are accumulations of external and internal signs, prevent man from reaching the essence of 'being', which is its leap toward Nothingness and its pursuant return to 'being'. Structures create the illusion that the Nothingness is "human," inhabited by social structures and epistemes. In fact, the difference between American and European society lies precisely here: European society is based upon the existence of "benevolent" and "malicious" structures, supported by which man's life forms a trajectory that follows the various roles available as mythical models. Via modalities man masters the Nothingness, by rejecting it within particular modal structures. Structuralist thought contains many variants of this basic situation. For Lévi-Strauss, the structures were indifferent phenomena, like natural law—even when they threatened the destruction of entire ethnic groups, as occurred during World War II. According to Lévi-Strauss, the American Indians did not know which structures organized their myths, forming "fugues" and "symphonies" from them. Even Michel Foucault initially thought structures were relatively benign and neutral "epistemes." Later, and guided by his own existential situation, he came to investigate the malicious, destructive structures in European punishment and carceral systems. Thereafter, he believed in the existence of "bad" structures. Yuri Lotman and his school were subsequently inspired by a belief in "benevolent" structures that make possible man's social life. Culture makes people happy, by generating structures like the "Sampo" of Fennougrian mythology or the Germanic horn of plenty.

Only a few thinkers in the European tradition have had the courage to step beyond the structures and dare to start from the concept of Nothingness: Nietzsche, Wittgenstein, Sartre. Nevertheless, it is typical of Europe that the moment previous structures are destroyed and an empty space created, it starts to be filled by new structures. After the second World War emerged existentialism, which "reinvented" the concept of Nothingness (Sartre, Camus, Marcel, Heidegger); however, existentialism was soon replaced by structuralism, which was none other than the world view of "benevolent" and "malicious" structures, now elevated into a doctrine (Lévi-Strauss, Lotman, Goldmann, Barthes).

In contrast to the European situation, the basic mood of America is one of existence without structures. America is based directly upon Nothingness and is controlled by no structure. No wonder that Baudrillard declared the desert to be the symbol of America: "American culture is a remnant of wilderness. Deserts do not represent a nature understood as a contrast to city, but the emptiness and radical nudity looming behind all institutions created by man. At the same time they show how human institutions are metaphors of that emptiness, the achievement of human work as the continuation of a desert, culture the mere reflection and stability of simulacra." This explains why in America everything is "possible" and there is no hindrance to unlimited fantasy, growth, and activity. In a culture based on Nothingness, everything develops on an exaggerated, irrational scale, as seen from a European point of view. No *harmonia praestabilita* is there to regulate matters as regards the whole. In America, the fantasy of an unmitigated Disneyland is a reality.

In such a world, the individual *sign* has its particular value. Amidst the Nothingness some symbol can suddenly emerge as a gift, completely irrational, without connections to anything else. In America, there is no Otherness, since there also is no Sameness, in the sense of a compatibility with dominant structures. In America, a *Bildungsroman* like Goethe's *Wilhelm Meister* would be impossible, a novel in which strange, romantic figures surface as voices and actors of Otherness (Mignon, the harp player). Disney's Mickey Mouse, in the animated rendering of Dukas's *L'apprenti du sorcier,* well depicts this world, in which the individual's most daring dreams can come true.

Nevertheless, as noted above, there are existential moments in which an individual sign emerges from the banal Nothingness and redundancy surrounding it. The slow theme in the middle section of Gershwin's *Rhapsody in Blue* is a good example. The music surrounding it is in a highly redundant, jazz-tinged style. Suddenly a hymn rises up amidst the repetitiveness and, in its overwhelming cogency of expression, appears as a symbol to the entire universe that envelops it, and elevates itself to the level of a reflection of that Nothingness. In a congenial way, this sign occurs only three times. Then the hymn-tune sounds no more, disappearing as mysteriously as it emerged. This theme's fortunes serve well as a metaphor for the existential emotion of America in music.

A society built upon the principle of Nothingness is a history-less society. History is possible only in relation to a structure. This structure is either hidden in the supra-individual, collective consciousness or in the narrative structures revealed by historians. Thus, one may understand why the further the Americanization of Europe and the rest of the world progresses, the more is said about the end of history. More precisely, what is involved is the disappearance of the structures that support history. "Structure" in this sense is always social reality. Existential semiotics, however, suspects any kind of communality. Does not the smallest unit of community, the family, already include the idea of excluding the others? Is it not so that *Gemeinschaft* is always possible only by excluding others? Is there a positive spirit of "community"? Certainly the American transcendentalists, Emerson and Thoreau, reacted strongly to such solidarity or communal interests. The latter thinker lived in his hut at Walden, and the former defended this act in his essay "The Transcendentalist": "It is a sign of our times, conspicuous to the coarsest observer, that many intelligent and religious persons withdraw themselves from the common labors and competitions of the market and the caucus, and betake themselves to a certain solitary and critical way of living, from which no solid fruit has yet appeared to justify their separation. They hold themselves aloof: they feel the disproportion between their faculties and the work offered them, and they prefer to ramble in the country and perish of ennui to the degradation of such charities and such ambitions as the city can propose to them." The situation described by Emerson has certainly reproduced itself in our own time, as is evident in certain environmental and ecological movements. Emerson saw in this withdrawal the essence of Americanness, and in his ideas I find support for my own theory of Nothingness.

The experience of Nothingness is always unbearable, anguishing. One seeks escape from it on both the individual and social levels. As the inevitable negation of 'being', Nothingness can be either accepted or rejected. Emerson's solution appeared in its most advanced form a hundred years later, in the Disney ideology. The community, the social structure—which helps Europeans see their way through the angst of Nothingness—is replaced in America by the belief in a common, universal spirit of human nature. Emerson called this nature the *oversoul:*

> I live in a society with persons who answer to thoughts in my own mind, or express a certain obedience to the great instincts by which I live. I see its presence to them. I am certified of a common nature; and these other souls, these separated selves, draw me as nothing else can. . . . Persons are supplementary to the primary teaching of the soul. In youth we are mad for persons. Childhood and youth see all the world in them. But the larger experience of man discovers the identical nature appearing through them all. Persons themselves acquaint us with the impersonal. In all conversation between two persons tacit reference is made, as to a third party, to a common nature. That third part or common nature is not social, it is impersonal; is god.

Beside this universal human nature or oversoul, all the achievements of art and science pale in comparison:

> There is in all great poets a wisdom of humanity which is superior to any talents they exercise. The author, the wit, the partisan, the fine gentleman, does not take place of the man. Humanity shines in Homer, in Chaucer, in Spenser, in Shakespeare, in Milton. . . . The soul is superior to its knowledge, wiser than any of its works. The great poet makes us feel our own wealth, and then we think less of his compositions. His best communication to our mind is to teach us to despise all he has done.

This utterance may seem paradoxical, but it should be understood as a particular form of transcendental experience. Emerson's reaction to the problem of Nothingness is to posit that Nothingness, or transcendence, represents a universe inhabited by the oversoul. From the latter's viewpoint, even the richest forms of being, on the level of manifestation or concrete reality, appear barren and banal.

Disney's fantasy world is based on the same hypothesis: Nothingness can be held back, at least temporarily, if you just believe in the "benevolent" structures that he has created. They are not European social structures in the positive sense, but as Dorfman and Mattelart stated, in them, pressing social realities fade into the background. Disney's "good" structures represent a higher degree of imaginary reality, which appeals to our inherent and universal infantility. Disney's animated figures represent precisely the other reality dominated by the Emersonian oversoul—the *secondary negation* in our existential semiotics, in which fantasy substitutes for Nothingness. As early as 1947, Robert D. Feild, in his *The Art of Walt Disney,* took this view when he said:

> If we are to understand the art of Walt Disney, we must abandon once and for all the contention that the fine arts of music, sculpture, and architecture were the last word in man's efforts to express himself with dignity; that they alone are *art.* We must awake to the possibility of entirely new types of creative activity more consistent with our immediate needs, expressions of a deeper cultural significance to us than their older prototypes. We must be free to enjoy ourselves, unconcerned by whether we are looking at Art or are participating in some form of entertainment that has somehow escaped from the generally accepted art categories and is under suspicion.

This freedom is possible if we find the universal youth and naiveté that is hidden within us all: "No one of us has really ceased being young. We can always evoke to our minds the once-upon-a-time of our childhood. . . . We only have to reject for a while our dignity, throw away our books and unashamed return to the paths of our youth, if we want to enter Walt Disney's fantasy world."

This return to childhood is an anthropological phenomenon that Lévi-Strauss calls the "archaic illusion." In his study of *The Elementary Structures of Family* (1947), Lévi-Strauss argues that the thinking of a child constitutes a kind of universal foundation whose crystallization has not yet taken place. While adult thinking is based on certain structures which it organizes and develops, these are only a small part of the original, unarticulated structures in the thought of a child. Every type of social organization represents a *choice* pursued by a group. Whereas adult thinking rejects and selects according to the demands of a group, children's thought is still polymorphic. One could therefore say that Disney portrays just this syncretic, "primitive" way of thinking, which results from the coincidence of several systems and from continuous vacillation from one system to the other. Disney's imagination precisely represents such a universal level. It is a completely different matter how, in Disney films, so-called primitive thought is represented and that which Dorfman and Mattelart so bitterly criticize. In Lévi-Strauss's view, primitive societies cannot be compared to the children of our culture. If we do so, we should remember that so-called primitive people do the same: They consider *us* childlike. In any case, Disney operates on an archaic level of mind, the one which is the meeting place of all forms of thought. I shall return to this later when discussing Disney's hidden totemism.

Disney's world is American culture's response to the fear and anguish awakened by the experience of emptiness. It is a counter-world, by which one rejects the Nothingness of the experience of a desert, a world where perhaps similar but controlled emotions are evoked in the spectator. In our earlier example, Mickey Mouse is rescued by the return of the Sorcerer. If the story of Goethe's poem and Dukas's symphonic piece were changed so that Mickey remained alone amidst the chaos, then the resulting ideological message would be that of accepting Nothingness. Such acceptance might be followed by a now-purified or transfigured return to one's semiotic self. As it stands, the result of the Disney-animated tone poem is a syncretic, musico-visual sign system, which does all it can to make us forget the roots of our existential situation. Yet we cannot be satisfied with mere philosophical reflections on Disney's semiotics. Let us analyze the phenomenon more carefully, taking the film *Fantasia* as our example.

Fantasia had its greatest commercial success as a reissue, on video tape, in recent years. This huge success reminds us of the strong position of the original film in Disney's output. Disney began making the film as early as World War II, a fact which brings us to remark on certain poetic aspects of the movie. In 1938 Disney, who had already created Mickey Mouse, Snow White, and his huge studio machinery, wanted Mickey to stage a kind of comeback. Disney met Leopold Stokowski at a Hollywood party, and at this meeting there emerged the idea of making a motion picture about Dukas's symphonic poem, *L'apprenti du sorcier* (*The Sorcerer's Apprentice*), itself based on Goethe's balladic poem, *Der Zauberlehrling*. The initial creative process thus involved a manifold media shift: from poem to music and from music to picture. Stokowski suggested that instead of using just Dukas's tone poem, they make an entire film based on various pieces of art music. To help with the project, Disney and Stokowski invited a popular music reporter of the day, musicologist and composer Deems Taylor of the Metropolitan Opera's broadcast performances. Together the three men listened to enormous amounts of classical music, until Stokowski was ready to supervise the process of recording the selected pieces. The result was a motion picture that consisted of a suite (a Toccata and Fugue by Bach, arranged by Stokowski), fragments from Tchaikovsky's *Nutcracker* ballet, Dukas's *Sorcerer's Apprentice,* Stravinsky's *The Rite of Spring,* Beethoven's Sixth ("Pastoral") Symphony, Ponchielli's *Dance of the Hours,* and Mussorgsky's *A Night on Bald Mountain,* culminating in Schubert's *Ave Maria.* Stokowski later related that *Fantasia* was produced mainly by persons without any musical education. They were nevertheless avid listeners, who "could find in music depths of expression omitted sometimes by musicologists."

In between the musical sections of the film, the orchestra was shown as a blue silhouette, an arrangement which allowed Mickey Mouse to greet Stokowski on the podium. The climax of the Toccata and Fugue was described by Deems Taylor as follows: "A flash of light against which the tensed, vibrating profile of the conductor is seen. The last chord. Bach has spoken" (Schickel 1968: 241). Yet one can justifiably ask: *Who has spoken*? Bach? Beethoven? Stravinsky? The answer is, Hardly any one of them, so big and radical were the changes made to their music in order to accommodate the animation. The *Fantasia* version does not correspond in any way to the original Pastoral Symphony, as little as *The Rite of Spring* does to Stravinsky's original. Stravinsky, who at the time was the only living composer of those whose music was used in the film, could have complained, but he did not. Disney's studio offered him five thousand dollars for the use of his music. At the same time, Disney said that even if Stravinksy refused his offer, *The Rite of Spring* would be used in any case: Since the copyrights to the work belonged to a Russian publisher, and the United States had not ratified the international contract which would have protected those rights, Stravinsky was forced to accept any changes made to his music. When Stravinsky saw the movie at a screening in Hollywood, Disney claimed that the composer was moved by it. However, the reason for Stravinsky's show of emotion lay elsewhere, as the composer himself stated in his diary: "The orchestration was changed, among other ways, [such that] the horns had been scored an octave higher [than the original] in order to play their glissandi. The order of the [movements] had been changed, and the most difficult ones were eliminated. This did not save the performance, which was disgusting. I do not say anything about the visual side, since I do not want to comment on such obvious idiocy."

Fantasia's "subject of enunciation," to use more technical language, is therefore none of the aforementioned composers. Is it, then, Stokowski and his orchestra? It is interesting that the performers are shown as physical beings—even if silhouetted and made mysterious by the dim lighting. We recall that Wagner, in his own "Disneyland" of Bayreuth, wanted the orchestra to be hidden in order to create a completely sonorous illusion. Why, then, in Disney's movie do the musicians remain visible? When Mickey Mouse greets Stokowski, this signifies an emphasis on the position and autonomy of the implicit musical "narrator," or "enunciator." On the other hand, the subjects of both enunciation and enunciate occur in the same picture, both the protagonist of the story and the narrator. The situation is made more complicated by the fact that Deems Taylor, the speaker, addresses his narrative gestures directly to the theater audience, although he is not shown directly. These direct addresses in the film correspond to the conative function of communication. At the same time, the content of the speech manifests the metalinguistic function, since musical codes are pondered therein: "Now we shall hear a composition, with a quite obvious plot."

One may well ask, however, why only the subjects of the *verbal* and *musical* enunciate and enunciation are foregrounded. Why not the cartoonists or even Disney himself? Is it not Disney who has "spoken" in this film? Even this is questionable, if one thinks of the whole production process of the movie. The implementation of each sub-field of the narration, in Disney's studio, is assigned to a special department in which hundreds of people work. The completed film is always the product of a carefully orchestrated cooperative effort. When one sees the structure of Disney's studio and its division into hierarchical compartments, with Disney himself as the supreme supervisor (who, incidentally, drew very poorly)—all this may evoke an Americanized version of the supervision and punishment system described by Foucault. This "fantasia," which seems to be a product of wild abandon, in fact emerges from a careful and detailed division of labor. Hence, "Disney" is by nature a sociosemiotic "folk" phenomenon, inasmuch as the narrator is an anonymous entity. One may wonder how such a production system holds together in practice, when relying on so many people and so wide a variety of opinions. The integrating force is the planning sessions and strategy meetings in which all matters are dealt with together. Yet the codes and channels of the senders of the messages are not engaged by the film itself.

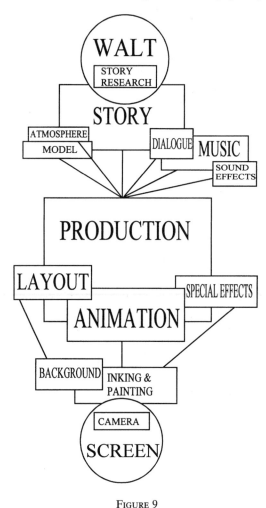

FIGURE 9

We therefore find the Disneyan subject situated firmly in the Heideggerian *das Man,* since all work in the studio aims at the supposed addressee of the message. What is this Disney "public"? On the ideological level, it is the universal infantile ego that inhabits everyone, the "archaic man" discussed by Lévi-Strauss, who, regardless of his society, is still on the polymorphic level of free imagination preceding its articulation. But in reality, this public is none other than the citizens of small-town America.

In studio strategy meetings, this hypothetical addressee becomes well-defined: He is honest, impatient, and has no time to ask too many questions. Disney liked an audience which owned up to the fact that it did not catch the point of a movie. Such an addressee is immediate, since the spectator has no chance to think about what happens on screen or about how the characters develop. When the curtain rises on the big screen, there is no longer time for reflection. Thus, a moving picture cannot be based semiotically on anything other than pre-existing codes that are completely identical with the message, for a picture is much more difficult to receive unthinkingly than is music.

I quote next from a studio strategy session about the production of Mussorgsky's *A Night on Bald Mountain.* Mussorgsky's music had already been recorded and several animation drafts drawn for it. At the meeting these drafts were projected as still-pictures along with the music, to assure that they coincided with key points in the music:

B: I think it seems all right.

J: It seems a little incongruous.

Walt: We have to have a little more chance for the audience to understand what this whole thing is about on Bald Mountain. The result now is confusing.

D: If you stuck to a simple theme like having the graveyard spirits come out instead of going to the town, that might simplify it.

Walt: You mean you worry about the town?

D: Yes.

Walt: It sort of symbolizes something. The forces of good on one side and of evil on the other is what I'm trying to see in the thing. What other reason can there be for it?

D: Well, the devil convokes all these spirits in the air and also brings them from the ground.

Walt: Everything comes from the town, doesn't it? The same as the good comes from the town?

D: The music seems too strong for just what there is here on the town. It seems to me it would be more appropriate if you stayed on the mountain and showed wild things rushing about and stormy skies—instead of cutting into a placid town with all this racket going on.

B: You can get a lot of interest out of the town.

J: I don't think the town will be placid when the spirits come down from the mountain. Everything is active. The shutters on the windows and everything will be alive as though bewitched. Then when you come to the end of the town, here is the graveyard and you follow up with those spirits. I think that will be cleared up as soon as it is properly represented.

D: I was just thinking of a simplification of it.

J: I think it's well.

Walt: I think you should do more with the spirits retreating, too. The devil pulling all the stuff out of the mountain doesn't seem to mean anything to me, now. (At this point in the conference a silence ensues. There is an ominous feeling that all is not quite as it should be. There seem to be too many divergent viewpoints as to the treatment of the subject. The tension increases. Suddenly . . .)

Walt: If anybody has any thoughts, speak out. If you think it stinks, say so. If you think it needs something, well what about it?

Studio disputes such as these reveal much about Disney's attitude toward music and image. If some circles at the time of the creation of *Fantasia* considered it Disney's admittance to certain intellectual groups (Finch 1973: 228), such documents as the one quoted above suggest that such was not the case. Still, it is paradoxical that the music's closest union with picture was not designed to increase the fantasy of the addressees but rather to limit it. If music is, as Lévi-Strauss says, "language without sense," then the picture inserts itself into the place of the empty signified.

On the other hand, Disney wanted to create the impression that his visual fantasies emerged organically and inevitably from the music, as if they were the music's natural, self-legitimized meanings. Hence, in relation to music, the pictures were not its interpretant; rather, the connection between the two is a much closer one—that of an indexical relation. The conversation below, about the animation of Stravinsky's *The Rite of Spring,* shows this relation quite clearly. The studio decided that, although Stravinsky perhaps wanted to describe a pagan ritual, in music there were points in which man loses control over primal natural forces. Therefore, the studio substituted another plot, and instead used Stravinsky's music to depict the evolution of the earth and the origin of life:

H: The music here is a little too long.

Walt: . . . I would like to see a sensational blow-up there.

A: A terrific explosion . . .

Walt (comparing continuity to what he hears): This fits right to a tee, doesn't it? I'm afraid Stravinsky wouldn't recognize himself. (Loud crash in music) Ooh, gee-hooray! That's swell! We can bring this out as strong as we like.

A: It really gets beautiful and everything sort of calms down, and you get the feeling of shooting stars.

H: You can pull back on the earth all the time and watch all the things flowing over and causing steam.

A: Sparks and lava slide into the sea . . . this is really pictorial . . . this is the rough stuff . . . triumphant . . . the lava is all freezing now. . . .

H: Part of this has been cut . . . this is the silence before the storm. . . .

Walt: That's wind! . . .

J: A wave effect. . . .

D: Wind and storm. . . .

H: Water spouts soaring. . . .

J: Enormous breakers. . . .
A: . . . that sock the cliffs! . . .
B: Big things swooping down. . . .

The Disney commentator Robert Feild, states: "Stravinsky may not have seen it that way, but he cannot escape responsibility for having caused other people to have such visions. It all came out of his music in the first place. Even the idea of the bully must have originated in some peculiarly aggressive note, a harsh phrase perhaps from some particular instrument, which aroused a latent anti-fascism in some hitherto peaceful soul. The subsequent downfall of Tyrannosaurus is an inevitable sequel under such conditions—both musically and in real life" (1947: 167). Feild's comments also point to another problem, which is most obvious in film segments such as *The Sorcerer's Apprentice* and Beethoven's Sixth Symphony. Namely, after Disney's story-research team had created a new character, how did it become a visual, on-screen person? How does the signified find its proper signifier? How does a protagonist in a narrated story become a *sign* to be perceived? *Essere est percipi*—the being is to become observed. This holds true in Disney's world as well as in "real" life. The protagonist must be visually complete since the spectator has no time to cogitate about the development of characters. As early as its first occurrence, the identity of each personage must be clear; each must have a unique character. Such clarity is attained in each final drawing, as the result of innumerable preceding drafts.

Semiotically speaking, what is involved is the process of actorialization. In a music-movie, the relationship between visual and musical "actors" is even more complicated, because the picture must correspond to the image already in the listener's mind, which has arisen in response to the music. This situation is obtained when the listener is musically competent and knows his Beethoven and Stravinsky. Yet for those lacking this competency, music provides its own image when the spectator sees its animated counterpart. In Wagner, it is largely the task of musical leitmotifs to "actorialize" a mythical story. In Disney, the myth as a visual drawing activates the music. In this way he forces the spectator to actorialize the theme of the Pastoral Symphony as centaurs, Zeus, Vulcan, Bacchus, Mickey Mouse as the sorcerer's apprentice, and certain aggressive motives of *The Rite of Spring* as *Tyrannosaurus rex.*

Accordingly, Disney's visual actor may represent modes of narration different from those of the music. According to Northrop Frye, a storytelling mode is *mythical* if the actors in the narrative are above us and perform supernatural acts; the mode is *realistic* if the actors are on our level as to their emotions and actions; it is *grotesque* if the actors are beneath us in social or moral status. In Disney's animation of the Pastoral Symphony, one encounters visual figures corresponding to all of these three kinds of actor: Zeus and Vulcanus (mythical level); girl and boy centaurs (realistic level); Pegasus, small donkeys, Bacchus and amore: (comico-grotesque level). In *The Sorcerer's Apprentice* segment of the film, only the upper (The Sorcerer) and the lower (Mickey) are present.

A typical feature of Disney is that in each movie there is one element which actorializes the narration, both music and picture, in relation to the real world of the spectator. This actorialization takes place by some marginal element that is intended to move the spectator and to make him identify with it. For example, even in *The Rite of Spring,* a lizard mother tenderly returns the lost youngster to her nest; the goldfish in the sub-aquarian world of the *Nutcracker* wrinkles its eyebrow in a seducing way.

According to Sartre, "the imagining consciousness is always the consciousness of something." Similarly, Disney's unique ability is that of realizing his fantasy precisely via certain concrete figures, as a kind of *bricolage* or concrete logic. It is thus appropriate to scrutinize some problems in the light of particular scenes. Below we shall consider reasons why Disney's *Fantasia* was never received without reservation. Disney himself even said that he would not remake the film, or even make it in the first place, should he be faced with such a choice again. Finch states, "Fantasia is a film which has its great advantages and great weaknesses" (1973: 243). Frank Lloyd Wright, the famous architect, considered the idea of illustrated music to be senseless. Although some films are bound with the special time of their production, *Fantasia*'s enormous success in video markets suggests that it has a universality that transcends the time of its creation. Indeed, watching *Fantasia* one also notices how little the medium has progressed in fifty years. The following analyses might reveal some critical points in this film.

THE NUTCRACKER SUITE

From Tchaikovsky's ballet, Disney chose to illustrate the "Dance of the Sugar-Plum Fairy," the "Chinese Dance," the "Dance of the Flutes," the "Arabian Dance," and the "Waltz of the Flowers." This selection of music already displays a fundamental problem, which is connected with the combination of music and picture: What was secondary musically becomes primary in the film; and, contrarily, what was musically primary becomes secondary in the movie.

The setting of the "Arabian Dance" in an underwater world can be visually congenial, and it also corresponds in a way to the general color and movement of the music. But in this setting, the spectator's attention is shifted to secondary musical ornaments, which are made visually central by the sudden darting movements of the goldfish. Similarly, in the "Dance of the Sugar-Plum Fairy," a descending melodic pattern of a subordinate theme is made to seem like a human sigh, a semblance which was further emphasized by Stokowski's conducting it in such a way as to prolong this pattern. Such changes are naturally part of Disney's "actorialization process," whereby music is made an object of identity for an average listener. Nevertheless, Tchaikovsky's music is for the ballet, and should therefore express the movements of the human body. It is precisely such "kinetic" energy which distinguishes Tchaikovsky from other, more mediocre composers of ballets. In his ballets, bodily motion is inscribed deep *within* the music itself. This is finely illustrated by the following example from *Swan Lake,* which contains a combination of movements typical of the human body:

MUSIC EXAMPLE 2

One could speak here (adapting Barthes) of a *phenodance* which the abstract figures of picture movie can express when roughly following the rhythm and sectioning of the music. Yet behind it looms the *genodance,* in which the original body, the physical movement, appears. Most obviously such disappearance of the body in Disney can be seen in the "Dance of the Russian Cossacks." There all the physical motions realized in the film are not meaningful from the viewpoint of the original, bodily nature of the ballet music.

THE SORCERER'S APPRENTICE

Paul Dukas's tone poem *L'apprenti du sorcier* (1898) has been considered a model example of narrative music. It appears as such, albeit problematized, in Carolyn Abbate's essay "What the Sorcerer Said," a chapter in her *Unsung Voices* (1991). Comparison of the Disney version to Goethe's ballad, *Der Zauberlehrling,* itself based on stories that one can trace back to antiquity, shows that the former differs from the ballad mainly by the fact that, besides (or rather, inside) the story of Mickey Mouse and the Sorcerer, another story has been embedded. In this grafted-on tale, Mickey is not satisfied with merely mastering the broom and carrying water for his boss, the Sorcerer. Instead Mickey imagines himself the omnipotent ruler of the world, who with his magic wand can even displace the stars from their course. This supplementary tale was Disney's response to the problem of musical *repetition.* Similar to Ravel's *Bolero,* Dukas's work consists of the gradual growth of a rhythmic ostinato. Visually such repetition would soon grow boring. Therefore, the music had to be illustrated with another, embedded story that draws attention away from the rhythmic monotony. In Goethe's version, the first stanza of the ballad is followed by the apprentice's magical incantation, which Mickey repeats in the film: "Walle! Walle

Manche Strecke, Das zum Zwecke Wasser fliesse, Und mit reichem, vollem Schwalle Zu dem Bade sich ergiesse!" [Hear ye! Hear ye! Hence! your spritely Office rightly, Featly showing! Toil, until with water clear, ye Fill the bath to overflowing!] In the music, the chant has its own leitmotif. In the Disney film, the repetition of the incantation underlies the shift of magical power from the sender (Sorcerer) to the subject-hero (Mickey); this power is symbolized by the master's hat, the very emblem of Magic. Yet Mickey is soon revealed to be a false hero, for, in the film, as in Goethe's ballad, the master returns to claim his rightful place. Upon the sorcerer's return, the situation is calmed by a new chant, with which the poem ends. Only the quotation marks in this final chant indicate that the words come from the mouth of the sorcerer: "In die Ecke, Besen! Besen! Seid's gewesen! Denn als Geifter Ruft euch nur zu seinem Zwecke, Erst hervor der alte Meister!" ["Broom, away thee! To thy nook there! Lie, thou spook, there! Only answer, When for mine own ends I want thee, I, the master necromancer!"]

Abbate demonstrates that the problem of Dukas's piece lies precisely with this final comment, which intrudes upon the story as if in the voice of an unseen narrator, whose presence is hinted at only by quotation marks. After the sorcerer's words, this narrator might have added, "he said." Therefore, in the story there is a third, invisible person, who follows the tale but enters only at the end. The slow coda of Dukas's music, in which the main motifs return transformed, corresponds in Abbate's mind to the unspoken words—the unheard "he said"— of the unseen narrator. Disney may have provided an even better interpretation, by letting the musical coda describe the repentant apprentice, and the last chords of the final bar accompany the indignation of the sorcerer, who casts out Mickey. The Disney version has no third narrating voice; nevertheless, this lack has been ameliorated by the fact that the whole story shifts to the viewpoint of Mickey.

THE RITE OF SPRING

The animated version of Stravinsky's ballet brings new issues to light, perhaps the most important of which is the condensation and acceleration of time. In all Disney's films, one expects the pacing of events to be fast, otherwise the spectator gets bored. In Disney's movies, we find the clearest example of the myth of American speed and efficiency—a myth, because anyone who has visited America knows that nowhere else are everyday matters carried out at such a tranquil pace as on that continent, whose very expanse induces the feeling that one has endless time and space at one's disposal. In keeping with this sense of America "on the go," the prehistory of the earth has been shortened to a few minutes in Disney's version of Stravinsky's *Rite*. To analyze this segment of *Fantasia,* it will first prove helpful to consider a semiotic method apt for the task.

The German scholar Walter Koch, creator of so-called "evolutionary cultural semiotics," developed a theory of "memes." These are the smallest, self-generating and recurrent units of *memory.* Memes are as important to cultural evolution as genes are for the evolution of biological life. He presents the development of life on earth in the light of this gene/meme theory, in diagrams such as the following:

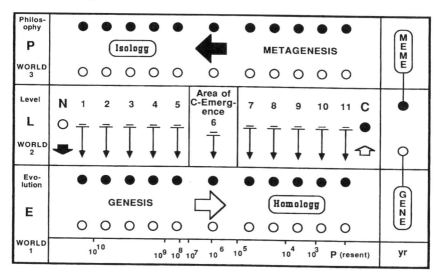

DIAGRAM 11. Evolution in the Light of Genes and Memes, according to W. A. Koch
(1986: 12 and 26)

In a somewhat humorous way, one could take Disney's story of the earth's evolution as an illustration of Koch's theory. The only difference is that, in *Fantasia*, even the dinosaurs and tyrannosaurs seem to have memes suited especially for their functioning.

In any case, the problem of condensation and acceleration of time has deep connections with our present-day, visually oriented civilization. Some time ago, the French academician René Huyghe noted, in his *Dialogue avec le visible*, how in the age of the picture an enormous acceleration of tempo takes place in communication. A climax to this accelerando has already been reached in contemporary video art, in which the plot is furthered only by quick flashes. Even the cutting of music in Disney's *Fantasia* seems to be completely justified, since video is a product which can always be repeated. The addressee can always sink into the world of Disney's *Fantasia* by turning on the video again and again. In contrast, the most powerful effects of Stravinsky's and Beethoven's music have relied on the idea that such music is heard only once, and then a day, week, or even a year passes before one hears it again. For such effects to take place, the music must have a certain redundancy, with climaxes only after long, steadily intensifying developments. In our time, the impressions of endlessness, unlimitedness, and infinity no longer require a six-hour hearing of *Parsifal*. It suffices merely to repeat the stimulus as many times as one likes by the push of a button.

THE PASTORAL SYMPHONY

Disney's version of Beethoven's Sixth Symphony exhibits problems in the compatibility of music and picture. The most essential connections between the two are the diegetic sounds, that is, sounds which belong to the story world of the visual narration. For instance, the horn signals of the centaur are arranged so as to parallel the *Hirtengesang* in Beethoven's music; Zeus's lightning bolts correlate with the timpani strokes; the rustic dance corresponds with the "folk" music in the third movement; and so on. In these passages, the unity of music and picture is completely motivated. Yet the greater part of the music is non-diegetic: It is strictly background music that does not take place in or emanate from the story world, but only creates the basic atmosphere of the story.

Although the animated imagery in Disney's version of the Pastoral Symphony was from the start oriented to a completely different kind of music than Beethoven's, it goes even further in this work, pushing the Disneyan mythology to its highest limit. Disney's version involves the reconstruction of ancient Arcadia, only with colors that evoke art deco and symbolist painting. The island, with its mountains rising from the water, is related to Böcklin's "Isle of the Dead," while the palette of colors alludes to Gauguin's Tahitian exoticism.

Now mythicism in Disney has a quite particular function, which might best be seen by a comparison to Wagner, who also creates a complete mythical universe. In the *Ring of the Nibelungen* and elsewhere, the task of the myth is to detach the narration from realism and elevate it to a universal level; Wagner thereby seeks to negate structures typical of European society. In Disney, however, the mythology functions to shift the spectator to the exotic "heterotopos" of an entirely new world, in which there prevails complete harmony, sustained by the Disneyan demiurge. From the American society of emptiness, one is shifted to a universe that is not a positive negation of Nothingness, but rather its suppression and surrogate. Disney's world literally fulfills the Emersonian doctrine of the *oversoul*, which supports all being. In Disney, the oversoul, itself the real agent of history, is none other than the "narrator." To Emerson's mind, only the one who understands this universal mind can comprehend all that exists or all that can be done, because the oversoul is the only true agent. It is precisely the universal character that gives value to individual persons and affairs. All the explorations of antiquity, of pyramids, ancient cities, and lost treasures manifest this desire to omit the wild and inconceivable There and Then, and replace it with the category of Here and Now.

Disney aims precisely for such a replacement, for his goal is to humanize antiquity. The flirting of the centaur girls in the slow movement of the Beethoven symphony is perhaps the best example of Disney's endeavors. In Emerson, the crucial point is that a connection exists between life's hours and the centuries of history (p. 124). Everything tends to brevity, and there is no age that does not correspond somehow to the course of our own lives (p. 126). Here Disney fulfills the Emersonian philosophy, in that one of the his basic devices is precisely the condensation and hastening of time that is emblematic of America, the culture of abridgment. The idea of "illustrated classics"—major literary works, shortened and in cartoon form for the public-on-the-go—would be impossible in any other context. From a musical point of view, the abridgment reaches its most catastrophic level in Disney's version of the Pastoral Symphony. Only the programmatic peasants' fest and the thunderstorm have escaped cutting, but among other things, the development section of the first movement has been entirely deleted. The pastoral euphoria of the slow movement has been shortened by more than half the original length—it ends as soon as it makes the centaurs yawn from boredom. The finale suffers the worst. Its huge culmination in dominant ninth chords is completely banalized because in the film version, they occur far too soon to serve as a climactic point in any strictly musical sense.

The most striking feature of the first movement of the symphony is its high redundancy. I know of no other classical work in which the same one-bar motif is repeated ten times at first and then 36 times, unchanged except for small differences in harmonic content. Disney illustrates these passages by a continuous galloping of the pegasus. The diatonic euphoria after the chromatic storm scene, as the "thanksgiving song" of the rescued, doesn't find its proper visual counterpart in Zeus's merely turning and glancing to his side, as clever and funny as this idea is in itself. When in music an entirely new actor appears, this should also happen in the visual narration.

Fundamentally, all of Disney's motion pictures deal with communication between men and animals, and all intermediate forms between the two. Yet such communication is not always as direct as when Mickey greets Stokowski in *Fantasia*. Most often it appears in the form of totemism. This anthropological phenomenon means that certain species of animals become totems, or benevolent and protecting creatures, to individuals and to groups. An Indian clan can call itself "beavers" because in its mythology the role of the hero is assigned to that species of animal. Correspondingly, the competing clan can consist of "bears." In its extreme form the totem becomes more important than the person, group, or thing which it symbolizes. Durkheim mentions as an example a fight for the flag in a war: On the battlefield this symbolic artifact can become much more important than what it represents (quoted in Lévi-Strauss 1969, p. 22).

Disney's universe relies largely on totemic relationships. If American civilization is based upon the phenomenon of nothingness, then totems must compensate for the lack of social structures, such as those prevailing in Europe. First, the mere viewing of a Disney movie constitutes a totemic event. The psychology of Mickey Mouse and other Disneyan protagonists is actorial in the sense that the average American can identify with them. In this case, the totemic relation obtains between the enunciate and enunciation, or addresser and addressee. Moreover, the movie itself often represents totemism on the level of the enunciate. In the Pastoral Symphony, a pegasus couple and their tiny ponies—emblematic of a perfect marriage—serve as the totem of the girl and boy centaurs and their group. In the *Nutcracker* segment of the film, both the Chinese-Russian mushrooms and the goldfishes are transformed into totemic animals, as are the ostrich and hippopotamus clans that compete against each other in the "Dance of the Hours," and the fighting dinosaurs in *The Rite of Spring*.

Lévi-Strauss supposed that both totemism and the primitive or savage mind were universal phenomena. Disney's movies show that he was right. If Disney represents the essence and philosophy of Americanness, and manages to "universalize" this basic experiential view of man's existential situation, then it is no wonder that his movies succeed even beyond the United States. The right way to approach Disney is not to disapprove of his films from the standpoint of certain moral codes, but to explain his movies in their philosophical, anthropological, and semiotical sense.

REFERENCES

Abbate, Carolyn. 1991. *Unsung Voices: Opera and Musical Narrative in the Nineteenth Century*. Princeton: Princeton University Press.
Baudrillard, Jean. 1986. *Amérique*. Paris: Éditions Grasset et Fasquelle.
Dorfman, Ariel and Armand Mattelart. 1980. *Kuinka Aku Ankkaa luetaan*. Helsinki: Love-kirjat.
Eco, Umberto. 1984. *Semiologia quotidiana*. Milan: Bompiani.
Emerson, Ralph Waldo. 1950. *The Complete Essays and Other Writings*. New York: Modern Library.
Feild, Robert D. 1947. *The Art of Walt Disney*. London and Glasgow: Collins.
Finch, Christopher. 1973. *The Art of Walt Disney: From Mickey Mouse to the Magic Kingdoms*. New York: Harry N. Abrams.
Foucault, Michel. 1970. *The Order of Things. An Arcaheology of Human Sciences*. London: Tavistock.
Frye, Northrop. 1957. *Anatomy of Criticism. Four Essays*. Princeton: Princeton University Press.
von Goethe, Johann Wolfgang. 1953. *The Permanent Goethe*, ed. Thomas Mann. English trans. Gustav Arlt. New York: Dial Press.
———. 1956. *Valituteokset* II. Finnish trans. by Otto Manninen. Helsinki: Otava.
Huyghe, Réné. [1959]. *Dialogue avec le visible*. London: Thames and Hudson.
Koch, Walter A. 1986. *Genes vs. Memes: Modes of Integration for Natural and Cultural Evolution in a Holist Model*. Bochum: Studienverlag Brockmeyer.
Lévi-Strauss, Claude. 1949. *Les structures élémentairs de la parenté*. Paris: Plon.
———. 1969. *Totemism*. Trans. Rodney Needham. Aylesbury: Beacon Press.
Sartre, Jean-Paul. [1943] 1993. *L'être et le néant: Essai d'ontologie phénoménologique*. Paris: Éditions Gallimard.
Schickel, Richard. 1968. *Walt Disney*. London: Weidenfeld and Nicolson.
———. 1969. *The Disney Version: The Life, Times, Art and Commerce of Walt Disney*. New York: Simon and Schuster.
Uspenski, Boris. 1991. *Komposition poetiikka: Taideteoksen sommittelun periaatteet*. Finnish trans. Marja-Leena Vainionpää-Palmgren. RT-Paino: Orient Express.

13

" . . . and you find the right one"
A NARRATOLOGICAL ANALYSIS OF AN ADVERTISING FILM

What kind of communication does advertising represent? According to Roman Jakobson's classical scheme, advertising is a communication that emphasizes the addressee; that is to say, it operates primarily by the so-called conative function. The term "conative" denotes the desire to change or control the conduct of the addressee. (A politician's speech at a civic gathering is perhaps the model example of someone exercising the conative function.) In Jakobson's view, every communication is intentional, and can stress any one of the six members of the communicative chain. Yet emphasis on one of the functions does not mean that the others cease to operate. Rather, they remain in the background, as subtle analysis shows to be the case with modalities. For example, 'will'—in this case, the "'will' to influence the addressee"—can be foregrounded without its entirely negating other modalities such as 'know', 'can', 'must', 'believe'. The present theory of advertising, however, assumes the dominance of one function—that of forcing products upon a customer. Though more subtle forms of influencing people have been developed, the basic truth about the discourse of advertising remains its conativity, in the same way as the only "truth criterion" of a politician's discourse is whether the citizen votes for him. In advertising, the only truth criterion is whether a customer buys the product being marketed.

One may also speak of "emotions" in advertising as an exchange in which the emotive function moves from the sender, where it originally belonged, to the receiver. The feelings of the advertiser (addresser) are not crucial to the advertising exchange, but rather the kinds of emotions stimulated in the addressee. These last should of course be positive toward the marketed object, and unsympathetic to all competing products. The key to the emotional world comes from the advertiser's knowledge of the value models of individuals and of communities, whether those models are articulated in the Greimasian way by categories of life/death, nature/culture, or by some other criteria. In other words, the discourse of advertising must penetrate into the *monde naturel,* the world of natural, mostly unconscious semiosis. What is more, advertising must mask its own identity as a suasive discourse, and instead present itself as iconically similar as possible to the "natural world" in which the objects of advertising—the consumers—live. Iconicity is therefore the basic sign category of advertising—not just any iconicity, however, but a magical, mythologized iconicity. Advertising strives to blend with the universe of human actions and thoughts, so that the indexical shift to the universe of advertising takes place unnoticed, as it were, by the addressees in the "real," in this case economic, world.

Despite such masking attempts by advertisers, the customers' guerrilla war of semiological retaliation has already begun. Customers are more capable than ever before of rejecting the iconic-indexical illusion offered by advertising, and this capability results from their being conscious of its nature as a discourse. The medium has become the message, in the sense that consumers no longer pay attention to the "what" aspect of advertising, but rather to its mechanics or "how." Before people even start to think about the content of an advertisement, they make a quick taxonomic operation by which they classify the message as a discourse of advertising.

As a semiotician, I take no position on the question as to whether we should use our knowledge to help advertisers out of their dilemma or let them negotiate their own escape. Personally, advertising irritates me, and particularly the use of classical music therein. On the other hand, as a scientist, I am too prudent to take a moralizing position. First, I am not an economist, and thus cannot speak with authority about the consequences that would follow should advertising suddenly cease. Second, a case can be made in favor of even the most annoying instances of advertising. For example, one might reason that people in whose lives art normally plays no part may come into at least some contact with it by means of advertising. (This argument has been made on behalf of the movie *Amadeus,* which is nothing less than the marketing of Mozart to the masses.) Instead of pursuing such axiological reflections, however, here I shall introduce some tools, which advertisers may use to open up new dimensions of their craft. I am not an advertising specialist, but in what follows I shall try to describe what I would do as a semiotician *if* I were such a specialist, beginning with the question of what theoretical position from which to depart.

Advertising operates with signs intended to evoke certain kinds of emotion. There are two semiotic theories for the analysis of such operations. If one wants to study mainly the sign-complex of the advertisement itself, then the *realist* sign theory of Charles S. Peirce is probably best suited for the task. However, if one's interest lies in the structures of signification behind these signs, then the semiotics of the Paris school might prove more useful, since it is more *nominalist* in nature. In my view, the first-mentioned approach risks leading to trivialities, to the behaviorization of meaning, and to emotional phenomena. Unfortunately, and especially when popularized by mass media, semiotics many times adopts such a form. For instance, in a Danish instructional film on semiotics, one sees a series of images in which actors use facial expressions to project various feelings, while the narrator's voice provides those expressions with verbal interpretants; thus the facial mimicry serves as a kind of sign. Yet detached from its context, such mimicry represents a most trivial kind of psycho-semiotics. Many people think, however, that all semiotics deals with such banalities, when in fact true semiotics attempts to show the complexities and plurivalencies behind such trivial signs, as well as to interpret as signs certain objects which a layman would never construe as such. For instance, nationalism is usually approached only via its most conspicuous, almost trivial, *marked* signs (anthems, flags), without consideration of its ordinary, *unmarked* signs.

These observations hold true extraordinarily well for the semiotics of advertising. While the naive addressee may experience an ad as a "true story," the semiotician is instead fascinated by the arbitrary and artificial nature of its signs. A central task of semiotics, ever since the Russian formalists such as Boris Eichenbaum ("How Was Gogol's Mantle Made?") and Mayakovsky ("How to Make Verse"), has been to destructure the semiotic object in order to look at the complexities of its functioning. In turn, French scholars, such as Roland Barthes, have concerned themselves with how advertising becomes a mythical discourse whose content is a certain ideology. One task of the study of advertising has been to reveal hidden ideologies and to show how ads act as social forces (Umberto Eco). In such a case, semiotic analysis performs an emancipative function, which few find objectionable. On the other hand, such extra-semiotical interests can restrict one's ability to extend the semiotic analysis to its logical conclusions. Whereas it is sufficient for a mythico-semiotic analysis to show a mere opposition or to determine the functioning of a "semiotic square" in the object, a true semiotician wants to penetrate deeper into the object's structure. This is made possible by the other pole of semiotics, which is an extremely rigorous and formalized methodology.

It seems to me, however, that between the extremely scientific and the populist approaches there remains an area in which a semiotician can operate when faced with a task such as ours. The semiotician simply uses sound reason and chooses those tools appropriate for analyzing the particular situation. This is how I shall proceed below, in my Greimasian approach to the analysis of advertising.

THE ADVERTISING CAMPAIGN FOR THE FAZER CHOCOLATE TUBE

As the object of my study I have chosen the Fazer Candy Company's advertising campaign for four new chocolate tubes, which were introduced in the autumn of 1989. More particularly, I shall concentrate on one 45-second television ad from that campaign. It would be quite sufficient for a semiotician to study only the television commercial, but it also proves interesting to relate the television ad to the goals of the designers of the ad campaign. Comparison of the campaign's "goal text" to the "text" of the television ad shows that the final product, the ad itself, is considerably more complex semiotically than the advertisers' specified goals would seem to require. Taking into account the global socio-semiotic situation of advertising, as outlined above, and that of Fazer's campaign to market chocolate, one can determine how the goals of the latter are realized in the television ad. Of course, all eight goals of the campaign are not stated directly in the advertisement; to do so would lessen the impact of the ad by displaying its "constructedness" and suasive intent. Therefore, only in the roughest sense can the goals be considered a "generative program" or even the basic isotopies of the advertisement in question. The stated goals of the advertising campaign, as such, are a kind of map for semiotic action of the type represented by Greimas's mythical actant model. As is known, this model consists of the paired oppositions of six roles: sender/receiver (or addresser/addressee), subject/object, helper/opponent. We shall be interested in how the campaign puts these roles to use for its own purposes.

The chapter called "Starting-Point" of the ad campaign says: "The market for chocolate bars is at the moment dominated by Marabou, which rules over two-thirds of the entire market. Products closest to the chocolate tubes are, among others, the Toblerone [chocolate] triangles." The next chapter, entitled "Goals," starts with the programmatic statement, "To elevate Fazer to the level of an outstanding producer in Finland also in the category of chocolate tubes. This means that we have to take over the markets from Marabou." In our model, the "starting-point" statement defines the actantial "opponents"—Marabou and Toblerone—and notes that the first of these possesses the "value object" of all subjects acting in the field (i.e., the markets). In semiotic terms, the point of departure for every action consists of two basic situations. First, a subject possesses, or is conjuncted with, the value object. This situation is represented with the following logical symbols: $S \wedge O$. If in our case the subject (Fazer) already had the object ("the markets of the chocolate tubes"), then the situation would represent the basic modality of 'being' and no action would be needed. Unfortunately, the situation is such that the subject's (Fazer's) opponent (Marabou) owns the markets ($S2 \wedge O$), which results in the situation $S1 \vee O$; that is to say, subject $S1$ is disjuncted from the value object O. Such are the basic operations of every action and every story: the elimination of disjunction and the attainment of conjunction. Hence, the starting-point for a "narrative program" is action, or the basic modality of 'doing'.

In addition to the basic modalities of 'being' and 'doing', there are five additional modalities, which more closely determine and characterize the quality of being and action. In Greimas's theory these modalities are 'will', 'can', 'know', 'must', and 'believe'. Thus, the initial moment of the advertising narration above can be expressed by the following scheme:

$$E(dys)(S1 \vee O) \ \& \ (S2 \wedge O); F(v)(S1/(S2 \vee O) \ \& \ (S1 \wedge O)$$

The scheme may be read as follows: The subject S1 (Fazer) of being E (*être*) is in a dysphoric state, a state of general unwellness. Dysphoria refers to a central emotive category—the "thymic"—in Greimas's theory; the opposing state would be dysphoria. S1 is dysphoric because it is disjuncted from the value object O ("the markets of the chocolate tubes"), and because the subject S1 wants (v = *vouloir*) to do (F = *faire*) something that makes S2 lose or become disjuncted (∨) from the value object O, and causes S1 to become conjuncted (∧) to it.

The reader may ask, Of what use is such a complex scheme? Are all these things not immediately clear when Fazer states that it wants to expand its own markets to the detriment of Marabou's? The semiotician would reply, No. For in order to be able to study carefully and objectively all connections of this *seemingly* simple course of action, events must be conveyed in a "neutral" metalanguage that is detached from everyday experience. This metalanguage shifts the scholar from the discourse of advertising to the impartial ground of semiotic analysis, to an entirely different conceptual network, in which the notions involved take on new connections. These new connections, expressed in theoretical metalanguage, reveal aspects about the object of analysis (here, Fazer's ad campaign) that a more naive or simplistic approach would not show.

To continue the semiotic interpretation of our goal program:

"Fazer has produced traditional chocolate candies, but so far no chocolate candy tubes. As a package such tubes have to some extent a more European image, which refers to the international 'world at large'. Fazer's chocolate tubes will be launched simultaneously in a series of four different tubes: Blue, Geisha, Dark Brown, and Crunchy. . . . The Dark Brown and Crunchy are new flavors; the Blue and the Geisha are already familiar to customers. . . . The Blue and the Geisha have their own individual concepts and product images."

In this programmatic statement, the auxiliary object, or tool, is determined by which the aforementioned conjunction can be realized. Oddly enough, Greimas's mythical actant model does not account for such auxiliary objects, though on the surface level, such an adjunct object, in many stories, can be as or more important than the object proper. In this case, the semiotic object we are analyzing is an auxiliary one—Fazer's chocolate tubes—rather than the principal object of the enterprise, which is the "markets." We indicate these by the symbol "O," and reserve the small letter "o" as the logical symbol for an auxiliary object. Let us take another case in point. In Wagner's *Ring of the Nibelungen*, the Object in the proper sense is "power," the domination of the world aspired to by both Wotan and the Gibichungs. The ring is a magical object by which that power can be achieved. Thus, the quest in Wagner's tetralogy is for the ring and not so much for the power, which, however, is the ultimate goal of the actants. In the same way, Fazer and Marabou do not fight for the chocolate tubes—to which both of these "subjects" are probably indifferent—but for control of markets and profits.

As noted earlier, however, the real goal of the chocolate companies, and of their advertising, must not be revealed to the receiver. Rather, it must be masked as an entirely different narrative program which only the designers of the ad, semioticians, and some social scientists know represents the category of 'seeming'/ 'not being': something that looks like something it is not, that is to say, a "lie." From the standpoint of the active subject S1 (Fazer), the situation involves the veridictory (or truth) category of 'not-seeming'/'being', which is the target in the proper sense. The true designs of this agenda must not be seen; it is the category of the "secret." Depending on whether we look at the matter from the viewpoint of the mythical actant model or of the addressee, we obtain various truth values within the Greimasian veridictory square. Perhaps the category 'not-seeming'/ 'not-being', or untruth, would equal the final result of our analysis, in which both the goals ('being') and the tools (the television ad, or 'seeming') prove to be completely artificial, arbitrary products, which we could just as well do without. In other words, on the level of both 'seeming' and 'being', the analysis "negates" its object. Semiotic analysis shows that the modality of 'believing', which is based on ignorance or the negation of the modality of 'know', becomes impossible. This is why semioticians have often been branded as anarchists or iconoclasts, in their overturning of deeply and commonly held convictions.

A closer definition of the auxiliary object (the chocolate tube) shows that it mostly operates with the modality of 'know', and particularly with the opposition new/traditional. Of the four auxiliary objects, two have been given traditional names (Blue and Geisha) and two have received entirely new ones (Dark Brown and Crunchy). As to the modality of 'know', one can say that an object contains more 'know' the more unexpected that object is; the more it produces or contains new information, the less familiar or traditional it is. Why then have these two extremes—the new and the traditional—been purposely mixed in the product at hand? The answer lies in the goals listed in point 3 of the campaign agenda: "To provide the product image of Blue and Geisha with youthful features, but in such a way that basic modern concepts would not be questioned." Hence, the subject (S1) wants to appear to the addressees (the customers) on one hand as guardian of the old, and on the other "to show that Fazer's chocolate tubes are more modern and at least as international as the competing products." "Modernity," "internationality," "Europeanness" are all positive values of the modality of "know" in its various denominations.

In fact, the complex isotopy 'know'/'not-know', or old/new, also appears in the only verbal text of the television ad, as the motto of the company as a whole: "Fazer, and you find the right one." The correct interpretation of this motto presupposes knowledge of another subtext, and therefore a certain advertising competency. This subtext is Fazer's earlier motto: "Say Fazer—when you want something good." In the later ad, with which we are concerned, this previous phrase has been condensed into one, mythic and magical word—"Fazer"—which is followed by the choice of that which is "right" (the "good"). Thus, an indexical connection obtains between the two slogans: In the former, the phrase is directly united with the modality of 'will' ("when you want something good"); in the latter, with the modality of 'know', upon which basis the right chocolate is chosen from among all the alternatives. As we shall see from the analysis of the advertising film, even this expression contains a complex isotopy: The "right one" alludes to both the right girl or boy—and him/her at a more general level—as well as to the right chocolate tube. This constitutes a genuine Bourdieu-like distinction among the masses, whether human beings or chocolates.

The goal of the advertising program is to increase "interest" in Fazer's chocolate tubes. Thus, a cognitive category comes into play, which is furnished with the euphoric semes of the "modern" (temporal articulation) and the "international" (spatial articulation). The most important cognitive task, however, is to create a particular "topos of chocolate tubes," a fictive world or place that is "wonderful," "surrealistic," "dreamlike." Here one is moving within the modality of 'believe'—gliding away from mere 'know' and into a completely fictional world whose existence is based only on belief.

The written advertising agenda proceeds to remark on the channels of communication; these remarks are quite brief, and thus give much latitude to the producers of the advertisement. There follows a lengthy discussion of the actantial role of "receiver." People in the age group 14 to 16 years old are determined to be the receiver or addressee. This age group is then expanded in both directions, to take into account consumers aged 12–13 and 17–24. In this context, the modality of 'must' emerges. Indeed, the only normative limits or obligations that the campaign imposes upon itself are derived from analysis of the addressee-actant (customers). This involves an actant who in turn has been provided with the modalities 'know', 'can', 'must', 'will', and 'believe'. The subject-actant S1 (Fazer) must necessarily know what content or import the receiver-actant allots to these modalities and how he organizes them hierarchically. This organization constitutes something like the receiver's "world view" (" ... the ideas and world closest to the target group"). To gain this knowledge, painstaking statistical research was made into the consuming behavior of the group, in order to make explicit the addressees' "opinions." This research enabled the advertisers to take the target group's way of living as a predetermined entity, and thereby to ascertain the 'must' that would guide the whole marketing project. The results of the inquiry can be grouped according to the modalities as follows:

'Will': "The youngest target group wants to live in the world of the older group, but it does not have enough resources." That is to say, the youngest group has 'will' but it is "not able" to do something. However, as regards the auxiliary object, the 'will' of the addressee-actant is guaranteed ("chocolate is bought regularly").

'Can': In general semiotic analysis this modality designates the ways of doing something, the techniques and concrete devices that enable an activity (such as "buying"). This modality influences the structure of the auxiliary object, or sales package—"too long a tube easily falls out of the pocket"—as well as the content—"it is important to get a mouthful of chocolate." Thus, the quality of the taste experience is not as important as the affirmation of the modality of 'can': The chocolate must produce a powerful feeling. On the other hand, inasmuch as the act of buying is understood as a semiotic activity, it is limited also by the negation of 'can', in relation to the amount of money available. This last has a certain upper limit, beyond which the modality becomes that of 'not-can'; this in turn prevents the main object O (the markets) from being reached by the subject S1 (Fazer). "Speed and power," or a certain 'can-do', is characteristic of the addressee-actant.

'Know': The target group is aware of its own limits to realizing its 'will' and 'can'. But it also knows that it wants alternatives. In other words, the product must provide new information, thus the modality of 'know' must be relatively high. A basic hypothesis of the project is that looking for "something new" is connected with other things commonly taken as "new" (internationalism, Europeanness, and so on).

'Must': If the addressee-actant, with all its modalities, forms the 'must' of the subject-actant to which it is subordinated, then the addressee—the group—in turn has its own norms. Some of these come from inside the group, as a kind of peer pressure: "You can eat chocolate alone, but real players enjoy it with the crowd." Other norms are imposed from outside the group: "the amount of money in your pocket," "five marks was considered the upper price limit." As a behavioral norm—and norms are part of any activity—this 'must' together with 'know' constrains the other modalities.

'Believe': What is involved here is a particular "fantasy world of chocolate." As such, it is a 'seeming'/'not-being': something that seems to be true but is not, yet whose existence the leader of the project assumes the addressee-actants to believe in. Here we have a distinction between two "topoi": chocolate fantasy/real world. The aim of the advertisement is to make the spectator believe in the existence of the fantasy—but not too much, lest such a belief inhibit the spectator's return to the real world, in which the shopping actually takes place. The advertisement thus serves as a kind of transitional passage between the sacred and the profane, between the fictive and the real.

THE REALIZATION—"A SHADOW DANCE"

Most advertisers believe that a good ad must fit with the lifestyles of the consumers. From this viewpoint, the analysis of modalities is necessary if one wants to get to the semiotic core of the problem. The question is whether the inner modalities of the advertisement somehow correspond to the modalities of the real world. Very often in ads, some protagonists, by their actions, fulfill certain modalities, and the addressee "accepts" the advertisement insofar as the modal structure is similar to his own. Nevertheless, as noted before, what is taken as the modal competency of the target group (aged 12–24) is even then a hypothetical creation of the mythical subject of the advertising (Fazer's project group). Yet the pragmatic "truth" criterion of this hypothesis is paramount in advertising: If the product sells, then the hypothesis and the modal model are correct.

Now let us consider the advertisement itself, a 45-second music video. What can one receive and cognize in such a short time? Not much, if it is a strictly verbal communication, for in such a time-span one cannot tell a long story. But with pictures and music the situation changes. The present film, lasting less than one minute, contains 26 scenes, which draw together plot, colors, movements, and music. Most of these scenes, several of which last only one or two seconds, go by too fast for conscious observation, but they nonetheless take root deep in the (passive) observer's consciousness. There follows a description of each scene of the ad.

Scene 1: In the foreground a pretty teenage girl glances to one side. Youngsters are standing in the waiting line of a movie theater. It is a dark night, with bright lights shining in the background. The girl stands on the left and is distinguished as the main figure, by her position apart from three other youths standing to the right (boy, girl, boy), and by the blue light that bathes her face.

Scene 2: A boy walks down the street toward the camera. It is night and car head-lights are shimmering, in the style of an American movie from the 1950s (see, for example, the dazzling lights of the police cars in the final scene of *The Young Rebels*). The dim lighting leaves the boy's face in darkness, and we do not know who he is—an effect that lends the image a sense of unreality. The asphalt is glittering; on the left shines an intense red light. The boy's left side, where he keeps his hand in his pocket—in which it will later be revealed that he is keeping a Fazer chocolate tube that he has just bought—is brightened with blue white, animated lines, which seem like a kind of magical emanation.

Scene 3: The girl takes off her overcoat, helped by someone. In the foreground shines a bright yellow arc of light, behind the red metro. There follows a shot of the street.

Scene 4: Shot of the boy's face, his eyes turned toward some object. The left side of the picture is bathed in blue "radiation"; the right side of his face blends to-gether with a yellowish-greenish light. The boy's head turns to follow his line of sight.

Scene 5: The girl turns away from where she was previously looking. On the left is another girl, whose attention is elsewhere; and on the right, the back of an-other boy, with light-colored hair. The girl is again the main actor, due to the focus of the lighting, but she is alone in a metropolis, amidst an anonymous, faceless mass. She does not perceive herself as distinguished from the crowd; only the camera lens highlights her individuality.

Scene 6: The girl's face is again shown from in front, glancing pensively to one side, as if absent-minded. In the background continues the bright yellow advertising light of scene 3, which resembles the glow of the "golden arches" of a McDonald's hamburger restaurant. The girl raises her head as if looking at someone. All movements in the scene are fluid and graceful.

Scene 7: Close-up of the boy's face. From his left eye emanates a pale blue "radiation"; another ray of light beams out from the space between his left eye and nose, in the direction of the object his gaze.

Scene 8: Again the girl, in the setting of scene 6. Now she turns her head to the left, as if expecting someone whom she does not know.

Scene 9: Against a shadowy and gray wooden fence, a black figure appears, completely covered with white-purple diagonal lines. In the right corner of the screen is the black shadow of a kind of scaffolding. The dark figure moves quickly to the right. The picture flashes by so quickly that one cannot know whether the scene is meant to depict the girl's thoughts or if it has some other significance.

Scene 10: The girl again, on the right side of the picture. The light spreads dramatically from below, creating a dark shadow on the left side of girl's face and dress. She seems a little amused. She moves, and again her look is directed toward something which is not shown. Finally she looks up proudly, tilting her chin and closing her eyes. She turns her head away abruptly, to the left and behind her.

Scene 11: At the same time, in the doorway the figure of the boy appears, wrapped in a radiant blue halo. The boy steps all the way in, not looking at the girl but toward the right rear. The camera zooms in on him. He is followed by a thick blue circle of radiation, and a blue light penetrates the hall from outside. At the door the boy turns directly toward the girl, whose entire body is revealed, her left side bathed in radiant light.

Scene 12: For the first time the boy's face is shown up close. He has short-cut hair, his forehead wrinkled quizzically (in the style of James Dean). His lips are pressed tightly together, and, with no apparent emotion, he looks directly at the girl. He turns his face to the right, still wearing the same, almost bored expression. On the right a round yellow lamp shimmers, as the doorway frames the blue, mystic light; the foreground remains black. The boy steps in and looks directly at the girl, and his face immediately takes on a natural color, reflecting the warm inside lighting.

Scene 13: The boy looks up suddenly, as if struck by an idea, and while his facial expression remains unchanged, the rest of his body seems to register surprise.

Scene 14: The girl and boy are shown in profile. The girl has turned completely away from the boy, obviously pretending not to know him. The boy's profile is on the right, and he approaches the girl. Though no words are spoken, the girl looks up as if "astonished," even though she has sensed the boy's approach. She raises her shoulders and chin, looks at the boy; she seems a little frightened, and steps away from the boy as if rejecting him.

Scene 15: The camera focuses on the boy's hand. Only his fingers are shown, in which he holds a light-blue, glittering "tube." The tube radiates *white* and the hand *blue* lines. The hand moves and the tube is completely revealed. Words on the edge of the object identify it as a chocolate tube. In close-up, the fingers of another hand grasp the tube and open it, and we get our first glimpse of the chocolate candy, bathed in a strong white radiant light. In the right corner of the screen appear thick yellow lights, as though in a kind of unrealistic drawing.

Scene 16: The center of the boy's face is shown from afar. His eyes are open, his look keenly directed forward, as if questioning either the girl or the spectator/addressee (causing a syncretization or conflation of the subjects of enunciation and enunciate).

Scene 17: The girl's fingers grasp the first chocolate candy. Her movement is somehow ritualistic, her fingers clearly lit with many white and blue lines.

Scene 18: Eyes closed, the girl puts the candy to her mouth. The chocolate disappears and her eyes open. She moves a little, as if taken aback by an inner experience. She looks up, still a little frightened, toward the boy—and also toward the spectator.

Scene 19: An abrupt shift, a peripeteia, to a completely different narrative topos. Against a white background appear the profiles of the boy and the girl—now with the boy at the right and the girl at the left (their positions reversed from the beginning of the film). They are holding hands and standing on what appears to be a roof terrace. The girl seems to rise into the air. On the left, the wall of a house is covered with a large Fazer advertisement. The girl and boy approach each other and jump into the air, as if freed from gravity's bonds.

Scene 20: Girl and boy arm in arm, completely surrounded by a mystic radiation, which forms an almost heart-shaped ring around them. Their faces are now clearly recognizable. The lighting becomes a deep red, which forms a contrast to the blue of the radiation. The light becomes "normal" when the couple dances around the floor. Then the light again turns red.

Scene 21: An abrupt montage: In the foreground appear what are either railroad or motorway guardrails; in the background are a sea and beach, all in blue and pink coloring. A silhouette of the girl and boy: The boy keeps the girl's hand in his as their dark profiles are seen jumping along the guardrail.

Scene 22: Girl and boy again, now dancing. On the left shines a yellow arc of light, similar to that of the beginning of the commercial. Girl and boy take a dance step.

Scene 23: Flashback to scene 21: landscape with motorway, now with the profile of city roofs behind it, all bathed in the light of a purple sunset. The girl jumps up, her hair fluttering in the air.

Scene 24: The girl and boy celebrate by dancing. Now they are surrounded by a multicolored radiation, with blue dominating.

Scene 25: Three Fazer chocolate tubes are shown horizontally so that the text of each is easily seen. In the upper corner is Fazerina, with toffee-colored candies, then the yellow Tofferina, and the mirror images of all three tubes. Blue radiation lines project toward the spectator. Handwritten text appears: "The New Fazer Chocolate Candies."

Scene 26: Girl and boy sitting arm in arm on the roof. The boy holds the girl protectively. Both of them look toward the spectator, their facial expressions now quite normal, indicating a return to the basic topos of the "real world." They turn their faces toward each other. To the left appears the word "Fazer"—the logo of the enterprise—followed by these words, written in white lines and underlined: " . . . and you find the right one!" The text starts to shimmer more strongly, as does the blue logo. The scene lasts a relatively long time, as girl and boy kiss each other.

INTERPRETATION

In closing, I shall interpret each scene, using the semiotic method whose most important elements and operations were introduced earlier, and are summarized here:

Subject, Object, and other actantial roles;
Operations of conjunction and disjunction;
Modalities, with bold-faced initials as abbreviations of the French terms: 'being' (e) and 'doing' (f); and additional modalities: 'will' (v), 'can' (p), 'know' (s), 'must' (d), and 'believe' (c);
Spatial, temporal, and actorial disengagement and engagement;
Aspectual semes: insufficient /excessive (too little/too much), inchoative, durative, terminative, imperfect/perfect;
Topos: here/elsewhere (or topos/heterotopos);
Thymic category: euphory/dysphory (wellness/unwellness).

We analyze the semiotically relevant content of each scene starting from its basic mood or feeling—the "emotional isotopy" that it tries to express—since this aspect is probably the most essential in the advertisement. The chain of emotional states formed by these 26 scenes constitutes the narrative program in the proper sense, by which the spectator is guided.

The roles of music and image are reversed in this narration. The visual expressions are extremely differentiated, paradigmatic, full of metaphoric expressivity, of "signs" and "symbols"; whereas the task of the music is to bind these discrete elements of the visual paradigm together into a syntagm, or linear continuum. In fact, listening to the text of the pop-tune soundtrack by Ressu "Redford" (a Finnish rock star), one immediately notices how the words of the tune also provide the rough framework for the visual narration. The impact of the music is thus unifying, though the visual narration contains many contrasts—for example, between the two topoi of the "real world" in scenes 1–18 and the "chocolate fantasy world" of scenes 19–26. The first world is characterized by the narrative functions of search, lack, and dysphory; and the latter by compensation of the lack, achievement, and euphory. During all this the music lends the entire commercial a softly sensual, slightly nostalgic atmosphere. Romantic "longing" forms the basic mood of the music. In this sense, the music follows the goal of the advertisement, which is to reach via music the two extremes of the target group: those who are too young to belong to the main group, ages 14 to 16, and those who have grown too old for it.

Scene 1: Introduction of the main actor or subject, S1. There are other actors as well, but they are too ill-defined to be helpers, opponents, or representatives of other actantial roles. Their purpose, by standing in line, is only to emphasize the loneliness of the girl. The girl seems to be waiting for something indefinite.

Therefore: $eS1m(dys)(v,-s,-p,-d,c)$.* We have here the subject of 'being' (e), whose modal (m) state is dysphoric (dys), consisting of positive values of 'will' and 'believe' (v, c). That is to say, the girl waits for or wants something, and believes that it is attainable, regardless of the negative values of the other modalities of 'know', 'can', and 'must' ($-s,-p,-d$). What is involved is the dysphoria of a "lack"—the archetypal beginning of any narrative plot. Temporally, this does not represent the initiation or closure of a state or activity, but rather a durative state, which could theoretically last forever. The basic modality is 'being'. Actorial articulation: 'I'; spatial topos: "elsewhere," "outside," "among strangers." Temporal articulation: "now"—the action is not taking place in the past or future, as it would in a "realistic" narrative mode.

Scene 2: The boy is introduced. He cannot, however, be taken as the main actor, or 'I' in the proper sense, since his face remains in the shadows. He is thus subject S2, who has been provided with a miraculous property, as in fairy tales where a

The lowercase letters in italics here refer to original French terms: $e = \hat{e}tre$ (be); $f = faire$ (do); $m = modalité$; $v = vouloir$ (will); $s = savoir$ (know); $p = pouvoir$ (can); $d = devoir$ (must); $c = croire$ (believe).

prince may possess supernatural powers, a magic ring, a sword of victory, or another quality of invulnerability. This heroic quality is not revealed openly, but is presented by indexical signs—the "radiation lines," which make this subject appear to be a half-supernatural creature. He belongs to a different topos from that of the subject S1 of the previous scene. The situation might be depicted as follows: $f\mathrm{S2m}(v,p,c,\text{-}s,\text{-}d)$. We have a subject of action (f), whose modal state cannot yet be defined as either euphoric or dysphoric. He is on his way somewhere, thus he wants something; and due to his determined gait he is able and believes himself able to do what he wants. Also, the magic radiation elevates his 'can' modality to a very high level.

As to the aspectual semes, this is a durative action, a virtual mode, characterizing "lack" and "imperfectivity" (to use Claude Brémond's terms). Actorial articulation: Though not the principal subject, the boy is sufficiently characterized in order to be some subject, that of "you." Spatial articulation: "outside," "elsewhere," especially in relation to the topos of the first scene. Temporal articulation: the "now" moment; this subject is in action, thus the basic modality is 'doing'.

Scene 3: The situation of the first scene seems to be repeated, but since what was introduced above has remained in the memory, the basic scheme of narration starts to take shape. One can already see that the girl is a subject who has been disjuncted from a value object whose precise modal value has not yet been determined. Thus: $e\mathrm{S1} \lor \mathrm{O}$. Otherwise the modal constellation is the same as in the first scene. Spatial articulation: "elsewhere," but in a different "elsewhere" from before.

Scene 4: Subject S2 is put in a role of opposition to some object. The boy's attention turns toward something. From this one can infer that, of the modalities, at least 'will' is positive. On the other hand, the movement of the subject stops; thus to the spectator he changes from a subject of 'doing' to one of 'being': $e\mathrm{S2}v(\mathrm{S2} \land \mathrm{O})$. Subject S2 wants to become conjuncted to the object O, whose modal content is not determined. Actorial articulation: "you"; no spatial or temporal articulation takes place, because the scene takes place "beyond" time and place. The aspectual seme is one of inchoativity.

Scene 5: The 'I' of the narration returns. Her loneliness is emphasized by other persons, who as passers-by are completely unconscious of her presence. Here the subject of the musical enunciation is a male voice, who sings about having searched for "you" for a long time. Music thus puts the undeniable 'I' or subject-actor into the role of an object-actor "you," which is the searched-for object. Subject S1 moves as if directionless; her 'will' has no objective. She remains in a dysphoric state, but nevertheless in motion, so that she turns from a subject of being into a subject of doing. The narrative function could be described as "searched for": $f\mathrm{S1m(dys)}(v,\text{-}s,\text{-}p,\text{-}d,\text{-}c)$. Notice also that the modality of 'believe' has become negative. The girl turns her gaze away from the camera, and lets an unknown person take off her coat: She does not believe she has found "the right one."

Scene 6: Subject S1 engages the object with her look: $eS1v(S1 \wedge O)$. The heretofore virtual mode of narration shifts to a passage to action. The aspectual seme is inchoative.

Scene 7: The facial expression of the boy is emphasized by "magical" lines that stress his supernatural powers: $eS2v,p,c(S2 \wedge O)$.

Scene 8: The same situation as in scene 6, but it is no longer the beginning of the boy's waiting, but a continuation of the latter; thus the aspectual seme is durative.

Scene 9: The human figure that moves in the foreground may be understood to exist only in the imagination of S1; it is a "nameless" person (the musical lyrics here describe a search for the name). Otherwise what is involved is a completely external, irrational, and incompatible element of the plot, which serves as a kind of anti-index, a factor that restrains or retards the forward course of events.

Scene 10: The modal situation of subject S1 remains unchanged: She is the subject of 'being', though inwardly she is in a state of waiting for someone. The constancy of her modal situation emphasizes a permanent state of lack—the basic state of man in Western postmodern society, a society in which all possible subjects and objects are available. Here reality is no longer shaped according to conventional narration, such that a subject searches for a certain object and is satisfied after having attained it. Quite the opposite: No longer can any object bring satisfaction, as sociologists have noted, and this keeps the subject in a dysphoric state of being. The seme of durativity prevails.

Scene 11: Subject S2 approaches and begins to act, in scenes that exhibit various degrees of inchoativity. At the same time, this subject is given physical properties: He is provided with a 'seeming' equivalent to the 'being' of the addressees of the message. But the blue radiation also underlines his belonging to another, mythical-magical isotopy; he is simultaneously from "elsewhere" and "here." He has high modal content of 'will', 'can', 'believe', and perhaps 'must', insofar as he has been sent from another universe in order to perform the task of a mythical "rescue."

Scene 12: Continuation of the previous scene, which is now, as it were, enlarged. His aloof facial expression indicates that the boy is neither euphoric nor dysphoric, but in an athymic state. The lighting tends to situate him in the topos of the "real world," where he starts to take on traits of the (real world) addressees.

Scene 13: A sudden change of modalities takes place in S2. The boy recognizes the girl, which provides his modality of 'know' with a positive value. At the same time, there occurs a change in the actorial status of S1. From her earlier position as the 'I' actor of the narration (as opposed to the 'I' of the music soundtrack, who is the boy), the look of Subject S2 changes her into an object. It has often been argued in the semiotics of advertising that the male objectifying look transforms the woman. Here this cognitive operation is a part of the plot in the proper sense. In other words: fS2(S1–O;S2–S1; S1$v \wedge$ O). S2 acts in such a way (by his gaze) that S1 becomes O, S2 turns into S1, and the new S1 seeks conjunction to the newly-produced O.

Scene 14: This narrative function can be characterized as a "rejection." S1 (now, the boy) approaches O (the girl), but O suddenly makes the epistemic interpretation of "denial," which corresponds to the pathemic state of being frightened. The girl's earlier behavior was one of "flirting"—which, according to Finnish theater semiotician Kari Salosaari, can be portrayed as: ve(O+)—and exhibited the aspectual seme of inchoativity, or eS1vS2cS1(S2m). Here her modal state is "fear"—in Salosaari's terms: $ve + de$(O); inchoativity eS1cS2d-(S1 O-).

The next scene explains this unsuccessful activity (in Brémond's terms, a *non-passage à l'acte*). Namely, Subject S1 lacks the mediating auxiliary object, a mediator which is quite central in mythical narration, as studies by Lévi-Strauss and Elli-Kaija Köngäs-Maranda have shown.

Scene 15: If earlier the emphasis went to modal states rather than to activities, this section fulfills the first real act of the commercial. S2 is represented by fingers that take hold of the auxiliary object and thereby enable further action. This is a virtual phase in the form of a narrative sub-program.

Scene 16: The gaze of S2 expresses nothing more than a questioning, interrogative modality. Such is the force—Desire—that launches any action.

Scene 17: The sub-program opened in scene 15 continues. Subject S1 takes a piece of the auxiliary object, and thereby takes it into her possession. A decisive turn takes place in the whole narration, from the lack of an object, or a state of disjunction, to possession of the object, a state of conjunction. Yet this decisive act is not modalized in any way—which provides it with a special solemnity. No expressions of emotions are shown on the face of the subjects—such expressions would be as inappropriate here as they would be at any ceremonial occasion.

Scene 18: This section attempts to describe the consequences of the acts from the perspective of the modality of S1. She is in a state of astonishment—the modality 'know' unexpectedly receives a positive articulation. At the same time she makes a quick semiotic reasoning, which is a shift from the "secret" to an openly 'seeming'/'being' situation that necessarily leads to other modalities. This is a true "modulation" of passions, in Fontanille's sense. The girl's frightened look indicates her realization that, having reached the auxiliary object, she will unavoidably proceed to another, perhaps even more euphoric state, in comparison to which the enjoyment of chocolate will pale. This represents a strong expectation of the future.

Scene 19: An abrupt change of topos, a shift to "elsewhere," to an illusory world of teenage love. Subjects S1 and S2 have found each other and have been freed, as it were, from the chains of material need. The spectator realizes that a completely different narrative program is beginning, yet without being connected by any mediating bridge to the previous sections. A gap or an implication is thus created, and one remains waiting for it to be filled or realized. It is characteristic of this new narrative program that interoceptive, or inner subjective, modal states change into those of exteroceptivity. The subjects are seen essentially from the outside. The emphasis of the modalities shifts from inner mental states to the cosmos surrounding the subjects. The latter half of the film thus contains two overlapping sub-programs, both of which describe the achieved euphoric state. The first of these sub-programs suggests a wandering in an outer space, under the open sky; the other, beginning in the next scene, represents dancing.

Scene 20: In this dance hall scene, the modal element appears by virtue of the change of the lighting into the symbolic form of a heart.

Scene 21: A shift to the "outer." The addressee-public of this scene, one with competency in other films of teen lovers in the city, might even provide it with a dysphory that links the railway and motorway railings with an indexical reference to the protagonists's intent to commit suicide.

Scene 22: Repetition of scene 20, and flashback via the yellow arc-lamp. Such cyclicity suggests the mythic realms of "before" and "after."

Scene 23: Repetition of scene 21. The narration starts to become more redundant, which undeniably strengthens the conative, or "command," function. The spectator-subject no longer receives new information. Rather, he is led to reflect on earlier information and its significance.

Scene 24: Return to the dance hall topos. The definitive interpretation of the film is not yet given to the spectator. So much redundancy, however, creates a tense expectation of resolutions; these would include, for instance, the heretofore missing mediation of the abrupt contrast between scenes 18 and 19.

Scene 25: If the previous, recurrent scenes have underlined the modalities of 'can' and 'do', then here 'know' is suddenly emphasized. At the same time, this scene constitutes the mythical act of "naming," in this case, the almighty auxiliary object—Fazer.

Scene 26: The synthesis and mediation of all previous narrative programs. The topoi of "here" and "elsewhere" blend together in such a way that, in spite of the blue background evoking illusory teenage love, the actors are presented realistically, without the magic lines that covered them at the beginning. The name of the auxiliary object is projected onto the lower edge of the picture, as a causal index of the mediation. Although the auxiliary object appears in reverse order in narrative time—first the mediation, then its cause—the spectator cannot fail in his/her interpretation. The arches of the advertising film close, and the spectator is ready to make his own semio-economic decisions.

REFERENCES

Ejchenbaum, Boris. 1965. *Aufsätze zur Theorie und Geschichte der Literatur.* Selected and translated from Russian by Alexander Kaempfe. Frankfurt am Main: Suhrkamp.
Jakobson, Roman. 1963. *Essai de linguistique générale.* Paris: Minuit.
Mayakovski, Vladimir. 1959. *Pilvi housuissa.* Helsinki: Tammi.

14

Senses, Values—and Media

Den Sinnen hast du dann zu trauen,
kein falsches lassen sie dich schauen,
wenn dein Verständnis dich wach erhält.
—Goethe

Was Goethe right when he advocated trust in the senses, which never fail—provided one also knows how to use one's understanding? What would he have said of the sensibility of the contemporary world, in which man has extended his senses almost without limits, so that the difference between "original experience" and "virtual reality," created by electronic and other means, has become so very vague?

The power of semioticians to intervene in the course of the world is very modest. They can perhaps comment on present developments, which include the movement into total semiosis thanks to media extensions of the senses. Paradoxically, a semiotician sees many of the phenomena and concepts he has discovered swell into those uncontrolled, immoderate, and Dionysiac proportions of which Jean Baudrillard warns us, when speaking about the "ecstasy of communication," the cancerous growth of information, the "bubble world" created by electronic means, and the transparent society in which privacy no longer exists. Have mass media and other forms of communication increased the goodness of mankind (a question for which one might have Rousseauian answers)? The following are some theses that address these topics.

Thesis 1: *The representation of representation.* The common denominator of the video, television, computer and media worlds is the *simulacrum*. What "bad" might there be in that? Has not art, at least since Aristotle, always been a kind of representation, a "simulation" of reality? In our time, however, representation involves something else, perhaps something more dangerous. Today we encounter the phenomenon of "representation of representation" or "double represen-

tation." In music—which as an art form does not rely much on representation—
the invention of recording led to a new kind of concert, in which listeners began
to require the same qualities from a live performance as from a recording. This
led to live musical performances that began to sound like studio products. It was
no longer important to have authentic interaction between performer and listener; such interaction was overshadowed by technical perfection, which pushed
aside the *signified,* or content, of music. Such a phenomenon forms a species of
modern mythicism, as Roland Barthes would say.

Think, for example, of speech acts at political conventions, ceremonies, interviews, and almost any public occasion. In television news, reviews and articles,
broadcast recordings, and other creations of the mass media, verbal exchanges no
longer take place on their own terms and for their own sake, but rather for the
manner in which they (are imagined to) look good as *simulacra* of reality. The
"performers" no longer have in mind the authentic audience of the situation, but
rather the anonymous receiver or "reader" of mass media. On televised and radio interviews, the interlocutors all speak the same standardized and "mediatized" language: Nobody stutters, speaks a dialect, or uses other original signs
that might be considered "noise" in the channel of communication. Opera performances are made for theaters so that they look excellent when videotaped,
and can be sold to millions of customers. In the much-acclaimed production of
Tristan, by Heiner Müller in Bayreuth some years ago, the stage was even framed
by an electronic light, which made it resemble a huge television screen.

In these and innumerable other phenomena, authentic reality has faded
into a representation of representation. The human spirit deliberately restricts its
own expressions so that they fit into subjective categories of representation.
Thus, we have a double representation of reality.

If the model is always a reduction, and accordingly more defective than the
represented reality itself, then in the universe ruled by mass media, the reality
always abandons itself beforehand to the limitations of the model. The vicious
circle of the continuous stupefaction of mankind awaits us.

Thesis 2: *"Specialists."* Control of the bubble world of mass media belongs to the
"specialists." There is a common belief that information is a kind of object which
can be distributed via personal computers (at home, the office, etc.), that everything can be done without stepping outside the electronic system. One forgets
how information—the modality of 'knowing'—is connected to *other* modalities
and to those concrete situations in which it emerged. The interrelationships between information and desire ('want'), technical ability ('can'), norms ('must'),
beliefs, affects—which together form a complex of values—disappear.

Above all, information becomes a message in the communication system,
and in McLuhan's famous phrase "the medium is the message." When the new
broadcasting building in Helsinki was inaugurated some years ago, a government
minister said that the medium is *not* the message. When the third speaker, the

director of the European Broadcasting Union (EBU), Albert Scharf, stated that the medium *is* the message, it became obvious that the medium really is a message, and more particularly a message reflecting the beliefs, capacities, and wishes of its sender, the information specialist. *Whose* message is the medium, and to whom is it a message? "The media activities of a public service cannot be limited to Shakespeare and Sibelius, to teaching programs or to elevated philosophical discussions, in a word, to all that does not appeal to the majority."

But who is this supposed majority? For the Heideggerian analyst it is the typical *das Man*. But how does a semiotician answer this question? The great audience—the "majority"—is satisfied with what it is offered, in the belief that everything else is too difficult. However, the majority does not always know to want something better without the help of "specialists."

On the other hand, the audience clearly knows what it does *not* want *in any case*. Yet, between what the majority believes itself to want (a belief manipulated by officials of mass media) and what it does *not* want, there remains a vast area of matters and programs, which the majority would want if it knew such a region existed. This area can be discovered and charted by the semiotician.

Thesis 3: *The civilization of the image.* Have we shifted irrevocably to the civilization of the image? If yes, then have we moved closer to (the represented) reality itself? As an icon, the image or picture is always more of a *First* (in Peirce's sense) than is a letter of the alphabet or some other symbolic sign. Nevertheless, the authentic reality escapes, in the same way as the picture eludes the letter, into a world in which signs basically refer to each other and in which nominalism is the dominant epistemology. In semiotic terms, there is a zero-point of reality, in which I (the subject) am here and now, a place where no narrative "disengagement" has taken place. What is involved is a concrete, qualitative, local, and authentic experience of reality, which of course can be enriched by the traces left by the history of humanity, but is nevertheless something evident, really existing.

Yet the reality of mass media is based only upon mutual references. The truth criterion of an argument, image, or word now lies not in its correspondence with some *hic, nunc,* and *ego*—the zero-time of avant-garde art, that of John Cage, for example. Rather, the truth value of images and the like is whether they are supported by other media, and by what other media say about them. A society produces, via its "research," the information it needs in order to support certain axiologies. Yet people believe more in the color and sense appeal of mass media realities and media "specialists" than in their own understanding.

René Huyghe, in his *Dialogue avec le visible,* almost prophetically foretold the coming of the civilization of images and its dangers. Huyghe quotes Abbé Lamennais, who wrote as early as 1819: "One does not read any longer, there is no time for it. The attention of the mind is trapped from every side; [a matter] must be spoken of quickly or it disappears. But there are matters which cannot be comprehended so quickly, and precisely they are the most important for man. In the end, this acceleration of movement, which does not allow us any time for reflection, entirely destroys the human intellect."

Huyghe, in turn, argues: "In our days everything is understood via sense perceptions, since they are not, unlike thoughts, in a dialogue with their objects; [sense perceptions] are identified with [objects], [sense perceptions] register and comment. . . . Undeniably we have moved from a civilisation of the letter to that of the image." There is nothing new as such. . . .

Thesis 4: *Critics, the priests of Sarastro, and semioticians.* Of course, literary communication has maintained its position to some extent. Yet even there the medium becomes a message. Few experience the original event—theater performance, movie, concert, other spectacles—and a thousand times more people read mass media opinions on it. The value of the written word varies in different cultures. In our own, art criticism is taken as a natural entity: "He got good reviews," it is said, yet few ask who wrote the review, in what sense it was written, or why it was written.

Mass communication always follows the research of its own area, in order to find arguments for its *raison d'être*. Deconstruction, the most influential semiotic movement of the last two decades, teaches that the marginal can be the most important. Like deconstructionists, journalists look for the strangest, most marginal aspect of a situation, and use that aspect by which to characterize an entire phenomenon. This is called the "point" of the article, and it lures the reader into the story by means of a seductive title.

We live in the limitless power of mass media and sensory reality. What, then, should we do?—as Leo Tolstoy asked one hundred years ago. Should one withdraw and step aside? Should universities become places that accept only the "right" intellectual clientele? Would a monastery be the ideal of a university? The Japanese anthropologist Masao Yamaguchi has founded a meditation university in a remote village in his country and donated his whole library to it. But the idea is old—recall that the Germans liked remote mountain schools and brother- and sisterhoods (see Goethe's *Wilhelm Meister,* and also Klaus Mann's autobiography, *Wendepunkt*). Can semioticians be compared to Sarastro's priests, the guardians of sacred knowledge, in Mozart's *Magic Flute*? Hardly, since the knowledge semiotics offers is open to anyone. In addition, semiotics constitutes almost the only analytic knowledge by which to grasp the sensory nature of the mass media, and to do so without forgetting values.

Thesis 5: *On "virtual reality."* One of the most debated novelties in the area of media technology is that of so-called virtual reality. Adherents of virtual reality claim for it two, very attractive things: interactivity and immersivity. It may be precipitous, however, to claim interactivity for a virtual simulator. One should perhaps talk about *intra*-activity, since in the simulator, the subject does not meet another type of reality. The channel and code are determined by the machine, and the subject only plays with new syntagmatic combinations. Such is the case, for instance, in the virtual art work *The Legible City* (1989) by Jeffrey Shaw. In it the receiver wanders through a town which is like a huge collection of books. In this and in similar cases, the artwork does not bring enough "resistance" to the person who enjoys it. The "reader" remains as ignorant or as wise as he or she was before being exposed to the work.

"Immersivity" denotes the fact that, in a virtual simulator, we "dive" into another reality. In fact, one only dives into oneself. Communication again is fruitful only if its participants remain themselves. They must not always adapt to one another's wishes (although paradoxically this is what man has longed for in art ever since Wagner: Tristan and Isolde wanted to have immersivity via music: *Ewig einig . . . sinken . . .*).

In semiotic terms, the problem of virtual reality can be articulated as follows. In it the subject of enunciation wants to become fused with the subject of enunciate, which is a logical impossibility. One seeks to obliterate the limit between the represented and the representer. If this were to succeed, then it would be a triumph for iconicity. The user of a virtual reality machine would become iconically and indexically the object of the artwork.

Most probably man's development relies on the fact that he encounters various, different realities, models, and ideas. Virtuality, in turn, is based upon the category of similarity. Its world view is extreme solipsism.

Thesis 6: *The stories in computers.* One might easily believe that computer games reveal to us the life of signs as if from the inside. Such games seem to fulfill the avant-garde idea of an "open work," in which the receiver assumes an active role. It is claimed that such games are educational, since nothing is given beforehand and everything must be learned along the way. Thus, an illusion of activity is created, which is one of the epistemes of the American, pragmatic world view— "learning by doing." Computer games do not put this principle as such into question, but yet they are texts so strongly oriented toward the receiver that they no longer communicate anything. In traditional narratives, the reader is "immobile" and the movement takes place inside the text. In computer games, the "reader" moves, but the alternatives of the player are less than when one receives an immobile text. The player blends together with the plot as one of its actors, but his movements are not based upon the disengagement of place, time, and actor. The games take place in the present, and they take their players prisoner in a kind of eternal synchrony. In no case do such games have a qualitative duration in the Bergsonian sense. In computer games, there is no narrator at all, yet they are still kinds of quasi-narratives or fragments of stories. They operate undeniably with mythical materials, and the players easily identify themselves and the game itself according to something like the Greimasian mythical actant model (as Leif Åberg has shown). In any case, as a motor activity, even the simplest act of playing a traditional instrument remains a more complex event than moving the mouse on a computer desk.

REFERENCES

Huyghe, René. [1959]. *Dialogue avec le visible. Connaissance de la peinture.* London: Thames and Hudson.
Mann, Klaus. 1976. *Wendepunkt.* München: Edition Spangenberg.

INDEX

Abbate, Carolyne, 185–186
Åberg, Leif, 213
Adorno, Theodor, 89, 99, 119
Agoult, Marie d', 159
Ahmad, Aijaz, 150
Albeniz, Isaac, 165–166, 169
Alembert, Jean le Rond d', 32
Ansermet, Ernst, 106–107
Antonioni, Michelangelo, 103
Apollinaire, Guillaume, 100–101
Appia, Adolphe, 139
Aristotle, 209
Arom, Simha, 125
Asafiev, Boris, 88–89
Ashcroft, 138, 141, 150
Attali, Jacques, 119–120
Augustine, 7, 168

Bach, J. S., 25, 126–128, 130, 178–179
Bachelard, Gaston, 171
Bakhtin, Mikhail, 68
Bankov, Kristian, 152
Barthes, Roland, 3, 9, 29, 60, 73–74, 103, 105,
      107, 143, 175, 185, 193, 210
Bartók, Béla, 22, 99
Baudrillard, Jean, 3, 18, 88, 140, 146, 173, 175,
      209
Beauvoir, Simone de, 106–107
Beethoven, Ludwig van, 22, 65, 81, 105, 107,
      144, 178–179, 183, 187–188
Behar, Lisa Block de, 74
Berger, Peter, 20
Bergman, Ingmar, 91
Bergson, Henri, 22, 59
Berio, Luciano, 104–105
Bernanos, Georges, 6, 108–109
Bhabha, Homi K., 142
Blixen, Karen, 130
Bloy, Leon, 59
Bocuse, Paul, 130
Boissier, Madame, 126
Borges, Jorge Luis, 59, 74
Boulez, Pierre, 102–104
Bourdieu, Pierre, 3, 18, 126–127, 197
Brahms, Johannes, 92, 144
Braque, Georges, 100, 105

Brecht, Bertolt, 99
Brelet, Gisèle, 107
Brémond, Claude, 78, 204
Bresson, Robert, 109
Breton, André, 101–102
Broms, Henri, 10
Bruckner, Anton, 92
Büchner, Georg, 99
Busoni, Feruccio, 125, 170
Butor, Michel, 165
Böcklin, Arnold, 188

Cage, John, 91, 119, 211
Camus, Albert, 11, 108, 174
Čapek, Karel, 99
Carlyle, Scott, 59
Carnap, Rudolph, 9, 51–53, 69
Cassirer, Ernst, 166
Cellini, Benvenuto, 96
Cézanne, Paul, 100
Chagall, Marc, 12, 110, 155
Char, René, 6
Charbonnières, Georges, 112
Charles, Daniel, 107
Chateaubriand, 130, 159
Chatwin, Bruce, 126
Chaucer, Geoffrey, 176
Chausson, Ernest, 22
Child, Julia, 129–130
Chomsky, Noam, 8, 29–30
Chopin, Frédéric, 71, 126
Claudel, Paul, 78
Cocteau, Jean, 100
Coquet, Jean-Claude, 25
Custine, Marquis de, 157

Dahlhaus, Carl, 98
Darzins, Emil, 90, 91
Davies, Peter Maxwell, 80
Dean, James, 200
Debussy, Claude, 10, 105, 170
Delacroix, Eugène, 157
Derrida, Jacques, 3, 15, 76, 120
Diderot, Denis, 14, 32
Disney, Walt, 107, 172, 175–190
Dorfman, Ariel, 172, 177

Dostoievsky, Fiodor, 99
Duchamp, Marcel, 101
Dufourt, Hugues, 104
Dukas, Paul, 175, 178, 185–186
Dumas, Alexandre, 130
Durkheim, Emil, 189
Dvořák, Antonín, 170

Eckermann, J. P., 168
Eco, Umberto, 3, 8, 57, 71, 88, 90, 104, 112–114,
      116–117, 123, 125, 130, 147, 173, 193
Edelfelt, Albert, 162–163
Eichenbaum, Boris, 193
Eisenstein, Sergei, 103
Emerson, Ralph Waldo, 118, 176–177, 188

Feild, Robert D., 177, 183
Fichte, J. G., 34
Filippot, Michel, 107
Finch, Christopher, 182
Fontanille, Jacques, 87, 206
Foucault, 3, 18, 106, 174, 180
Freud, Siegmund, 30
Frye, Northrop, 14, 183

Gallén-Kallela, Axel, 162–163
Gauguin, Paul, 157, 188
Geigges, Werner, 38
Gentil, Jules, 126
Gerico, 100
Gershwin, George, 175
Gide, André, 66–67
Gilels, Emil, 88
Glazunov, Alexander, 90
Goethe, J. W. v., 12, 151, 155, 159, 168, 175, 178,
      185–186, 209, 212
Goldmann, Lucien, 28, 47, 58, 175
Gould, Glenn, 93
Greimas, A. J., 3–4, 6, 18, 24, 26–30, 35, 42, 63,
      71, 76–77, 87, 89, 106, 108–109, 114, 117–
      118, 140, 147, 154, 158, 164, 194–195
Grund, Cynthia, 55
Guerrero, José Manuel Briceño, 140

Hahn, Reynaldo, 128
Harnoncourt, Nicolas, 127
Hegel, G. W. F., 14–15, 18, 32, 35, 39, 51, 53–54,
      73, 106–107, 167, 173
Heidegger, Martin, 4, 13–15, 18, 40, 47, 71, 74,
      76–77, 80–83, 88, 107, 117–118, 174
Heraclitus, 77
Herrmman, Jörg M., 38
Hesse, Herman, 89
Hindemith, Paul, 100
Hocevar, Drina, 152
Hoeg, Peter, 22
Hoffmann, E. T. A., 99
Hoffmann, Jan, 126

Hogarth, William, 157
Hollander, Hans, 99
Homer, 176
Honegger, Arthur, 101
Hume, David, 64
Husserl, Edmund, 21, 45, 60–62, 64, 69–70, 74
Huyghe, René, 187, 211–212

Indy, Vincent d', 169
Ives, Charles, 100, 105, 144, 170

Jahrnach, Philipp, 125
Jakobson, Roman, 102, 162, 191
Jameson, Fredric, 150
Janáček, Leoš, 99
Jankélévitch, Vladimir, 61, 69, 71–72
JanMohamed, Abdul R., 141–142
Jaspers, Karl, 4, 13, 18–20, 27–28, 101, 107, 165,
      167
Johansen, Jorgen Dines, 23
Joyce, James, 99

Kafka, Franz, 99
Kandinsky, Vassily, 102
Kant, Immanuel, 4, 18, 20, 26, 35, 71, 91
Kaurismäki, Aki and Mika, 14
Kierkegaard, Søren, 5–7, 12, 14, 18, 41, 50–51,
      79–81, 93, 107
King, Larry, 145
King, Martin Luther, 105
Klotins, Arnold, 91
Koch, Walter, 186–187
Koivunen, Hannele, 152
Kraus, Karl, 99
Kristeva, Julia, 3, 20, 28, 30, 40–41, 63
Kukkonen, Pirjo, 152
Kuusamo, Altti, 55
Kuusimäki, Mikko, 152
Kwiek, Marcel, 73
Köngäs-Maranda, Elli-Kaija, 206

Lacan, Jacques, 106
Lahier, Bernard, 73
Lamennais, Abbé, 211
Landowska, Wanda, 127
Langer, Susanne, 44
Le Corbusier, 138
Leibniz, Wilhelm v., 18
Leibowitz, René, 106–107
Levinas, Emmanuel, 22, 26
Lévi-Strauss, Claude, 18, 28, 37, 59, 103–106,
      112–113, 116, 139, 161, 166, 174–175, 177,
      181–182, 189–190, 206
Ligeti, György, 80, 92
Lima, Luiz Fernando de, 152
Lindberg, Magnus, 80, 170
Linn, Denise, 43
Linné, Carl, 157

Liszt, Franz, 18, 22, 71, 126, 159–160, 170
Locke, John, 64
Lotman, Yuri, 5, 13, 18, 28–30, 41, 76, 89, 119, 142, 167, 174–175
Luckmann, Thomas, 20
Lucretius, 6

Mâche, François-Bernard, 90
Mahler, Alma, 89
Mahler, Gustav, 29, 89, 105, 144
Majava, Heikki, 74
Mallarmé, Stephan, 59
Mann, Klaus, 212
Mannerheim, Carl Gustaf, 68, 130
Marcel, Gabriel, 166, 168, 174
Marcus, Solomon, 124
Margolis, Joseph, 3, 5
Martinů, Bohuslav, 22
Mattelart, Armand, 172, 177
Mayakovsky, Vladimir, 99, 193
Mazarin, Jules, 130
McLuhan, Marshall, 210
McTaggart, J. McT. E., 40, 42
Mead, George Herbert, 38, 68–70
Mendelssohn, Felix, 25
Merleau-Ponty, Maurice, 21
Merrell, Floyd, 23, 41, 167
Meyer, Leonard B., 105
Milhaud, Darius, 100, 165–166, 170
Milton, John, 176
Minkus, Léon, 164, 170
Mishima, Yukio, 81
Moore, G. E., 93
Morris, Charles, 38
Mozart, Wolfgang Amadeus, 14, 52, 93, 125, 192, 212
Müller, Heiner, 210
Munsterhjelm, Hjalmar, 132
Musil, Robert, 67
Mussorgsky, Modest, 81, 169, 178, 181

Napoleon, 68
Nattiez, Jean-Jacques, 67
Nietzsche, Friedrich, 14, 58, 65, 107, 174
Novalis, 118

Ortega y Gasset, José, 98
Ortoli, Cecile, 14

Paderewski, Ignace, 126
Parland, Heidi, 131
Parland, Henry, 13
Pascal, Blaise, 47, 58
Pasolini, Pier-Paolo, 103
Pasteur, Louis, 162
Pavese, Cesare, 5
Peirce, Charles S., 3–4, 7, 11, 14, 17–18, 21, 23, 26, 28, 30, 33–35, 38, 41–42, 48, 64, 74, 76, 109, 121, 137, 167, 173, 192, 211
Pergolesi, Giovanni Battista, 125
Petrov, Vladimir, 67
Picasso, Pablo, 10, 100, 105
Pirsig, Robert, 14
Pivot, Bernard, 145
Plato, 21, 141
Poncielli, Amilcare, 178
Ponzio, Augusto, 150
Poulenc, Francis, 100
Poussin, Nicolas, 155–156
Presley, Elvis, 167
Prokofiev, Sergei, 88–89, 103
Propp, Vladimir, 6, 27
Proust, Marcel, 22, 33, 91, 117–118, 120, 128–129, 131, 165
Puccini, Giacomo, 167
Pärt, Arvo, 93

Queneau, Raymond, 137

Racine, Jean, 6, 47, 58
Raffler-Engel, Walburga von, 61
Rauhala, Lauri, 45, 47–48
Ravel, Maurice, 107, 127, 170, 185
Rawls, John, 64
Redford, Ressu, 203
Renoir, Jean, 103
Richter, Sviatoslav, 93, 128
Rickards, Guy, 144
Rosen, Charles, 7
Rossi-Landi, Ferruccio, 150
Rougier, Louis, 103
Rousseau, Jean-Jacques, 156
Royce, Josiah, 137, 152
Rubinstein, Artur, 96
Rüdlinger, Arnold, 99
Runeberg, Fredrika, 131
Runeberg, Johan Ludwig, 131–132
Ruskin, John, 26, 93, 116, 118, 120–123
Russell, Bertrand, 64

Saariaho, Kaija, 80
Salosaari, Kari, 206
Samuels, Robert, 29
Sand, George, 159
Sartre, Jean Paul, 7, 11, 14–15, 18–19, 40–41, 53–54, 105–106, 106–109, 174, 184
Satie, Erik, 100
Saussure, Ferdinand de, 17–18, 28, 137
Scharf, Albert, 211
Schelling, Friedrich W., 18–19, 39, 49–51
Schiller, Friedrich, 65
Schnabel, Artur, 82
Schoenberg, Arnold, 80, 103
Schopenhauer, Arthur, 25
Schubert, Franz, 178

Schumann, Robert, 107, 169
Schütz, Alfred, 61, 69–70
Schweitzer, Albert, 106
Scriabin, Alexander, 100
Sebeok, Thomas A., 3, 11, 17, 38, 73
Seidlhofer, Bruno, 128
Sénancour, Etienne de, 158–160
Sesemann, Wilhelm, 61
Shakespeare, William, 176, 211
Shaw, Jeffrey, 213
Shostakovich, Dmitry, 52, 88–89
Sibelius, Jean, 22, 71, 89–92, 143–144, 151, 165, 211
Sisley, Alfred, 9
Slemon, Stephen, 138, 145
Smetana, Bedřich, 165
Snellman, Johann Wilhelm, 114–116
Soloviev, Vladimir, 11–12, 19, 69, 152
Souris, André, 99–100, 106–107
Spenser, Herbert, 176
Stallone, Sylvester, 128
Stokowski, Leopold, 178–179, 184, 189
Strauss, Johann, 119
Strauss, Richard, 13, 164
Stravinsky, Igor, 99–100, 178–179, 182–183, 186–187
Strindberg, August, 99
Swingle Sisters, 105

Tarasti, Eero, 90
Taviani, Paolo and Vittorio, 119–120
Taylor, Charles, 46, 105
Taylor, Deems, 178–179

Tchaikovsky, Piotr, 165, 178, 184
Thoreau, Henry, 116, 118, 176
Toller, Ernst, 99
Tolstoy, Leo, 22, 68, 87, 92–93, 116, 212

Uexküll, Thure von, 38–41, 46, 67
Uspenskij, Boris, 28–29

Verdi, Giuseppe, 167
Villa-Lobos, Heitor, 101
Voigt, Vilmos, 62–63
Voltaire, 14
Välimäki, Susanna, 74

Wagner, Cosima, 93, 107
Wagner, Richard, 6, 8, 65, 79, 88, 91, 93, 107, 167, 179, 188, 195, 213
Wahl, Jean, 18–19, 44, 48, 107
Watteau, Jean-Antoine, 170
Waugh, Evelyn, 165
Weber, Max, 145
Weiss, Peter, 15
Westermarck, Edward, 40–41
Wittgenstein, Ludwig, 108, 174
Wittgenstein, Paul, 107–108
Wright, Frank Lloyd, 184
Wright, Georg Henrik von, 4, 28, 34, 39, 67, 73–74, 92, 140

Yamaguchi, Masao, 212

Zweig, Stefan, 10

Eero Tarasti holds the Chair of Musicology at the University of Helsinki. One of the world's leading semioticians, he is founder and President of the Semiotic Society of Finland, Director of the International Semiotics Institute at Imatra, and author of numerous articles and books, including *A Theory of Musical Semiotics* (Indiana University Press).